0304327271

Other titles in the Cassell Education series:

Education and Meaning: Philosophy in Practice

Paddy Walsh

CASSELL

Cassell Educational Limited
Villiers House   387 Park Avenue South
41/47 Strand   New York
London   NY 10016–8810
WC2N 5JE   USA

First published 1993

British Library Cataloguing-in-Publication Data
A catalogue record for this book is available from the British Library.

Library of Congress Cataloging-in-Publication Data
Walsh, Paddy.
    Education and meaning: philosophy in practice/Paddy Walsh.
       p.   cm. – (Cassell education)
    Includes bibliographical references and index.
    ISBN 0-304-32725-5 — ISBN 0-304-32727-1 (pbk.)
    1. Walsh, Paddy. 2. Education—Great Britain—Philosophy.
    3. Education—Great Britain—Curricula—Case studies. I. Title.
    II. Series.
    LB880.W26E38   1993
    370′1 – dc20   92-42792
                                          CIP

ISBN 0-304-32725-5 (hardback)
     0-304-32727-1 (paperback)

Typeset by Colset Private Limited, Singapore
Printed and bound in Great Britain by
Dotesios Ltd, Trowbridge, Wilts.

Contents

Introduction

This is not the short introduction to philosophy of education that I thought I would write. The need to rethink issues for myself – including, at a critical time, the defining issue of what philosophy is *doing* in education (where does it go on? who needs it? what is its 'constituency'?) – saw that intention off gradually. So, this book is not particularly short. So, also, it will be found to relate as much to the general discipline of education as to philosophy of education – I think of it as a philosophical offering to educational theory. So, again, it will lack some of the attributes of the introduction. Thus, it both skips more lightly over some areas and digs others up more intensively than an introduction should. On the other hand, it remains the case that it presupposes little or no specialist knowledge of either philosophy or educational theory, and is intended to be accessible to all who have learnt, in whatever field of study, the patience needed to read a complex text – thus, say, to graduate and final-year undergraduate students in education, say, to the experienced teacher whatever his or her specialism, to the educated and interested layperson.

It has grown slowly and somewhat painfully. One or two of its ideas were there rough-cut from the beginning but most declared themselves only in the writing, and the idea which gives it some coherence, and its title, grew into that role almost retrospectively. That idea is that the ideal of education, under the haunting aegis of which teachers teach their particular subjects and age-groups, and parents and others do a great range of things for young people, requires *inter alia* relating one's teaching tasks of the moment and of one's particular role to some overarching scheme of things (however defined), or to the quest for such a scheme. Such a relation, it may be said, makes the very practice of education a philosophical practice.

I was first alerted and sensitized to this by the linguistic analyses of the uses of 'education' and its cognates that now constitute Part 1. I had not thought to find much new here, but I was wrong. Previous analyses, I was to realize, had been diverted to shallow waters by methodological prejudices, and I found a more open approach yielding a good dividend, exposing, indeed, what I came to think of as the 'geometry' of the concept of education. Already in this geometry the outline shape of developed educational discourse can be discerned, as well as the deep involvement of education with the ideal of a coherent life. Part 2 develops these hints into an analysis of the requirements of a proper educational theory; that is, of a theory which seeks to be adequate to the good educational practice in which it is 'emergent' and, in particular, to that practice's aspiration to coherence. The relationship of theory to practice is, of course, an academic, institutional and public issue of the moment, and the argument here engages more than glancingly with those debates.

In Part 3 the book switches from a formal to a substantive mode. First remarking on our cultural question marks against the ideal of a coherent scheme of things – and noting that something more than piecemeal cross-curricular initiatives is at issue – it goes on to develop substantive points of view on two of the main requirements of an educational vision. It proposes, first, a particular classification of educational values and an ordering of them that accords primacy to what it calls 'love of the world', and, second, a particular pluralist approach to the analysis or mapping of cognitive and cultural capital for educational purposes, which it relates to the previous ordering of values.

Part 4 acknowledges the 'sub-practices' of education and its three case studies might be said to represent that substantial proportion of educational theory which is sub-curricular. These also counterpoint the book's discussions of whole education and whole curriculum. Education is, indeed, more than the sum of its parts and hence there is a need for a theory of the whole, but unrelieved diets of general theory tend to homogenize the parts, which in reality are quite disparate and, also, more than parts – unlike machine components, they have lives of their own and studies of them do not combine without remainder into some ordered theoretical whole. Finally, these case studies exemplify and test the book's views on general educational values – test as well as exemplify, weigh more soberly as well as make more vivid.

Philosophy of education in Britain remains nervous about its future. Undoubtedly, the hard-nosed insouciance of government is partly responsible for its downturn of recent decades. It is important, however, that it examine its own conscience: does it also have itself to blame for being seen as a luxury that is dispensable in hard times? The view of this book is that its present situation calls for theoretic and institutional development in each of three directions (which are quite often acknowledged singly but need to be taken together). First, as already intimated, it should see itself as in integral relationship with educational practice, such that practice is a source and not just a target of philosophy, and philosophy is already a significant element *within* the discourses and deliberations of practice. Second, it should see itself as much more than an outpost of general philosophy to which independently achieved arguments and positions can be 'applied'. In the recent past it has been quick to admit a duty to keep pace with developments in general philosophy but slow to see how well placed it is to contribute to such developments. Third, it should see itself as firmly located within the general discipline of education. This would imply less sensitivity about its boundaries (which are inherently fuzzy anyway) and a positive, as opposed to a primarily critical, orientation towards the other sub-disciplines of education and the forms of research employed by them. Dewey, we might ruefully note, believed in all three of these outreaches. My attempts to practise them remain a deal less assured than were his at the start of the century!

More recently it is educational theory generally that has come into question, particularly in Britain, and this does seem more than anything else a politically engineered thing. There are the extraordinarily ignorant, and well-publicized, comments of some pundits of the Right. There is the dismal narrowing of the terms of political debate about education. A greater involvement of education with the technological and the vocational is defended at some length in this book. But it is another matter to regard that involvement as education's primary obligation and then take that view as read. There is, finally, the questioning in high places of a continued role for the university and the academy in teacher education. This goes beyond a sensible enlargement of the role of schools in teacher education to threaten the academic dimension – and, one might say, the very idea – of teacher education. Of course what is ultimately threatened by this tide is the idea of education itself. This book is addressed to the teachers, educationists and others who continue – and who will continue whatever happens – to be moved by the idealism implicit in that idea.

I am deeply thankful to those who have helped me along the way. These include my colleagues and students, past and present, of the Curriculum Studies Department of the London University Institute of Education; colleagues and students, also, of the Institute's Philosophy Department, especially John White and Graham Haydon; audiences in the UK, Ireland, Australia and Spain, and the editors of several journals, who gave a fair wind to versions and drafts of various sections; and the ESRC who awarded me a two-year studentship that first got me going on many of these reflections. In more personal terms I thank Denis Lawton for his quiet and patient support, Ruth Jonathan for reading a draft of most of the text at a crucial time and for her thoroughly encouraging comments, Ray Elliott for his critical assurance at key points, and Paul Hirst, Margaret Meek, Peter Lee, Peter Mortimore, Malcolm Skilbeck, Lynne Chisholm and Hazel Francis who read and commented on individual chapters. Most of all, I thank Pat Walsh, who – often at a cost to her own studies in philosophy – read draft after draft of section after section and forced countless clarifications of both substance and style. I thank, too, Conal Walsh for sometimes disguising his disbelief in the thing ever being finished, and Aoife Walsh – who does not remember a time when I was not engaged with it – for forgiving my too-frequent absences from her life. Finally, I thank very particularly my own graduate teachers in philosophy, Richard Peters and (again) Ray Elliott – inspirational men both, to whom this book is dedicated.

NOTES

Papers relating to various parts of this book have been published previously in the *Journal of Philosophy of Education* (three), the *Journal of Further and Higher Education*, *Irish Educational Studies* (two) and *London File*.

I use 'he' or 'she' randomly in this book. To have adopted the more common practice of using the neutral plural where possible would have seemed to me needlessly to sacrifice a lot in the way of colour – and philosophers can ill afford to sacrifice colour.

Part 1

The Meaning of Education

Chapter 1

Rethinking Linguistic Analysis

Every concept that can ever be needed, will be expressed by exactly one word, with its meaning rigidly defined and all its subsidiary meanings rubbed out and forgotten. Every year, fewer and fewer words and the range of consciousness always a little smaller.
(George Orwell, *Nineteen Eighty-Four*)

What can we hope to gain from occupying ourselves, as we shall in the first two chapters of this book, with words – with 'education', 'educational', 'educated', 'educator', etc.?

A measure of reflexive attention to words is, of course, an everyday matter. So a perfectly ordinary conversation might pause over 'education' – a word with many senses, and some that verge on the technical – to identify the particular sense being used and distinguish it from some others. In that same clarifying spirit a book on education might more systematically offer a glossary of uses, perhaps even reproduce the *Oxford English Dictionary*'s entire entry on 'education'. But we harbour larger, and more specifically philosophical, ambitions than clarity and easy reference. What we are after is a kind of self-knowledge, knowledge of our shared 'social self' to start with, and some knowledge of our personal selves as well.

At some very general level, our language tends to shape the contours of our thoughts, to give not detailed destinations but some general directions to our enquiries. We can speak even of a 'knowledge' that is embedded in language, for there is no knowing our language that is not also a tacit knowing, or thinking we know, an enormous amount beyond language. 'If language is to be a means of communication', Wittgenstein famously remarked, 'there must be agreement not only in definitions but also (queer as this may sound) in judgements' – a sharing, he went on to say, not so much of 'opinions' as of 'a form of life'.[1] For agreement on definitions or word meanings itself depends upon some degree of consensus and some limit to dissension over particular applications of those words in judgements. (How, otherwise, could we learn the meanings of words in the first place? How could we break in?) The sense of queerness arises here because we can *ordinarily* distinguish between disagreements over matters of fact and disagreements over the meaning of words. Factual disagreement is perfectly compatible with sharing a language – presupposes it, indeed, if it is ever to become a defined disagreement. But *in the limit* this distinction falters and fails. Thus, far beyond everyday disagreement, well beyond even 'radical' or 'pervasive' disagreement, there is a Kafkaesque hypothesis: an inability to agree so total as to suggest that linguistic communication is not actually taking place and that this common-sounding language is not, after all, common. It is only the obverse of this very creepy hypothesis that really sharing a language involves sharing assumptions and knowledge as well.

If language makes assumptions and sets directions and contexts, then, by attending reflexively to the relevant parts of it, we can hope to make explicit for ourselves the ones that bear on our enquiry of the moment – in our case those which frame the form of our educational life. That is the hope in which we shall labour over the word 'education' and its cognates.

Revealing ourselves to ourselves in this way should have some intrinsic fascination. Beyond that, it may nourish our substantive non-linguistic enquiries about education – and that at two levels. First, we shall find that among the things to be articulated and displayed are certain questions which live in the very grain of the usage of 'education'. These are questions that are 'always with us', if elusively. When we dig them out we 'recognize' them, and they are likely to strike us as 'fundamental', as having shadowed a multitude of our everyday deliberations in this field. At a fairly conventional level, then, linguistic analyses can contribute to the general coherence and satisfaction of our substantive enquiries. But, more subversively, these analyses may put us in a position to cast a cold eye over the habits of thought they reveal, not excluding our sense that certain questions are the right and fundamental ones. Sometimes it is claimed that analyses of this kind 'leave everything as it is'. Of themselves, they do perhaps. But they enable, and may incline, us to *go on* to challenge and change, or (*pace* Orwell) to defend more discriminatingly, what they reveal – including the very linguistic usages themselves.[2] This is not to assume that we can somehow stand right outside language and reconstruct from there our whole thought and language. It assumes only what is obvious, that language is sufficiently many-layered, reflexive and adaptable for us to employ it even in its own development or reform – as is attested, for example, by the eloquent effectiveness of the feminist critique of sexist usages.

There has recently been some marked reaction against linguistic analysis, for decades the domineering technique in Anglo-Saxon philosophy. The critique[3] that is one component of this reaction (ennui being the other) seems well judged to me as directed at standard practices of the recent past, and I shall give my own account of it as I go along. But linguistic analysis is ancient in philosophy – as one technique among many – and not lightly to be abandoned. What we really need to do is rethink its goals and strategies (as well as leave room for other techniques). This is a process on which we are already embarked, indeed, for that we are to place some emphasis on the reformability of language and its associated mind-sets will already distinguish our analyses from the run of previous analyses. An equally significant departure will be an insistence on the full range of the meanings of 'education', and on the mutual bearings and relationships of those meanings, and to this we now turn.

A MULTIPLICITY OF USES

It is not difficult to evoke this range of meanings. For example, such questions about education as 'is it necessarily a good thing?', 'can we have too much of it?', 'can we ever be done with it?' invite the reply that it depends on which sense of 'education' is intended. Sometimes the word functions, like 'virtue', as a term of commendation, as naming something worth having *by definition* (if it is not worth having it isn't 'education'); but at other times it quite lacks this implication. Again, we may be as ardent as William Morris in believing that 'we learn to live and live to learn', yet still admit a sense of 'education' in which it does typically come to an end – one graduates or drops out finally. In *this* sense the process may eventually yield a product, the educated adult – as car assembly yields the car – but that need not inhibit us from insisting in *other* contexts that education is a lifelong process with an internal point of its own and no finished product.

The uses of 'uneducated' can be rehearsed to the same effect. Most commonly the word is applied to one who has not been to school (or has learnt nothing there) and who has not otherwise learnt the kinds of things that schools teach: to read, write and calculate, a smattering of literature, history, science, etc. The peasant Platon Karatayev in *War and Peace* is certainly uneducated in that sense. But now note that Tolstoy can credibly depict him as one who by upbringing, experience and grace has been rendered uncommonly resourceful and marvellously wise. When the chips are down and he and Prince Pierre Bezukhov are prisoners of war together, struggling as much for their souls as their lives, it is the cultivated Pierre who feels himself exposed as (could we not well say?) the 'uneducated' one. 'No, you just can't understand what I learned from that illiterate man – that simple creature,' he later exclaims to Natasha.[4] In still more studied paradox, schooling has sometimes been *contrasted* with education and rejected in the name of education: education is what begins when schooling is over; school is an interruption in a child's education; worse, it is positively miseducative. Put plausibility to one side here. That we even understand such quips turns at least partly on our grasp of a use of 'education' that embraces kinds of learning not associated, nor ever likely to be associated, with school.[5] And to these two uses of 'uneducated' we can add a third. Whole societies have been, and are, uneducated in the first sense of being unschooled in literacy and its products. Yet anthropologists may discuss the educational ways and systems of these societies, alongside their kinship, economic and political ones. The sense of 'education' they then imply is unlike the second sense in not conveying any endorsement of what it describes. And, unlike either of the previous senses, only children could be described as 'uneducated' in this sense, by which would be meant 'not-yet-educated'.

These various uses of 'education', 'uneducated', etc. are not generally in competition with each other – to employ one does not usually commit us to eschew others. Our language invites us, rather, to avail of all of them as they suit our changing purposes and contexts. We could even find ourselves switching among them within a single discussion. Suppose that two parents (perhaps middle class, perhaps not) are deliberating on the choice of a school for their children. Let us say their relevant interests include:

- what the schools in question have to offer in the way of academic, but also of social, development;
- this in relation to what they can provide at home themselves and get other agencies to provide;
- and in relation to what higher education and the job market expect on the one hand, and to their own values and ideals in life on the other hand;

- the present as well as the future happiness and well-being of their children;
- what might best suit the particular temperament and aptitudes of this or that individual child;
- and what might be best for their children – or, more narrowly, for their children's advancement – as against what might best express their own wider social commitments.

Now, as the parents discuss this angle and that, we can easily imagine them employing 'education', 'educative', 'educator', etc., first in one sense and then in another, matching the complex criss-cross of available senses to the clash and interplay of their interests. 'John's education' may at one moment refer to what some lucky schools will provide him with in the way, especially, of formal and publicly endorsed curriculum; at another time to his 'education in the widest sense', a more general enterprise which will include much that is elusive and much that is highly personal and which will be serviced by a whole array of agencies (John's family itself not the least of them). Again, they may use 'education' in connection with what a school is actually providing ('a lively education', 'a rather traditional educational diet'), and then in connection with what the parents think it ideally should provide ('education in the true sense, dear'). Yet again, they may employ it at one time in an open-ended, heuristic way as a marker of something they are still trying to get clear about – like 'X', as the still uncertain quantity – and then at a later time in some more loaded way to encapsulate a set of pretty definite ideals, perhaps as shorthand for 'a liberal education'.

We are in the main remarkably sure-footed in negotiating transitions among these uses of 'education'. (Our practical skill here, our tacit knowledge, ordinarily far outstrips our ability to give it articulate definition – in the same way that long familiarity with a place ensures we will rarely lose our way in it, but not that we can draw good maps of it.) Suppose, however, that the parents did now and then find themselves at cross-purposes. That might be thought to suggest some practical advantage in an agreement to limit themselves to just one of these uses. But then, if they were not as drastically to curtail the range of their perspectives on the choice of a school, they would have to cast around for either synonyms or paraphrases for the excluded uses, and these might be, respectively, hard to come by and prohibitively prolix. This remedy might prove a greater strain than the original problem! In any case, the parents have a more natural remedy to hand in those qualifying expressions, like 'true', 'so-called', 'in the widest sense', by which particular uses of 'education' can quite adequately be identified when the context does not do this already.

It is not really a matter, however, of the parents being able to 'cope' despite the 'limitations' of language. In deliberations like theirs the versatility of 'education', we may go on to surmise, is a *positive asset*. Somewhat intuitively and sketchily, and for elaboration throughout this first part of the book, it contributes notably, and may even be indispensable, to that *conjuring and marshalling of manifold considerations* which is typical of educational deliberations. Parents' tacit knowledge of the uses of 'education' enables and inclines them, does it not, to approach the choice of school as the complex matter that it really can be? For their general sense of the ramifying connections of these uses braces them for a wide trawl for relevant factors. Specific uses and combinations of uses prime them with many of those particular perspectives on the choice of a school which we found it natural to ascribe to them. And at the same time as they multiply their

deliberations the uses start them on a marshalling and ordering process. What they provoke in the parents are semi-organized clusters of ideas and aspirations: a sense of
arguments to be joined, of *balances* to be struck, of *reconciliations* to be effected –
between home and school, academic and social, individual and common, present and
future, ideal and actual. Finally, none of this bracing and priming, multiplying and
ordering is particular to the business of choosing a school. The themes just mentioned
are ones that recur, and concur, quite generally in educational discussion.[6]

   To suggest in this way that the various uses of 'education' have some power to structure that considerable manifold on which collectively they draw is to raise the questions
of what kinds of relationship they have with each other, and what kind of whole, if any,
they add up to. Let us begin to address those questions.

SIMILARITIES AND DIFFERENCES

One way in which the uses hold together is by virtue of similarities between them – they
are not straight homonyms. As common threads,

(a)   learning is implied in them all; indeed it would seem both
(b)   rather a lot of learning (education is a protracted business), and
(c)   unlike training, learning of many kinds.

Thus when 'educational' and 'educative' are applied to single learning episodes, they
invoke a wider and variegated whole of which these episodes are parts. Going on, all
uses might further be said to make some kind (we have to be vague to cover all the cases)
of implicit reference

(d)   to the learning being of value (the uncontroversially trivial or evil, as such, would
      not qualify) and
(e)   of a value that promised to be not just short-term, but lasting.

Most uses imply a learning, further,

(f)   that is more a (possibly creative) catching up on, than a forging ahead of, a tradi-
      tion or a culture considered as a social deposit of knowledge and skill.

Finally, most uses also make some more or less substantial reference

(g)   to tradition as a process, i.e. to some kind of instruction or handing on.[7]

Note that the purpose here is only to display *one* way in which the uses of 'education'
hang together. The light shed on individual uses by this exercise is a pale and uneven
one, and, were we now to 'total' these common elements, they would yield only an
unnuanced abstraction. They would emphatically not yield, though there is some temptation to suppose they might, anything that could happily be called either 'the concept'
or 'the definition' of education. For, whatever else, concepts and definitions should
include all that is essential. And we could not be happy to regard as just inessential what
we had to omit from the account above. Let us be sure of this. First, the conditions (b
and c) of volume and variety would have to be construed in such a way that they were
satisfied by the learning of any normal adult in any society, because all such may be
deemed 'educated' for anthropological purposes. The most this 'definition' could entail

is that amount of learning which one could hardly help acquiring through childhood, and that variety (some values and practical skills as well as some factual knowledge, some knowledge of the social as well as of the natural world, etc.) which this learning could hardly fail to exhibit. So, more stringent requirements, conveyed by time-honoured phrases like 'depth and breadth of knowledge', 'a balanced curriculum' and 'education of the whole person', would be incidental, extra-conceptual – despite being centrally intended in some uses of 'education'! Similarly, the reference in this 'concept' to tradition, whether as deposit (f) or as process (g), could certainly not be of the strong kind that summons up a picture of curricula, teachers and schools, still less any particular conception of the business of these. For such invocations, too, are confined to some among our uses of 'education'. Third, our uses of 'education' divide into committed or normative uses, which carry value judgements, and 'cool' or descriptive uses, which, so to speak, merely note value judgements. These opposed stances are not really reducible to some broader category or definition that can span both. Hence there is the vagueness (approaching vacuity) acknowledged above in the pair (d) and (e).

In sum, the various uses of 'education' are not mere homonyms but their differences are as much a part of the life of the term as their similarities. So, if it is definitions we seek then each category of use will require its own. Now, however, we may suspect that such multiple definitions would then fit together in some way to make a larger whole. Indeed, if we are to speak at all of a unitary concept of education it will *have* to be as of something revealed and articulated in the main uses of 'education' *collectively*, differences included. And if this concept is to have much coherence then the uses must diverge more systematically than randomly, must complement each other and, we might say, constitute together some approximation of an ordered set. Those marshalling and binding roles, which we earlier inclined to ascribe to these uses, would then be greatly facilitated. The hunch we shall pursue is that there *is* such a non-definitionally unitary and coherent concept of education.

CORRELATIVITIES

The first step is to notice more formally that we are not here faced with endlessly many distinctions but with just a few, which, by cutting across and compounding each other, generate all the main uses of 'education' and its cognates. There are, I suggest, three such seminal distinctions. First, 'education' as a *formal* enterprise (F) is to be distinguished from 'education' in the much *wider* sense (W). Second, in the case of each of these senses a further distinction may be drawn between *normative* (N) and *merely descriptive* (D) modes of it. Third, there then further applies to all four of the resultant categories a scale which runs from the very *open* (nominal, general; O) at one end, to the very *loaded* (substantive, specific; L) at the other. In the process this scale passes from standard usage, through semi-standard perhaps, to the stipulative and theoretical and, by the same token, from the widely assumed to the hotly contested – to the point, indeed, at which there are many *competing* uses, about equally but differently loaded.

So each concrete use of 'education' is either formal or wide in sense, is either normative or descriptive, and is loaded in one of many possible degrees and ways. (We shall

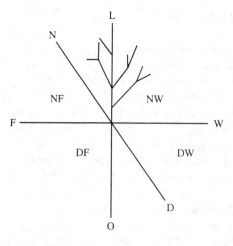

Figure 1.1

indicate later that there are other important words which also exhibit this triple pattern.) Some examples may help here. The use of 'education' to mean 'initiation into the best that has been thought and written', or the competing 'promotion of interest-based learning', would be at once formal, (usually) normative, and loaded beyond standard levels. On the other hand, the anthropologist looking into some previously unstudied society may stand ready with both the formal and the wide senses of 'education', each to be employed in a noncommital, descriptive way and each heuristically kept as skeletal as possible. Again, in deeming the illiterate peasant to be 'uneducated' we invoke something formal; we usually mean to convey, normatively, that she has 'missed out' on this; and in specifying literacy and suchlike we load it, more than when we play the anthropologist, but still lightly, standardly and much less than when we are working up our personal statements about education.

There is a further distinction to mention, between 'education' as a practice and 'education' as the second-order study of that practice. It does not, however, have the compounding effect of the first three distinctions. 'Education' as the name of a practice breaks down in the three criss-crossing ways we have noticed, but 'education' as the name of a branch of study does not – its organization into sub-branches follows different distinctions. (This fourth distinction has its own suggestiveness, however, as we shall mention in Chapter 3.)

Our multiple uses of 'education' begin to look like a network. What would now considerably enhance this impression is if we could go on to show, in respect of each of the three controlling distinctions, that its two or more members were not only all useful in their own rights but the necessary complements of each other, i.e. that they were *logically correlative* (akin to 'northerner/southerner' rather than to 'Scottish/English'). Do the formal and the wide senses, the normative and descriptive uses, and the different levels of openness and loadedness, coexist symbiotically in three such equilibria of meaning, each member referring implicitly to its partner or partners? It seems likely that they do and this is a hunch that, in the next chapter, we will attempt progressively to confirm for each distinction in turn. Before that, however, there is a comparison to be made with a different approach to analysis.

A QUESTION OF STRATEGY

We are engaged, recall, on the linguistic analysis of 'education' (and cognates) with a view to laying bare the most general contours of our thought and enquiry in this area. We seem now to have developed a definite strategy for this. It is one which inhibits us from letting some uses of 'education' drop prematurely from consideration, and which commits us to giving them all a good run. Beyond that, it inclines us to look for relationships between them which are not just common threads or similarities, but are ways in which they complement and feed off each other by virtue of their differences. What we are to suppose is that it is precisely in these relationships that the concept of education lives – and empowers and structures our thinking.

This strategy has not been widely adopted by analytic philosophers. Faced with a multi-meaning term like 'education', the tendency has been rather to anticipate that *one* among the meanings would turn out to be 'the' meaning, presupposed by all the others while itself standing by itself. They would hope then to concentrate pretty exclusively on this 'primary' ('paradigmatic', 'central') meaning in their analyses and to consign to footnotes the 'secondary' ('extended', 'derivative', 'parasitic') ones. The model which helps to explain this, and which I think they often have in mind,[8] is the relationship between literal and figurative uses of a word at its most straightforward. 'Sunny' said of a smile or a disposition, 'punishment' to describe what boxers hand out in the ring, 'law' in 'law of the jungle', 'deep' as a measure of trouble – these are all extended uses of terms. To understand them, at any rate fully, one needs to know the original literal uses of these terms (as well as some of those other terms that could provide a literal translation) – but not, it would seem, vice versa. 'Sunny disposition' is elucidated by reference to sunny skies and climates (as well as to ideas like cheerfulness and optimism), but skies and climates do not in turn require a reference to dispositions. The uses of 'education', it was hoped, would also break down in this way, leaving just one aboriginal category of use for the analyst's focus.

This approach shares with our own strategy an expectation of some order and relationship among the uses. But where it would anticipate an order based on the primacy of one use, we anticipate one based on the equilibrium of many uses. It would be content with dependence; we look out for interdependence. This is to make it clear, however, that our strategy is the more open in its sweep: it is better designed to catch *also* any one-way dependencies that happen to be around, than is the other to notice two-way ones. That would seem a good reason for preferring it.

Certainly we should not be seduced by any proposed analogy with the logic of metaphor. In the first place, and to digress a little, metaphor is not as simple a matter as was suggested above. In particular, its dependence on the literal is not its whole story. Consider the series 'deep lake', 'deep voice', 'deep remark', 'deep trouble'.[9] The first alone is fully literal. The rest are metaphorical uses, and to my ear progressively more so. But note that these metaphors are all of the well-established (though still faintly alive) variety as opposed to once-off poetic contrivances. Like thousands of other metaphors they are bits of English usage. As such, each of these 'extensions' has a certain unfrilly solidity of its own. Note, further, that not all metaphors can be 'cashed in'. In our series, 'deep voice' has no equivalent which is more literal, and perpendicular metaphors generally – such as high, low, soaring, etc. – are quite indispensable to our descriptions of sound and music, and indeed to our way of perceiving these.[10] Such necessary metaphors are not to be dismissed as epiphenomena. Note, finally, that the metaphors in our series may well have some backwash effect on the literal original, such that the echoes between metaphors and original reverberate in both directions. In general 'the deep' easily impresses (moves, troubles, unnerves): both literal depths (wells, seas, holes, valleys, etc.) and metaphorical depths (notes, truths, sorrows, attachments, etc.). It seems reasonable to suppose that the aesthetic impact of literal uses receives a confirmation and a reinforcement from the well-established coexistence of the metaphorical uses.[11] All in all, then, the undoubted extendedness of metaphorical uses would seem an insufficient reason for generally ignoring them in linguistic analysis.

In the second place, none of those uses of 'education' of which we have been reminding ourselves actually is metaphorical, daring or otherwise fanciful. They are all equally literal. Thus they *all* contrast with some uses that are fanciful, with 'well-educated Virginia creeper' for instance, or 'educated left foot', or, perhaps, 'educated palate'. Again, to speak of a romance as 'an education' is (often rueful) hyperbole. However remarkable, it could hardly constitute a whole education. By contrast, the more modest claim that it was (in the wide sense) 'educational', or 'a part of one's education', can be understood as quite literal. There would seem to be no ground, then, for a presumption that some one use of 'education' will emerge as 'the' use and, so, every reason for us to prefer our own more open strategy.[12]

We should mention, however, another *prima facie* possibility. Wittgenstein, in his later philosophy, likens our language as a whole to 'an ancient city: a maze of little streets and squares, of old and new houses, and of houses with additions from various periods; and this surrounded by a multitude of new boroughs with straight regular streets and uniform houses'.[13] He sees the variation in the uses of individual terms, such as 'game', as usually a similarly unsystematic business – like (a famous image) the patterns of resemblance in a large family.[14] This view runs directly contrary, of course, to the idea of a single 'primary' use grounding all the other uses of a term, which is ironic considering the respect for Wittgenstein in the analytic tradition. Might the uses of 'education' line up with this model, be so subtle in their variations as always to exceed the philosopher's ability to map them adequately, so that the mature language user's 'tacit knowledge' here could never be made fully explicit? It is a seductive supposition, but it too can be tested by our open strategy and we shall find that the evidence stacks up against it and for an articulable 'geometry' of those variations.[15]

THREE MAXIMS FOR LINGUISTIC ANALYSTS

We set out from the observation that the purpose of linguistic analysis is to discover embedded patterns in our own thought and enquiry regarding a matter like education. We can conclude with three maxims that should increase the scope and the power of our discoveries. These can be our antidotes to tendencies that have enfeebled the analytic tradition (from which, however, we shall be salvaging what we can).

1   *Treat different uses of a term as equal in status unless they are clearly shown to be unequal.* This is an expression of the point of strategy that we have just discussed. Its fruitfulness remains to be seen in the analyses of the following chapters.

2   *Respect the virtuosity of language in the adaptability of many terms to denomina-
tional and individual points of view.* The term 'education' is a case in point. Hence,
among our three seminal distinctions, there is the one based on a use's degree of
openness/loadedness. The meaning as well as the value of this maxim will become
clearer in our main discussion of that distinction in the next chapter.

3   *Treat usages, and the habits of thought and enquiry they embody, as subject to
criticism*; as subject, that is, not only to change – though many analysts have in
practice ignored even that much – but to deliberately pursued change, as to
deliberate endorsement. A language may embody the wisdom of a culture, but the
language, the wisdom and the culture are none of them beyond criticism, nor, as
Orwell reminds us, beyond the need of critical protection. So, for example, we shall
soon come upon a challenge to the whole business of 'education-speak' and, with
it, of education-mindedness and education.

NOTES

1.   *Philosophical Investigations*, para. 242.
2.   A more aggressive statement of this point: 'Language is not a neutral medium that passes
     freely and easily into the private property of the speaker's intentions; it is populated – over-
     populated – with the intentions of others. Expropriating it, forcing it to submit to one's own
     intentions and accents, is a difficult and complicated process' (M. Bakhtin, *The Dialogic
     Imagination*; cited in Giroux, 1986). But note that this omits to mention that the process
     in question will also be one of *self*-criticism!
3.   See, for instance, Rajchman and West (1985).
4.   Page 1324 of the Penguin translation.
5.   It may – and in some of these cases does – also turn on our capacity to envisage radically
     alternative kinds of *formal* education, e.g. Illich's 'learning-webs'.
6.   Compare Raymond Williams, in his justly regarded *Keywords*, on the different meanings
     of 'culture': 'Faced by this complex and still active history of the word, it is easy to react
     by selecting one "true" or "proper" or "scientific" sense and dismissing other senses as loose
     or confused. . . . It is clear that, within a discipline, conceptual usage has to be clarified.
     But in general it is the range and overlap of meanings that is significant. The complex of
     senses indicates a complex argument about the relations between general human develop-
     ment and a particular way of life, and between both and the works and practices of art and
     intelligence. Within this complex argument there are fundamentally opposed as well as effec-
     tively overlapping positions; there are also, understandably, many unresolved questions and
     confused answers. But these arguments and questions cannot be resolved by reducing the
     complexity of actual usage. . . . The complexity . . . is not finally in the word but in the
     problems which its variations of use significantly indicate' (Williams, 1976, pp. 80–1).
7.   Actually, figurative uses aside, there is one maverick in relation to most of these conditions,
     i.e. the use of 'education' to name a particular branch of study – that 'education' which is
     shorthand for 'the study of education'.
8.   It is explicitly invoked in Wilson (1981, pp. 8–9).
9.   To borrow and adapt an example from Wittgenstein's *Blue and Brown Books*.
10. They are indispensable at least in the sense that they are the only tools for the job that we
     have actually developed. Whether we might have developed different linguistic conventions
     (e.g. a colour-coding of pitch) is another question.
11. Similarly, 'sunny smile (temper, mood, etc.)' reverberates back on 'sunny day', I suspect.
     Note, too, that there can be reciprocity between metaphors, e.g. sunny smile, smiling
     heavens.
12. The blinkering effect of that presumption has, in fact, gone beyond a failure to look out

for balances and correlativities among available uses. In their impatience to get to their favoured 'primary' use analysts have skimped even their preliminary *listings* of 'secondary' uses. Thus Wilson (1979), in a whole book devoted to the analysis of 'education', takes two very hurried pages (17–18) to select his 'primary' sense and, inadequately, to list the others. R. S. Peters is another for whom the range of uses has been an invitation to spot the 'primary' or the 'interesting' one (e.g. Peters, 1966, Chapter 1). Generally, analysts have tended to overlook or misconceive the wide sense of 'education', to be perfunctory in their acknowledgement (or, in some cases, denial) of the normative/descriptive distinction, and, at any rate until pressure from critics of analysis forced it upon them, to neglect the phenomenon of different degrees of loading. One paradoxical result of this has been some lack of definition in the favoured use. But there has been enough definition for some competition to emerge for the title of 'primary use', (in particular between normative and descriptive claimants), which from our broader point of view is just what we should have expected!

13. *Philosophical Investigations*, para. 18.
14. *Ibid.*, para. 66ff.
15. I do not suppose, however, that all multi-meaning terms are similarly geometric in their deep structures. Thus 'culture' in Williams's account of it (see note 6) seems closer to Wittgenstein's model, though with an extra dash of conflict. And that, as much as Williams's particular interests, may suggest his more historical approach to analysis in this case. (Williams is rightly conscious, though, of the distinction between historical precursors of, and historical residues in, a meaning.)

Chapter 2

The Geometry of 'Education'

The complexity . . . is not finally in the word but in the problems which its variations of use significantly indicate.

> (Raymond Williams, *Keywords*, on the word 'culture')

What Williams says here of 'culture' is also true of 'education': its complexity is finally in such 'real-life' great issues as its aims, design, resourcing and feasibility, but the complexity in the word may be a significant way into such issues. Thus, in the first part of this chapter some persevering donkey-work on the pair of uses, '(formal) education' and 'education (in the widest sense)', will expose some of education's deep structures – and possible faultlines.

FORMAL AND WIDE

The formal sense of education

We encounter this sense widely: in everyday conversations about 'the state of education' and 'the educational system'; in references to certain professions and offices like 'educator', 'educationist' or 'the Ministry of Education'; when in a curriculum vitae we find it written that the subject 'received his education at schools x and y, and university z'; in assumptions about graduates being 'highly educated' and illiterate people being 'uneducated', and so on. All these cases involve our practice of unqualifiedly representing as 'education' that which, at other times, we qualify as 'formal education' and think of as but a part of education.

At its most conventional and common this '(formal) education' use is to be elucidated, as a little reflection on examples like the above would confirm, by reference to two familiar sets of institutions:

- schools and like establishments;
- the disciplines 'of the book', history, literature, science, mathematics, design, etc. – in general those areas of study for which literacy is a more or less indispensable condition of progress.[1]

These two are themselves related. At any rate, it is obvious that schools are to be identified in some reference to book learning. That is how we would distinguish them from some other institutions that are also concerned with teaching and learning, like driving schools, or that are also especially for the young, like playgroups and youth clubs. True, we sometimes throw open the question of curriculum, while continuing to take schools as given. What, we ask, should schools really be teaching? But, usually, we mean only what else should they teach *besides* letters (manual skills, political education, personal and social development, etc.) When the attack becomes more radical than this it tends quickly to engulf the idea of school as well.

The reference to 'letters' seems indispensable then. It might seem, however, that 'school' could be bypassed as a non-essential middleman. For don't we deem to be educated in this formal sense those who have acquired enough knowledge in these disciplines otherwise than at school, from parents perhaps, or by their own efforts? In fact, this would simplify excessively. First, in regard even to those cases, this use of 'education' implies more than a learning content. By the very nature of that content it also implies a more or less structured learning process. Thus parents deemed to be educating their children at home are assumed to be replicating in their home lives some of the typical features of a school. Do they not guide, monitor, even plan, their children's learning, engage in deliberate teaching, set times aside for study, accumulate appropriate books and other learning-aids, or, at any rate, do some of these and similar things? Even the 'self-educated' are thought of as having had to 'school' or discipline themselves to it in these kinds of way. So when there is not school itself, there is a *schooling* that resembles the learning process of school in some significant respects (while, of course, differing in others). Second, to be deemed 'educated' in this formal sense is to be judged to have come up to some *standards* in one's learning. By what standards, then, do we judge the self-educated and the home-educated? Is it not probable that here too a sidelong glance is being cast at school? Schools are too prominent in our consciousness to be omitted from an elucidation of our conventional '(formal) education'. A biped it remains, identified by reference both to a certain content (letters, etc.) and to a certain agency and process (school), for even when it stands on just one leg the other is contributing to its balance.

The foregoing analysis, like the examples from which we set out, was of '(formal) education' at one level of loading. There are also both more open and more loaded uses of it. On the one hand, we sometimes wire into the word extra conditions; for example, an exclusion of indoctrination or (more controversially) a limitation to interest-based learning. This we are particularly liable to do in discussing educational aims and values. On the other hand, there is a thin and open use of it to mean something like 'any kind of more or less sustained and systematic induction into some substantial proportion of whatever it is that is, or that is deemed to be, essential to know'. We may fall back on this in anthropological contexts, e.g. so as to include the organized oral transmission of the Koran and its world-view in traditional Muslim societies, and, again, when it is a question with reference to our own kind of society of accommodating proposals, like Ivan Illich's 'learning webs',[2] that run counter to the norm of 'schooling in letters'. We shall not forget these other variants of '(formal) education'. But it is right to pay special heed to the most conventional one, just because it is the most conventional: much the most frequently employed by us, best befitting everyday purposes in our kind of society, and expressing just about the extent of public consensus in this area, i.e. of what most of us take for granted most of the time.

Education in the widest sense

The contrasting 'education (in the widest sense)' we have already met in connection with the wisdom of Tolstoy's peasant, in the claim (intelligible, even if thought extravagant) that school is an interruption in a child's education, and in the idea that education should be lifelong (the point of which is not, or not principally, that people should still be taking degrees in their eighties). It is also to be found consorting with travel that broadens the mind, relationships that promote maturity, and experiences that involve significant discovery in respect of one's powers or one's limitations. It is the sense invoked in the familiar assertion that parents are the first and the chief educators of their children, for usually something wider and deeper is intended by this than that they instruct in the alphabet and help with homework!

'Development', 'upbringing' and 'socialization' are close relatives of this 'education (in the widest sense)'. At any rate some uses of these terms are. 'Growing up' is another member of the family, especially that use of it which occurs when 'he never really grew up' is remarked of a well-formed adult of the species. And of course 'learning' relates as intimately to this as to other uses of 'education'. None of these is actually synonymous with 'education (in the widest sense)'.[3] But we can play around with combinations of them and come up with quite reasonable definitions of it, as in, for instance:

> the whole sum of that *learning* of a person, and what promotes or has promoted it, which makes for (or, which is considered to make for) his becoming, or being, a *developed* human being;

or, more briefly:

> the sum of that *learning* that contributes to development.

But now we have to note that in this case there is something not altogether appropriate about a definition – at any rate an unaccompanied, bare definition. For education in the widest sense, though it includes formal education where it exists, is precisely *not* focused and landscaped as regards that in which it greatly exceeds formal education. Thus it does not have points of reference as convenient as the two kinds of institution by which we earlier pinned down '(formal) education'. To convey its flavour we should expect to have to resort to some more jagged and discursive account. So we might append to our earlier definition some lengthy gloss like the following:

> It embraces much of what is learnt outside and in no reference to classroom and school – as well as much of what is learnt inside these or in some reference to them; much of what is 'picked up' as well as of what is formally studied; a great deal of what is 'caught' as well as of what is taught; much that is only very broadly cognitive as well as much that is more narrowly so; a lot that is specialized and idiosyncratic as well as a lot that is common; and so on.

Interdependence of the two senses

It is significant that this gloss proceeds in constant reference to *formal* education, that it structures itself on its 'rival's' characteristic features: the classroom, study, teaching, the cognitive, the standardized. It comes quite naturally to us thus to describe education in the widest sense *in its relation to formal education*, as formal education along with its hinterland or, perhaps better, the iceberg of which formal education is only the most visible tip. This association accords with many, if not most, of those contexts in which we might put 'education (in the wide sense)' to work, e.g. when challenging the commitments of our own kind of society to schooling and to letters (do these help or hinder an education for life?); when issuing correctives to these commitments (there is more to maturity and competence, and so to education, than can be learnt from books or measured in examinations); and in bridging the gap between them and our concern with processes marked by wider and more primitive terms like 'growing up' (thus, in proposing to conceive of formal education itself in developmental or 'growth' terms and, on the other hand, when we scrutinize child-rearing practices for their effects on school performance).

It should now be getting clearer that these distinct uses of 'education' reinforce each other. Let us view the matter from each side in turn.

(1) Our formal use is at least significantly coloured by our possession of the widest-sense use. The effect of that possession, stated broadly, is to inhibit a tendency to see formal education as standing on its own and to provoke or confirm in us a view of it as having to fit in with, and to leaven, more general processes of nurture and development. But since to conceive what we are about with schools and curricula as a leaven seems already implicit in calling it '(formal) *education*', we can say that 'education (in the widest sense)', by acting as a bridge here, *facilitates the sense* of '(formal) education'.

This, of course, is still less than to say that it is essential to that sense. Might we not have managed to make the required connections directly, without this 'bridge'? Perhaps so, but it is at any rate difficult to imagine ourselves not devising this means of smoothing our way. Imagine a society which has hitherto employed formal instruction only with regard to very specific skills like cooking, weaving and spearmanship. Suppose it to be just now reorientating its training institutions towards much more general 'life goals' – creating thus for the first time a system of formal *education* for itself (or for some elite part of itself). Suppose, further, that it decides to mark the new purpose of these institutions by a new term (or a new use of an old term), '*x*'. Isn't it difficult now not to suppose that it will soon be observed, if indeed it is not at once observed, that if that is what '*x*' means then a great deal of '*x*' and '*x*-ing' goes on, and always has gone on, outside these new-fangled institutions?

At bottom the point is this: to conceive of a system of instruction in the arts of living in general is correlatively to conceive of a *learning* for life, a concept which is inherently applicable beyond the confines of formal teaching institutions, and one which it is difficult to envisage not being so applied once it has been conceived. Furthermore, anything that could be inhibiting this wider application of the learning-for-life concept would also be endangering at its birth the other new concept of an instruction-for-life. The formal use of 'education' stands in some need, then, of the 'widest sense' use. At the least it would seem to require the *admissibility* of that use.

(2) Contrariwise, we may doubt that the 'widest sense' use would arise at all without

the stimulus of the formal use. How is it to emerge from the crowd of related concepts like 'development', 'nurture', 'upbringing', 'knowledge', and so forth? It is a reasonable speculation that the high visibility of schooling, or something like schooling, is a normal condition of this.[4] But wouldn't education in the widest sense be going on, in its informal way, in a society which lacked formal instruction on a front broad enough to count as formal education? We perhaps could say this of it, but the issue of course is what its members could say of themselves. And it is not implausible to suggest that they could *not* so describe themselves – that they would lack terms in their language that we could comfortably translate as 'education' (just as we might legitimately wonder if the 'cave artists' thought of themselves as artists and of their paintings as works of art, assuming them to have lacked the institutional trappings with which we surround those concepts).[5]

What, it might then be asked, would entitle us to describe their activities in a term they could not use of themselves? This challenge may seem strange but is in fact perfectly fair. Much as the literary interpreter must start from the text itself, so the proper description of human activities must lean on the agents' own view of what they are doing – aerobics as opposed to waving, say – since this at least partly constitutes what they are doing. However, we can stay on the right side of this principle (an important one, which we shall meet again) and still defend a diffident use of our term with regard to a people who were not education-minded, on the basis that they would surely have all the ingredients of a concept of education, though without bringing them together. For on the one hand they would have concepts of development and maturity, of upbringing and nurture, and on the other hand concepts of knowledge, skill, teaching and learning. To deny them a concept of education is only to deny that they entertain certain interplays between those two groups of concepts (such as the one we lately retraced in defining education in the widest sense in terms of learning and development combined). They reserve 'knowledge', 'skill', 'teaching' and 'learning' for highly specific achievements and processes, and they are not led to make our sharpish discriminations between biological and cultural development and between physical, emotional and cognitive types of nurture. It remains, however, that they do have all the concepts from the interplay of which we derive our concept and our uses of 'education'.[6] This basic similarity of their way of life to ours might excuse our temerity in extending this one use of our term to them; we would, after all, be starting out from their own perceptions of what they were about. So the inclination to believe that pretty well any human society can be said to engage in education, that education is a transcultural universal, seems just about compatible with the claim that 'education (in the widest sense)' needs '(formal) education' to call it forth originally.

Questions

'Education (in the widest sense)' is called forth, we have argued, to be the bridge between '(formal) education' and more primitive and general notions like 'maturing' and 'rearing'. In the commerce that it facilitates we can now more deliberately notice two basic lines of challenge and enquiry, each of which comes in different weights corresponding to differently loaded levels of '(formal) education'. One – *the relevance question* – addresses the value and role of book learning in general human development (and may proceed in part through some enlargement of this latter notion). If we assume that it has some substantial role, as the conventional level of '(formal) education' encourages us to assume, then the challenge is limited to seeking some more just and precise view of what that role is and what it entails for how we go about initiating pupils into this knowledge. It might entail, perhaps, more integration of the curriculum, or a more practical approach to literacy and numeracy or – as was at one stage proposed for the new English and Welsh National Curriculum – 'profile components' in science in action and in the communication of science. But, standing back from the commitments expressed in that conventional version of '(formal) education', we might more aggressively enquire whether book learning has *any* role in a proper human development that is significant enough to warrant its usual central place in formal education, and whether there might not be a very different kind of curriculum with a much better claim to relevance.

Second, and related to the first, there is *the school question*, i.e. enquiry and query regarding the importance and role of the school among nurturing agencies generally – what can or should be expected of the school in relation to what can or should be expected of the family, the peer group, the workplace, the media, etc. (One is tempted to speak here of the rational division and coordination of educational labour. But this would mislead by suggesting that the educational functions of agencies other than school would lend themselves to precise definition and prescription, which would be at odds with their essentially informal character.) This issue too has its more aggressive formulations, as the deschoolers in particular have shown us. We might want to ask whether schools make, or could make, *any* contribution to growing up that is at all commensurate with their protractedly compulsory monopoly of the young person's time, and what radically alternative arrangements for formal education might better exploit and cohere with the educational possibilities of more informal agencies.

Some of our later enquiries will relate to these questions – though full answers to them are beyond our scope because of the amount and variety of evidence that they involve. The point here, however, is that our notion of education in the widest sense boosts their legitimacy as fundamental lines of enquiry. That our arrangements for schooling the young in their letters (or any alternatives we might come up with) have to be 'relevant', have 'life' in view, be justifiable by reference to some 'wide scheme of things' – this is already implicit in their claim to constitute a formal education. But it is a good deal more explicit in a claim to contribute seriously to education in its widest sense.[7]

(Of course, notions like 'relevance' and 'for life' need careful handling. Three clarifications can be given. (a) Everything depends on the view of human development and the 'wider scheme of things' that is favoured. Only with a rather special view of these (which we shall consider in a later chapter) could 'relevance' be interpreted in purely, or even primarily, economic and job-related terms. A broader viewpoint – a reaction, perhaps, to that one – would propose the ideal that all should be rendered fully able to participate politically, culturally and interpersonally, as well as economically. But now this might be thought to miss out rather on the individual, and to over-identify 'the person' with 'the participant'. One might want to appeal to the Socratic, stoic and Christian ideal of the care of the soul. And so on. The point is that although (both) our uses of 'education' imply relevance to a wider scheme of things, they do not, except in more loaded cases, imply any particular scheme. (b) The insistence on relevance does not mean that formal education has to be viewed as social 'reproduction', training people to 'fit in'. It is clearly just as open to the 'reconstructionist' ideal of a critical, creative and ameliorative kind of participation, or, for that matter, to some more revolutionary ideal. (c) 'Relevant to' does not mean the same as 'instrumental to'. So the idea that intrinsically worthwhile activities are peculiarly apt candidates for curriculum is not excluded. These might be thought of as basic, perhaps transforming, *constituents* of the good life – as such more directly 'relevant' than any mere means towards this life.)

There is a yet more radical line of enquiry that is also kept open by 'education (in the widest sense)'. Above, that notion provoked our historical and anthropological imagination into envisaging a society that did not think at all in educational terms but stopped at various more logically elemental concepts. From there it is a short step to asking whether our own 'education-mindedness' is benefit or bane to us, whether we should not recross the bridge of education in the widest sense to our more elemental concepts and blow the bridge up as we go. This challenge, laid down in particular by the second wave of the deschooling literature, is to the assumption, shared by all sides in the usual debates, that there is at any rate *some* form under which education is worth pursuing as a matter of conscious, deliberate policy. It is a fundamental philosophical challenge, which we shall take up seriously in Chapter 7.

NORMATIVE AND DESCRIPTIVE

In discussing the second and third of our seminal distinctions among uses of 'education', we shall continue our policy of attending to the connectedness of what is distinguished, to bring out the fundamental ways in which these distinctions structure our thinking. Broadly, what we shall find is that, as the dialectic between the formal and the wide senses of 'education' foreshadows the scope of educational enquiry, so these two dialectics foreshadow much of its complexity, its evolution of special evaluation and 'scientific' discourses and its ideological pluralism, for instance. In this section we tackle the normative/descriptive pair.

The distinction between uses that carry a positive value charge and those that do not, the committed or normative and the noncommittal or purely descriptive, is not unique to 'education' and its cognates. Indeed, the name of any well-marked practice or product in which there is a question of coming up to recognized standards has its normative, as well as its merely descriptive, uses. Thus: 'Now *that* is what I call an omelette (darning, a high jump, a stamp collection, etc.).'. Or Dan Maskell, commenting at a Wimbledon final, when the match is levelled at the end of the second set: 'We have a final!' But such normative usage seems to be an especially established feature of the lives of some terms, probably because of a combination of importance and difficulty reckoned to attach to the practices or products they name. Thus it is *very often* the case that to call something 'a work of art' is to praise it (though it remains that sometimes it is only to identify the kind of thing it purports to be). 'Literature' and 'democracy', – and 'education' – are further examples of terms often and very naturally normative.

This modest distinction is not to be confused with the wholesale and drastic fact/value distinction that Hume and Moore, between them, bequeathed to analytic philosophy. For one thing, it envisages not two kinds of word but two kinds of use of the same word. More significantly, it envisages not a gulf and two 'universes' of discourse, but, as we shall presently see, a strict logical symbiosis within a single 'universe' of discourse. Last but not least, it is clear and undeniable where the fact/value distinction is unclear and eminently deniable! (A properly nuanced critique of the conventional distinction will not deny that there are some distinctions in this general area. Rather, it will criticize the usual conflation of different distinctions and the usual assumption that distinction implies the absence of logical connection.[8])

The descriptive use and evaluation

In their purely descriptive uses 'education', 'educated', 'educational', etc. pick out certain systems, practices, institutions, persons, objects – and aims, ideals and theories – but without endorsing them. There is no implication that what they pick out is good, right, effective or otherwise commendable, though there remains the presumption that it is, or was, valued by someone. Thus we can neutrally refer to something as 'a system of education', implying not that it actually delivers 'a true education', but only that it purports to deliver this, and is valued as delivering this by some of those involved with it. Similarly, we can introduce someone as an educator, catalogue a toy as educational and address a letter to Anytown College of Further Education, and thereby cast them in worthy roles but not commit ourselves on how well they fill those roles. Note, also, that our identifications here usually derive from the ways in which the things in question identify themselves. The system, college, toy or person advertises itself as educational, and we follow suit. We accept the self-identification while declining any self-endorsement. In general, then, the point of view which the descriptive use mainly expresses and facilitates is that of *the detached observer of what already exists and already identifies itself as educational.*[9]

So far, so fairly commonplace. But we must not underestimate the range and power of this point of view. Usually its sustained presence in the human sciences and its much more casual employment in everyday referencing – making introductions, giving directions, etc. – will be noted. But its indispensability for the particularly basic business of *evaluation* has been rather overlooked. Yet this is really quite clear. Even if we speak frankly and definitely of 'good education' or 'bad education', it is the adjectives that carry the evaluation while 'education' identifies its subject quite noncommittally – otherwise 'good' would be redundant and 'bad' contradictory. Although this 'education' has evaluation in mind, it is itself noncommittally second hand. It marks the spot, as it were, where the evaluated may speak and the evidence be considered before judgement is passed, and where the professional evaluator could file the report that seeks to make judgement easier for others while making none itself.[10]

We should distinguish here *two levels of detachment and, so, of evaluation* according to whether what one is being for the moment noncommittal about is only the *efficacy of instruments*, the success of systems, practices, institutions, persons, objects and proposals at realizing the educational conception that fires them, or, on the other hand, extends also to the *validity of the conception*. Societies in which detachment of the second degree was never practised would be ones with a thoroughgoing consensus on educational values. It is likely that this would be uncritical, and that they would be largely unaware of alternative conceptions of education and have little contact with dissimilar societies. But even in such closed societies there would be room for doubt and debate with regard to the effectiveness of particular institutions, practices, teachers, etc., and hence employment for a neutral use of 'education' and cognates with regard to these instruments, whether in their evaluation or in referring casually to them. In pluralist and open societies, however, the more radical descriptivism will be forced upon thoughtful people. They will resort to it in referring to other and different societies (in whose views and practices they will tend to be interested) and to rival or alternative views in their own societies. They will use it for an 'objectification' of the views to which they themselves incline or are committed, a condition of keeping these inclinations and commitments critical. Even where the immediate reference is to some instrument of education, their detachment may embrace its aims as well as its efficacy. Unawed and casually, for example, they will identify X as a place of education without committing themselves to its conception of education (which they may not even know). And the evaluation of instruments in this open society will have a way of expanding to encompass aims. A school inspection or self-evaluation exercise, for example, will typically include some objectification and appraisal of the school's 'philosophy' and not simply take this as read. In sum, the merely descriptive uses of 'education', 'educational', 'educator', etc. in open societies can nobly serve that critical temper in which values as well as instruments, and the relationships between values and instruments, are laid open to regular scrutiny.

The normative use: two contexts

Used descriptively, 'education' leaves it open whether the education referred to is any good. Used normatively, however, 'education' might be said to mean 'good education'. We reach for the former, we have seen, mostly in reference to what already both exists and identifies itself as educational. The two contexts in which we tend rather towards the latter are those in which one or other of those conditions is missing. The first of these is where we wish to commend something (like romance or travel) that does not already identify itself as educational by relating it to education in the widest sense. 'Travel can be an education' is rather more natural than 'travel can be a good education'.[11] By contrast, where travel is institutionalized as education, as in the education tour, we quite naturally make adjectives like 'good' and 'bad' do the evaluative work. 'A good education tour' sounds fine.

The second, and very significant, kind of context is where one thinks and speaks, no longer as an observer or evaluator, but as in some way an *agent* of education. Used as a term of practical reason, a tool for the shaping and focusing of effort and enterprise, the name of something to be done, 'education' is naturally a charged word. It is enough for the school prospectus to proclaim as its overriding aim 'the education' – it is unnecessary to say 'the good education' – of its pupils. Parents select from the range of *outside* agencies those that will provide 'a good education' for their children, but as educators themselves they promote (simply) 'the education' of their children. Let us pause over the important case of the *utopian dream-plan*. In evaluating educational instruments and pronouncing them 'good', 'bad', etc., one is employing some set of norms. If one moves to reflection on these norms, precisely as norms, i.e. as what practice must measure up to, one speaks of education as it *ought* to be, implying a possible contrast with education as it is. But that contrast fades from the mind if one now goes on to think of the norms rather as *aims*, to see or to imagine oneself as plotting the broad outlines of the enterprise *de nouveau*. Then one will speak naturally rather of what ('real') education *is* and *involves*. Thus philosophers express their deliberated 'visions' of education in the indicative mood: education *'is* "conscientization" ', *'is* the development in depth and breadth of a caring understanding', *'is* interest-based learning', *'is* . . .'.

Interdependence

(1) It seems clear that 'education' considered as something valuable is in some way prior to 'education' as neutral. To apply it neutrally is still to invoke the *idea* of something worthwhile: to imply that this thing identifies itself as worthwhile, is believed or is supposed to be worthwhile, occupies the social space reserved for a particular worthwhile thing, offers, if not the reality, at least the illusion of this worthwhile thing, and so forth. In the light of the connection with agency and practical reason just noticed, the point might be made in the following way. 'Education' names an enterprise. Where enterprises are concerned the involvement of language is two-fold, once in conceiving, planning and executing them, then again in describing them as conceived, planned and executed. But the purely descriptive involvement has to presuppose the practical one, because without it there is simply nothing to describe. 'Education' as something to be accomplished logically precedes 'education' as something being accomplished.

Now this does not mean that one must oneself use the term normatively (and value education) in order to qualify to use it descriptively. The point so far is only that unless *some* people see a point in education, and so set about it, there will be nothing for any of us to be noncommittal about. So also with 'astrology' and 'safe-cracking'. Our ordinary descriptive uses of these terms imply that there are circles in which normative uses of them would be admissible and natural, or that there were once such circles – but it does not commit us to membership. And education, we shall see later, has its own conscientious and vigorous detractors.

On the other hand, dissociation from education is more startling than dissociation from the ranks of astrologers and safe-crackers. Why is this? And why is the normative use of 'education' so particularly ingrained and natural? Now the social standing of education is quite high, nearer to science's than to astrology's. It also seems relevant that, unlike safe-breaking, astrology, or science for that matter, it is an enterprise which casts a great many of us in the role of agents. As well as teachers, parents and sundry others regularly find themselves drawing a bead on it, and hence being locked into that practical, responsible perspective to which, as we said, normative uses naturally belong. Education, then, is both generally esteemed and widely engaged in. But it has a further involvement with value that is perhaps unique to it. As well as being an actively valued business it is, or it notably includes, the business of *communicating values*. In connection with much of what the pupil has to learn – at the least in the moral sphere, but on most accounts of education in other spheres as well – the aim is not only that she masters it but that she comes to care about it. It is this, I think, that is fundamental here, and that gives to the anti-educational position its air of paradox. What can it mean, we ask, this declaration in principle against education, assuming it is not just misanthropy or cynicism? How could one have some care for young people, believe certain things to be important in life, and not then want the young to be brought to care for those things?

Perhaps one places the freedom to choose one's values above any particular value. Then would one not have to be favourably disposed to the dissemination of at least that attitude? And how, in general, can it be supposed that people will be damaged by being helped to cherish what is worth cherishing? Now when we consider the deschooling challenge later we shall find that their objection is not, in fact, to the communication of values as such, but to a *manner* of communication that they (too hastily) assume that 'education' also implies, i.e. with overbearing systematicity and an overwhelming future orientation. But it remains that here is exposed a root of the idea of education, this connection with value communication, which goes some way to explaining its hold on us and the corresponding strength of the term's normative use.

(2) The separate functions and the necessity of the descriptive use remain, however. Consider such basic facts about education as that it is pursued under conflicting conceptions of what it involves, that it can be botched, that it throws up screens against those not directly involved (like the famously impenetrable classroom walls), that it has to be institutionalized, to the point that even its agents find themselves constrained by 'the System'. The need for a neutral form of reference to it, for both evaluative and more casual purposes, now becomes very clear. (Its further use in a 'science' of education is another matter, to which we shall return in a later chapter.)

Furthermore, we can go on to derive this need, insofar as it relates to evaluation, from the same practical logic as underlies the normative use. We may say that the felt importance of education dictates both uses. For precisely to the extent that a continuing or recurring enterprise is important, so is it important to monitor it, to observe, describe and evaluate what is going on in its name. Just as to will the end is to will also the means, so really to will to achieve something ongoing and recurrent is to will this check on how well we are going at it. And that requires, as we saw, a purely descriptive use of the relevant term. This, then, completes our demonstration of the tie-up between these two kinds of use. The descriptive use presupposes the normative and is in turn needed as its complement.[12]

OPEN AND LOADED: CONSENSUS AND CONTEST

At least in open societies, uses of 'education' and its cognates may be distinguished according to their place on *a scale that runs from the very open (nominal, general) to the very loaded (substantive, specific)*. This applies to all the kinds of use we have been considering. Thus in dealing with '(formal) education', we have seen that its most conventional version, 'schooling in letters', is intermediate in specificity. On one side of it there is the much more open '(formal) education', taken to mean 'the sustained, systematic induction of people into some substantial proportion of whatever is deemed to be essential to know' – which can comprehend, say, the organized oral transmission of the Koran in traditional Islamic societies. On the other, i.e. the loaded, side there is that use of '(formal) education' which carries a built-in contrast with 'indoctrination'. Further out on that side are those fuller and now competing uses (about equally but differently loaded) which we recognize as summing up particular educational traditions and philosophies – as meaning, for instance, 'the systematic promotion of interest-based learning', or 'the systematic initiation into the best that has been thought and taught', or 'conscientization'. Clearly 'education (in the widest sense)' also comes in less and in more loaded forms, from the heuristically skeletal in anthropology to uses that incorporate quite particular views of the meaning of life, e.g. 'all teaching and learning as it anticipates and prepares for the Beatific Vision'. Considering uses as either *descriptive* or *normative*, each category again yields its more and its less loaded forms. A detached account of education in Mao's China may begin with an outline of what it was essentially taken to be, and thereafter use 'education' sometimes as a shorthand for just that outline, and sometimes, perhaps in the author's factual comparisons with other times and places, in a much more global way. And normative uses can be as loaded as to require, say, 'interest-based learning', or almost as open as to leave it at 'valuable learning'.[13]

Let us start out to explore the logic of the open–loaded continuum from an obvious question about loaded uses. As uses become more loaded so do they become less standard, passing through semi-standard to non-standard. More exactly, as uses are perceived as loaded and in serious competition with other loaded uses, so do they cease to be standard. But linguistic communication requires standardness of use. There is, I think, no gainsaying this simple intuition. A private language, supposing there to be such a thing, would not do for communication. *How then is communication possible in the medium of loaded uses?* It must be possible, for it actually occurs. Loadedness of use may sometimes get in the way of communication, but certainly not always and insuperably. We understand many uses of 'education' from which, because they encapsulate points of view we dislike, we would ourselves refrain; we quickly get the hang of unfamiliar ones; and we find that our own tendentious uses are usually understood. But *how* are these things possible? In particular, how do rivals know of each other that each is speaking differently of the same thing and not, cross-purpose-wise, of some quite different thing?

A useful preliminary is to remind ourselves that standardness of use is no absolute notion. Usages, like whole languages, have histories and geographies. They become standard, 'struggle' to become or to stay standard, cease to be standard, are semi-standard, are standard only within a particular area, or social class, or age group, and so on. Thus there is already plenty of relativity – if nothing else the creativity of language, embodiment and instrument of our own creativity, would require it – in the world in which we must now situate the phenomenon of loadedness. Initially this merely generalizes our problem. How can there be communication across variations in usage? But it also suggests the obvious direction of a solution. We are, in general, able to cope with difference and impermanence of usage because of a much larger measure of agreement and stability, and because our learning of language does not stop in childhood. A stock of already shared usages and an ability to pick up new ones would seem to be the two conditions for, say, reading Chaucer, or eavesdropping on computer freaks.

Let us apply this to the particular case of loadedness. First, with regard to contentious terms like 'education',

- competing uses will have some features in common.

Users tacitly know this inasmuch as they can articulate these common features in other *shared (open)* uses of the same term. So differences, however serious, will be assumed to begin only above or beyond some point of specificity. Any two competing uses will be seen as like different superstructures built on similar foundations, or paths that diverge only beyond a certain point. Second,

- this going above or beyond is itself a standard linguistic process,

though its products are not standard products. It is one of language's built-in aids to development and learning, and a powerful one. (We shall enlarge on it first, below.)

To these two points we shall eventually add two more in explaining the intelligibility of loaded uses:

- uses ordinarily carry the imprint of some competing uses;
- all uses share the intention of truth.

A standard practice

One may wish to say with Richard Peters that true education is the development in depth and breadth of a caring understanding, or with Paulo Freire that it is 'conscientization', or, perhaps, that it is the process of incorporating the individual into the life of the collective. A society might be so wedded to one of these ideals that the use of 'education' to stand for it is a standard use in the language. But in our pluralist societies each of these definitions and uses, and in general any use loaded above some rather minimal level, is liable to be controversial and to face competition from other loaded uses. This is to say that such uses will not be standard for us *considered individually*. Yet something about them is standard, and that is the *general practice* they each exemplify of letting 'education' stand for one's preferred ideals in this area whatever they are. The ideals may not be widely accepted, but using the term 'education' to cover them is. Our language itself invites this tendentiousness.

This does not mean that our loaded uses must therefore go unchallenged. But challenges should be of a particular kind. *A* disagrees radically with *B* on education. She may indeed express this by saying that what *B* favours would not deserve to be called 'education', that 'education' would be a misnomer for it, that to call it 'education' would be a misuse of the term. This is to challenge a use as part and parcel of challenging a view. It is a feature of this kind of challenge that *A* can acknowledge that, from the point of view that *B* takes, *B*'s use is fine and it is her own use that becomes suspect. Contrast this with the situation where somebody whose command of English is weak is confusing 'education' with 'emigration'. His misuses are of a quite different order: he does not succeed in saying what he himself means. To correct him is not to challenge his views but to allow him properly to express them.

This nuance could be missed. *A*, let us suppose, goes further than she did above. Now she claims that *B*'s use of 'education' is wrong *quite apart from* the issue of substance between them. *B* ought to call the policies he advocates by another name, 'indoctrination' let us say, whether or not they are defensible – clarity demands as much. But to this a quick-thinking *B* could object: 'To express myself as for indoctrination instead of education (i.e. in one fairly common sense of "education") is indeed an option for me – and with the merit of extra shock value! But to present my proposals as a view of education itself, and thus to claim for them the cachet of this term, is also legitimate. It is backed by the open use of "education" which implies nothing as definite as your sharp distinction from indoctrination and is available to a wide range of positions, mine included.' And indeed the only way for *A* to discredit *B*'s usage is to discredit his view (that, however, *would* do the trick – as it may be politically important to insist).

Yet *A*'s mistake is an interesting one. We might guess from it that she finds *B*'s view extreme and repugnant. We might wonder, too, how much experience she has had of the range of views on education. This brings us back to the point that it is pluralism that forces on us the distinction and the continuum between open and loaded uses. Granted just two conceptions of education, we would need two loaded uses to express them and an open use to subtend the debate between them. Granted many conceptions, overlapping and diverging in a variety of ways and degrees, and different debates of varying intensity and degrees of generality, we need an extended continuum of uses between open and loaded. Then exposure to these debates will lead to familiarity with many of these particular uses. More significantly, it will lead to a tacit understanding of how they operate in relation to each other, of the logic of the open–loaded continuum. That understanding (which is what we are seeking here to make explicit) is a main condition of coherent participation in the debates. And it includes some agreement to disagree and some expectation of the unexpected – an implicit awareness of the paradox that here the non-standard *is* standard.

Common ground

The last statement is true only within certain limits! We shall focus now on the understanding that competing users have that there is common ground between them, expressible in shared, open uses of 'education'. It seems clear that they must have this. Without it they could have no assurance that they are speaking of the same thing differently and not of quite different things, like education and emigration. Of course the amount of common ground will vary from one set of disputants to another. Such and such a group see themselves as sharing, say, the ideal of a liberal education (they all tend to use 'education' as shorthand for 'liberal education'). If forced to a definition they could agree that it involves the following three strands: cognitive and curriculum breadth, the pursuit of knowledge and cultural activities 'for their own sake', and antipathy to indoctrination and authoritarianism.[14] But they disagree on the *relative* importance of these three strands. This emerges as they discuss such matters as the scheduling of specialization in secondary schools, or the Technical and Vocational Education Initiative, or the kinds of choice that students should be allowed to make for themselves. Perhaps they also find that they identify with different heroes of the liberal tradition – some with Socrates, some with Plato, some with Newman. Among themselves, then, uses of 'education' that rank-ordered the three conditions mentioned, e.g. 'education' as the promotion of autonomy above all else, would be contentious, while one that implied them but in no particular order would be open. But let them then be joined by Marxists, progressives, and New Right pundits and politicians (all groups with their own internal divisions), and then by a number of the uncommitted and of those who want to rethink education from the bottom up. Now only something very much more general will count as an open use – one that begs no questions, identifies the object of their competing claims and so confirms they are competing, and permits their (perhaps limited) communication.

What content survives in this limit case, *'education' at its most open*? We should remind ourselves that there will be one variant for 'education (in the widest sense)' and another for '(formal) education', and that each of these will have both normative and descriptive modes. With that caution, and harking back to an earlier discussion, we might say that at its most open 'education (in the widest sense)' must mean something like 'some sufficiently large, varied and coherent set of "catching up" (as opposed to "forging ahead") learnings that are (thought to be) of some lasting value'. And for '(formal) education' one would add some reference to systematicity and its institutions.

There is a more dynamic way of depicting this minimal general commonality. The various loaded definitions, each with its complement of energy and fuss, are so many specific responses to one basic and enduring human situation, whose universality is guaranteed by the truistic nature of the facts that compose it. H.L.A. Hart once famously argued that legal systems in all their diversity were alike in being responses to a combination of the following broad and unavoidable facts: that human beings are vulnerable, that even the strong among them must acknowledge their vulnerability (that, as Hobbes charmingly put it, they can be killed in their sleep by a child), that they are to at least some degree altruistic, that they are limited in both understanding and determination, and that their environmental resources are limited. Legal systems are precisely those institutions and practices, or those aspects of larger institutions and practices (e.g. custom, religion), by which people express and accommodate these undeniable facts in their social existence.[15] What truisms might similarly found educational institutions, practices and concepts in all their diversity? Some that we have already met, plus some others, are:

- that we are born ignorant;
- that some forms of ignorance are known to be dangerous or otherwise disadvantageous to ourselves and to others;
- that many things can be learnt more quickly and securely from those that already know them than by independent discovery;
- that many things can be more quickly and securely taught than caught;
- that our capacity for learning is immense;
- that we care for our young;
- that we can, and indeed cannot help but, think to the future;
- that we can, and sometimes should, think to the long-term future;
- that we can, self-reflexively, conceive of our lives as wholes.

There are perhaps some others. Education, then, is either that set of ideas, practices and institutions by which a society identifies and lives just this set of basic truths, or those aspects of other sets (nurture and development, teaching and learning) by which it lives them, without isolating them.[16] This roots the minimal unity of our competing uses of 'education' in human nature and the human condition.

Uses as polemical

Our picture is as yet ahistorical and, therefore, too polite. We need now to remind ourselves that positions on education are almost always *reactions*, of some kind and in some degree, to other positions. They are protestant, or counter-reformative, or ecumenical. Understanding them more or less depends on understanding their enemies, ancient or modern – at any rate, their view of their enemies. So, 'conscientization' takes much of its shine from the contrast with 'education as banking'.[17] The 'process' model of curriculum[18] is almost unintelligible save as a reaction against a 'behavioural objectives' model, itself a product of impatience with traditional 'content'. Progressivism, from Rousseau to Plowden, indignantly promotes the child who was suppressed in classical humanism – while that tradition hits back with reactionary reassertions of the primacy of 'standards' in Black Papers and White Papers, or ironically counters by affirming at once the learner, the 'Holy Ground' of knowledge, and a subtle interplay between respect for one and respect for the other, as in the work of a Richard Peters,[19] and so on. Perhaps there could be such a thing as a view that develops independently and is then surprised to find other views trying to occupy the same ground. But the common situation, one wants to say, is that views grow up fighting for that ground and have the scars to prove it.

Perhaps this last point overdoes the 'battle' metaphor. Certainly it fits many cases, to the point sometimes of almost ceasing to be a metaphor: there may be an antagonism between viewpoints that is undeceived and undeceiving; or the views and practices of opponents are misrepresented, their difficulties magnified, their motives doubted – whether in prejudiced good faith, or cynically and for political or other advantage.[20] But often the (overlapping) metaphor of 'debate' – again scarcely a metaphor in some situations – is the more applicable one. Views can interact and shape each other in the manner of the collaborative development of ideas among friends, or of a movement towards compromise or synthesis among those of different inclination, or, more bruisingly but still respectfully, of an argument in which we learn principally to reformulate our positions so as better to challenge and to block those of opponents. But from open warfare to conversation, the same phenomenon repeats itself of views *imprinting* themselves on each other. And this point needs to be added to our two earlier ones when we consider how users of differently loaded versions of 'education' can acknowledge each other. As well as sharing open uses of the term and accepting loading as a practice, there is the reference to some specific other views that is almost sure to be part of each one's own specific view.

Truth – a common intentionality

These conditions themselves imply a fourth. All users of 'education' are further united, and tacitly aware of themselves as united, in some kind and degree of acknowledgement of the ideal of truth (rightness, appropriateness). As well as starting out from a shared open use, they share, or make some pretence of sharing, this destination.

Open uses, loaded uses and the logic that relates open to loaded uses all refer forward to this. They all – as we might put it despite our tendency to become fidgety with solemn talk about 'truth', our suspicion that it can serve as a cloak for intolerance – legitimate the notion of the *true* meaning of 'education'. Open uses do so by their very openness. They suggest – hence their heuristic value – a question in brackets:[21] 'Whatever learnings (*and what may they be?*) meet such and such conditions'. So they look to answers, but of course to true (right, good) answers and to the true meanings that would embody such answers. Loaded uses in turn represent so many answers to that bracketed question. And each of them implicitly claims that it, rather than any conflicting one, represents the true answer and the true (best, right) meaning of education. 'Perhaps none of these claims is justified; certainly not all of them are' – which is to invoke the notions of falsity and contradiction and hence, again, of truth.

'Debate' and 'contest' also point firmly in this direction. In practice, debates may be as much occasions for bullying, obduracy and rhetorical display as for pursuing truth – thus the ambiguity of 'winning the argument'. But where there is not so much as a pretence of objectivity, not even that backhanded compliment to truth, we no longer think of them as 'debates' at all. Humphrey Bogart is not 'arguing' when he tells the crew of the *Caine* that things aboard will be done, neither the right way, nor the wrong way, but his way! Likewise, a 'contest', by contrast with a 'brawl', imports some order and coherence, some agreed ground rules and concept of victory. The runners start from the same gun, race on the same track and in the same direction, and acknowledge the first to the tape as the winner. Even where the contest is looser than this, as in the big-city marathons with their several grades of victor and their many less formal triumphs, there remain acknowledged rules and goals – different and overlapping sets of them for the different and overlapping sub-contests. With 'education', ground rules of the contests are suggested by its agreed open uses, but the very first rule is the intention of truth. So it happens that there is no 'victory' for a loaded view that does not involve the acknowledgement, whether sincere or not, that after all there is, or could be, some truth in it.

To sum up our findings: In the open–loaded continuum there is a dialectical interplay between openness and loadedness. Each occurrence of 'education' in discourse has its own point on the scale but also refers implicitly to other points. Uses as open look to ('intend') more loaded uses. Uses as loaded presume both more open uses and other loaded uses. This dialectic is strongly objectivist in its anticipations: it is crucially energized by the notion of the right or true use.

Essentially contested concept?

Many philosophers now suppose there is a class of concepts that are 'essentially contested', and that 'education' belongs to it, along with, for example, 'art', 'democracy', 'the Christian religion' and 'the British Labour Party (battle for the soul of)'. These are concepts of social life (and social science), of things that are unlike sticks and stones in being actually partly constituted by beliefs and intentions regarding what they are. Perhaps this reflexivity already makes for some instability in them (not that all such concepts could be thought contested, not, for example, a '£5 note' or a 'cheque', though perhaps 'the economy'!). In any case, while physical concepts, like 'space', 'time' and 'oxygen', are prone to dispute and revision, many of the most important social concepts seem prone to never-resolved dispute and never-agreed revision. More formally, there are concepts which have the following interconnecting features:

- they are normative, or, better, they have significant normative uses;
- they are complex;
- there is disagreement on some of their elements and/or on the order of priority among their elements;
- such disagreement is endemic in their history; and
- their variants are shaped or adapted for offence and defence against each other.

Such concepts, it is claimed, should be deemed essentially contested.[22]

Clearly there are affinities here with our own account. These concepts seem very much the ones in which we would be unsurprised to find an open–loaded dialectic. But we should be cautious about 'essentially contested'. In its reaction to an earlier autocracy, this label carries two excessively anarchic tendencies which our earlier account had the merit of overcoming.

The autocracy was that of 'standard usage' in Anglo-Saxon philosophy. Indeed it was a greatly reduced image of 'standard usage' that did the tyrannizing. In Chapter 1 we criticized an effective reduction of the different *non-competing* senses of terms to single 'primary' senses. Immediately relevant here is another reduction, that of the *competing* uses of some terms to single 'correct' uses, the others – if they were even noticed – being presumed 'aberrant'. The true claim about linguistic communication that it presupposes common usages in a common language was narrowed, it seems, to its presupposing that all (successfully communicating) uses would be common in all respects – leaving no room for the idea of legitimately, intelligibly, competing uses. From this it was expected that analyses of the terms of a philosophical issue in their 'correct' meanings would provide a usefully neutral clarification of it. What actually happened, of course, was that favoured loadings of terms like 'education' were proffered as neutral and insisted upon (the blunder we earlier noticed *A* to make with *B*), and the relevant philosophical differences came to intrude – uncomfortably – upon these 'neutral preliminaries'. Perhaps it was from this that some came by the even more cramping idea that philosophical problems *were* linguistic, and actually soluble by linguistic analysis, as though false philosophical doctrines were at bottom mistakes of the same order as the unskilled English user's confusion of 'education' and 'emigration'.

In this context the doctrine of essentially contested concepts came as a liberating event. It reaffirmed a broader conception of philosophy as concerned with ideological as well as linguistic matters, re-legitimated a pluralism of schools and doctrines, and suggested a more comparative, less sectarian, approach to issues. But, first, its exponents were understandably impatient with 'the standard' and tended to affirm 'con-testedness' simply *at its expense.*[23] They were long on contest legitimacy but short on inter-contestant intelligibility. What they missed was the dialectical interplay that we sketched above ('expecting the unexpected use', and 'agreeing to the disagreeable use'), between coexisting standard and contested uses. Yet on this absolutely depend both the tolerance and the heuristic power of language. Without it there could only be either fixed unanimity in meaning or Babel. That is one doubt regarding the description 'essentially contested concepts' and one reason for preferring 'open–loaded dialectical concepts'.

A second reason is the subjectivist leanings of the doctrine. Why was the con-testedness said to be *essential*? Actually there was some ambiguity about this. (1) At times the reference seemed only to what we have called 'imprinting' and the resultant network of internal relationships between competing views, to the historical and on-going debates as essential to the concept as we have it. (2) But at other times the reference was rather to the interminability of the debates, coupled with an implied explanation of this from somewhere in the range:

(a) there is, in principle, no way of demonstrating that a particular view of, 'educa-
      tion', say, is the right one;

(b)   there are no *irresistible* demonstrations of even the wrongness of views;

(c)   there are, ultimately, no rational grounds for preferring some views to others.

Fairly obviously (1) and (2) are different. Less obviously (a) and (b) do not entail (c), as we shall see later. Only (2c) is properly subjectivist and incompatible with the objectivist anticipations of debate. But by fudging these distinctions the 'essentially contested' position gravitated towards a soft subjectivism, and a project to legitimate a wider debate threatened to undermine debate altogether.[24] (A proper *defence* of objectivism is, of course, another matter – and a task for a later chapter.)

CONCLUSION

In Chapter 1 we sensed the complex power that accrues to the word 'education' from its multiple uses and we outlined a new strategy for analysing it. Now at the end of Chapter 2 we can see more clearly that this word power is a matter of a *triple dialecticity*. The ideas of formal education and education in the widest sense emerge together from nurture-type ideas on the one hand and training-type ideas on the other in the measure that a society espouses the ideal of a reflective view of life as a whole, and the dialectic between these ideas is what underwrites that ideal. The dialectic between normative and descriptive uses of 'education' contains the seeds of the dividing and recombining discourses of educational studies. It also allies itself with a third dialectic between open and loaded uses to underwrite, on the one hand, the development of conflicting substantive theories of education and, on the other hand, both mutual comprehension across theories and the drive for better and truer theory.

(We can see now how other multi-use words may exhibit part or all of this triple pattern. There will be normative and descriptive uses of the names of all practices and products with regard to which there is a serious question of coming up to a standard; there will be a contrast between nominal and loaded uses of the names of practices to the extent that their constitutive standards are differently conceived and theorized; and there will be institutionalized and wider senses of the names of those practices for which there are institutions which formalize (and heighten the profile of) the practice but without exhausting it. In fact all three distinctions appear in the uses of 'justice' and of 'art' for example.[25])

Further to their intrinsic interest as exposing structural features of our educational thinking, these linguistic analyses have had the broad purposes of, first, facilitating a critical scrutiny of those structures and, second, allowing us to take some direction from what survives that scrutiny. Those purposes remain to be fulfilled. By way of *scrutiny*, we have yet to test the assumptions that descriptivism makes a 'science' of education possible (Chapter 5), that objectivity in educational enquiry is possible in any real tough sense (Chapter 6), and that a desirable form of the pursuit of a coherent view of life is possible for us (Chapter 7). By way of *direction*, we shall presently (and while still assuming the ideal of a coherent view of life) exploit all three of the exposed dialectics in analysing the idea of an adequate educational theory (Chapters 3 and 4), and much later we shall develop some key elements of a substantive educational response to the ideal of a coherent view of life (Chapters 8 and 9).

NOTES

1. The point *here*, of course, is neither to defend nor to criticize this centrality of 'letters', but to note our common assumption of it.
2. Illich (1971).
3. 'Socialization' picks out either one aspect only of 'education (in the widest sense)' or one particular and controversially anti-individualist view of it. 'Rearing' includes too much (feeding, clothing, etc.) and 'bringing up' is often too emphatically behavioural, while both are more exclusively terms of nurture than this 'education', of which we ourselves and the impersonal are among the agents. On the other hand, 'development' and 'growing up' are a degree or two looser than uses of 'education' generally in their connection with agency of whatever kind (thus 'develop' is asymmetrical with 'educate' in having an intransitive as well as a transitive use), as well as being broader than them in their inclusion of the biological with the cultural. 'Development' qualified as 'physical', 'emotional', 'moral' or 'mental' retains, if in diminishing strength, this biological dimension while being, from another point of view, now narrower in each case than any use of 'education'. Finally, 'learning', as we have seen, has particularly close connections with 'education' in all its senses but could approximate synonymy with any of them only after complex qualifications in respect of volume, variety and significance.
4. It is important to remember that it is with our *present* uses of 'education' that we are concerned. Peters (1977b, Chapter 1) remarks that before the nineteenth century 'education' was used synonymously with 'rearing' or 'bringing up' and was employed in reference even to the training of animals. *That* use of the term, for all I know, may have preceded any use of it in reference to schooling, to which the term may first have been applied as to just one of the agencies of child-rearing. But that use is *not* our present 'widest sense' use, which is not synonymous with 'rearing' or 'bringing up' (see note 3), a fact to which Peters does not seem to advert.
5. I am borrowing ideas here from Wilson (1979, pp. 32–8) – though putting them to different use. 'People can do things for which they have no clearly differentiated linguistic markers – just as works of art can be created by men who see them primarily as religious rather than aesthetic objects, or who at least do not have the concept *we* mark by "a work of art". There are . . . good reasons for supposing that virtually every society must take seriously the question of what its children are to learn. But not every society has to distinguish this, in overt terms, from a more general question about what its children need to be able to do and to be (whether or not as a result of learning); just as, though every society uses and marks some concepts of what it is important to do and believe, not every society distinguishes sharply between (say) morality, law, etiquette and religious commandment' (Wilson, 1979, p. 32).
6. '[T]o say that these societies did not have our concept of education is not to say that they did not have what we may call the constituents of the concept. They had available, as it were, all the constituent criteria – human learning, deliberate enterprises, the making of a general policy, and so on; but they did not put them together into a single range of meaning marked by a single term' (Wilson, 1979, pp. 32–3).
7. So the prominence awarded to this notion in a philosopher's preliminary analyses and definitions is a likely index of the extent to which, and the level at which, he will take up these challenges. See Wain (1984) for a pertinent discussion.
8. For a critique of the fact/value distinction see, for example, Midgley (1979, Chapter 9) and Putnam (1981, Chapter 6). Putnam specifically exempts our normative/descriptive distinction from his general broadside against a dichotomy he regards as having the status of a cultural institution: 'Consider the terms we use every day in describing what other people are like, e.g. *considerate* or *inconsiderate*. *Considerate* and *inconsiderate* may of course be used to praise or blame; and one of the many distinctions which have gotten confused together under the general heading "fact–value distinction" is the distinction between using a linguistic expression to describe and using that linguistic expression to praise or blame. But this distinction is not a distinction which can be drawn on the basis of vocabulary. The judgement that someone is inconsiderate may indeed be used to blame; but it may be used

simply to describe, and it may also be used to explain or to predict. . . . And both the prediction and the explanation may be perfectly *correct*. . . . The use of the word "inconsiderate" seems to me a very fine example of the way in which the fact/value distinction is hopelessly fuzzy in the real world and in the real language.'

9. Of course, such formal self-advertisement goes only with '(formal) education' – to which alone, therefore, this part of the analysis relates. But there would seem to be few, or no, purely descriptive uses of 'education (in the widest sense)' outside the rather special context of anthropology. Generally when we wish to be noncommittal in this wider area we speak of, for example, 'formative' rather than 'educational' influences or experiences.

10. Thus it is misleading to refer to the normative (committed) kind of use of 'education' as the 'evaluative' or 'appraisive' use, for this is not the kind of use that is employed in formulating evaluations or appraisals of education.

11. This is again to suggest (see note 9) that 'education (in the widest sense)' is normally and naturally normative.

12. B. Williams (1972, p. 52ff.), following Geach (1956), has tracked the special behaviour of the adjective 'good'. Our argument accommodates, and allows us to extend, his observations.

    (a) A black cricketer is a black person but a good cricketer is not necessarily a good person. That is, the meaning of 'good' varies with the meaning of the noun it qualifies to an extent that the meaning of 'black' does not. 'Good cricketer' means 'good as a cricketer' – the phrase has to be taken as a whole. Williams speaks of 'good' as an adjective that is *logically glued* to its substantive, 'real' being another such. (Geach had earlier called these adjectives 'attributive' and ones like 'black' 'predicative'.)

    (b) Furthermore, the difference between 'good' and 'black' is not simply down to the comparative overtones of 'good'. True, a comparative adjective like 'large' is similar to what we have so far seen of 'good'. A black mouse is a black animal while a large mouse is not a large animal. But a large mouse *is* a larger animal than most mice (an animal large as mice go), while a good cricketer is not necessarily a better person than most cricketers (a person good as cricketers go). 'Good', Williams concludes, is *more* context-bound, *more* intimately 'glued' to its substantive, than are comparative adjectives.

    (c) On the other hand, it has to be said that the 'good' in 'good cricketer' (like the 'good' in 'good education') is genuinely additive or non-redundant. There are, after all, bad and mediocre cricketers. So what in the end, we may ask, does the connection metaphorically called 'logical glueing' amount to? This, I suggest: the 'good' in 'good cricketer' is bound to its noun *by an implicit reference in both to a normative use of 'cricketer'*. Their close link is, as it were, an echo of the situation in which they were fused. Thus we come again to the conclusion that the use of descriptive language in evaluation invokes a corresponding normative language for what is being evaluated.

13. 'Art', 'democracy' and 'marriage' are likely to be among other terms that have uses that are variously, and to varying degrees, loaded, as well as having open uses.

14. As plausibly argued in 'Ambiguities in liberal education and the problem of its content' in Peters (1977b).

15. Hart (1961, pp. 189–95). I was reminded of it in reading Care (1973).

16. So the unavoidability of these facts is consistent with the possibility of a society and a language that would have no concept of education. But it suggests that the practices of this society would be such as to allow *us* to describe them as 'educational' – what we supposed earlier in the chapter.

17. Freire (1970).

18. See Stenhouse (1975).

19. For example, Peters (1966), or, though using different philosophical tools, Maritain (1943).

20. Some would think here of the present press campaign in Britain against schools, teachers, local educational authorities and educationists.

21. More or less bracketed depending on the context. Where the common ground is being emphasized the question is in abeyance, noted but held over; where debate is joined it governs everything.

22. A definition distilled from a number of accounts: see Gallie (1955/6, 1964, Chapter 8), who first proposed this idea; Gellner (1967), a review of the former; MacIntyre (1973) and Care

(1973), a symposium; and Naish (1984), a recent, critically open, account.

23. So, too, they saw themselves as breaking with the tradition of conceptual analysis in philosophy, though in fact they were making a broadening new move *within* it.

24. At least one of its proponents realized the danger. 'Was not a kind of "essentialist illusion", the mistaken supposition that one unambiguous fully determinate notion or norm is "there" if only we could locate it, . . . necessary to keep going that ever-open and fruitful debate?' (Gellner, 1967, p. 55). (For further referencing of the 'essentially contested' position and a longer discussion of the relationship to it of the 'open-loaded' view, see Walsh (1988).)

25. These examples, and the general point of this paragraph, emerged in discussions with Pat Walsh.

Part 2

Practice into Theory?

Chapter 3

Education Is a Philosophical Practice

The most penetrating definition of philosophy which can be given is, then, that it is the theory of education in its most general phases.

(John Dewey, *Democracy and Education*)

Geology might have been called 'rocks', biology 'life', and sociology 'society'. The study of education *is* called 'education', as the study of history is called 'history' and of law 'law'. Might not these have been called instead, say, 'educology', 'historonomy' and 'legal studies'? This particular ambiguity in 'education' does seem more accidental than any of the three we have just considered. But it is at the least a happy accident, for it can suggest the *communicative continuity between the practice and the theory of education*. It may even reflect some common perception of this continuity, underlying that quite separate institutionalization of educational studies in higher education which we are only now beginning to think seriously about. In any case (and we shall not rely further on the linguistic point) this continuity – its manifestations, implications and limits – will be a constant refrain in this chapter.

A PARALLEL WITH HISTORY

History studies history; that is to say, lives and events that were *already* imbued with historical sense. First, and grounding everything else, there is the ordinary temporality of daily life: people in their own immediate circles mundanely act and suffer out of their past and towards their future, pervasively conscious – in relation to bodies, spiritual lives, friendships, careers – of change and stability, gathering and dispersal, disappointment and fulfilment, decline and progress. Then within that workaday temporality there occur moments of formal historical consciousness: birthdays and anniversaries, liturgies of remembrance, re-enactment and launching; awareness of 'history being made', or of oneself as 'making history' (which we all may do as members of movements and communities); even vainglorious attempts to catch the eye of the future historian. Next, there is the study of history, a concomitant awareness of a tradition and a community of scholarship, and some striking the pose of 'the historian'. Finally, this pose and quite specific historical knowledge complete the circle by feeding back into both mundane and historic living, into shopping for antiques and watching period TV, and into breaking world records and making wars or treaties. The point is the curve that underlies the (real) discontinuities between the temporality of ordinary human life, the historical sensibility of some of life and the study of history, between Man the temporal being, Man the sustainer and maker of history and Man the historian.

In the same slightly grandiose vein, the subject education theorizes about education, a practice already imbued with at least intimations of theory, and this duet has education in the widest sense for background chorus. So we may distinguish Man as educational being, as participant in educational systems and as educationist. As *educational being*, she has an immense appetite for learning, showing and informing, and these saturate her ordinary living. Much here is idle or pretends to only immediate importance. But some takes the long and the wide view and the learning duly gathers into competence, experience, world-view and wisdom. As *system participant*, she is a student and/or a teacher. We saw in Chapter 2 how this dimension of her life interacts with the first. Broadly, if, and only if, there is formal education in her environment will the educational dimension of her usual life become self-conscious and intensified as 'education-mindedness'. As *educationist*, she studies the system, and complains, makes plans and generally philosophizes about education. 'She' may be a professional educationist but is much more commonly a reflective teacher or student, or an interested bystander. For knowledge of education cannot be the preserve of the expert. Some understanding of it is actually intrinsic to educating and being educated.[1] Hence that democracy of educational comment, as we might call it, part reality and part ideal, which is an integral aspect of the larger democracy of education generally (along with education in the widest sense, the acceptance of universal educability and universal formal education).

OVERCOMING MYSTIQUE

There are two mystiques which limit this freedom of comment. One surrounds teachers and their 'book learning' and keeps students and the lay public at a distance. The other attaches to educational theory and educationists and keeps teachers at a distance. Both inhibit education itself, as well as educational comment. The stand-off from children's minds results in many of those minds remaining untouched. The stand-off from parents and other adults limits and disorients their contributions to the educational process. The stand-off from teachers inhibits grassroots innovation and development. These mystiques are connected historically with the class and educational differences between teachers and their pupils, and between teacher-educators and teachers. So they have been diminishing as those differences diminished, and many notable developments in educational theory have it in common that they may be seen as intellectual expressions of this demystification. In broad brushstrokes:

(1) There is *progressivism*. Put aside its radical form of an insistence on *nothing but* what interests the child. In its milder and more pervasive forms it still requires the teacher to be 'with' the child, on his side, to respect his language and allow him to work with it, to consider his experience in all things, and so on.[2]

(2) The *sociology of knowledge*, though from a different intellectual stable, complements this by its aggressive interrogation and deconstruction of traditional learning and its disciplines.[3] As actually organized and institutionalized and as then translated into curriculum courses and materials, these disciplines might be governed rather less by objectivity and logic than by powerful vested interests – professional, bureaucratic, race, gender and (particularly) class interests. This line has proved less apt for *reconstruction*, indeed left itself no base for reconstruction in some of its more relativistic early statements, and it is not without its own mystifying tendencies. But many who are alert to these drawbacks and disinclined to this relativism are, none the less, induced to be sceptical where they might once have been deferential. For example, the attractive Brunerian proposal of a series of 'courteous translations' of the key ideas in each discipline, 'spirally' arranged for revisiting at successive ages, has come to seem perhaps too trusting: the key ideas might be distorted by class, or other, interests. Real courtesy to students might entail deliberate rudeness to the discipline establishment! A critical programme of deconstruction and (somehow) reconstruction may rather be the way forward. And this thought gets added to the progressive idea of negotiation with the student.

(3) A still embryonic, and ambivalent, idea, associated particularly with the New Right, is that of a *free (i.e. deregulated) market of ideas, disciplines, curricula and schools*, with students and their families cast in the role of 'consumers' exercising their right of choice on the basis of accurate information about options.[4] It, too, advertises itself as demystifying. Now we may wish to remind ourselves here of the usual distance between consumers and manufacturers. Consumer choice is in fact heavily constrained choice, and consumer power, though it indirectly affects production, falls far short of co-production or any kind of partnership. This extended metaphor is then disturbingly hospitable to 'pre-packaging' in education, and inhospitable to participation. That is in addition to serious doubts about the reality, as opposed to the rhetoric, of choice and deregulation at a time when governments seem bent on both decreasing their spending and increasing their control. It remains that this philosophy, though deliberately reactionary in many other ways, is another to ride the demystification bandwagon.

(4) The mystique that separates educationists from teachers has also diminished. Thus, in the area of curriculum development the aspiration to 'teacher-proof' packages gives way to a fashion for associating specific in-service courses with curriculum projects (courteous translations for teachers!), which, in its turn, yields to the perception that *reflective practice and reflective practitioners* are the main thing, the centrepiece of curriculum development.[5]

(5) In educational research, too, the role ascribed to communication between the expert or the theorist, and the practitioner, progressively increases. Thus the popularity of case study, a research form which is particular about allowing subjects (usually practitioners) to speak for themselves,[6] and of action research, which is the natural correlative of reflective practice, indeed a form of research in which researcher and teacher might be said to meet half-way.[7]

Needless to say, these subversive ideas attract resistance, and overcoming this resistance is one reason why it is important not to overstate the ideas too provocatively. They are, in fact, broadly compatible with according a *measure* of authority, and even of mystique, to both professionals and disciplines. The good teacher can still be esteemed, the practices and traditions of an academic subject or a craft still provide inspiration and solid guidance, the independence of the outside researcher still be jealously valued, knowledge still be thought of, even, as 'holy ground' between teacher and taught. We may reasonably be quite confident of these points, at the same time that we recognize the democratizing trends that are forcing re-evaluations and reinterpretations of the traditional distinctions and relationships.[8]

THE ORGANIZATION OF EDUCATIONAL STUDIES

We can now remind ourselves that the study of education is not a monolith. It is commonly institutionalized as an assemblage of sub-disciplines, suggestive at least as much of looseness as of unity, which changes over time in its members and in the power relations among its members. These changes offer another perspective on the evolving theory–practice relationship. Let us first briefly review the recent institutional history of the subject, particularly in Britain and countries influenced by Britain, before evaluating the sense of the theory–practice logic that imbues present arrangements. Simplifying again, four phases may be distinguished in this history.

(1) Up to the 1960s, and despite the earlier establishment of history and of psychology of education, a quite *holistic* view of the subject prevailed, though with growing doubts as to its vigour and its rigour. This phase is sometimes lampooned as 'tips for teachers and thoughts of great educators'.

(2) It yielded, during the 1960s, to a *multidisciplinary* view. Educational philosophy, sociology and comparative study joined psychology and history, and for a time these 'foundation' sub-disciplines attracted all the interest and resources. Education was, in effect, being colonized and fragmented by other – stronger – disciplines, seen as its sources (as though it could not generate ideas and theories of its own and had to be content to be a field for the application of theirs), and by scholars whose original allegiance was to those disciplines. The previous period was now perceived, in the words of Richard Peters, as one of 'undifferentiated mush' relieved only by those early inputs from psychology and history. But, on the other hand, Peters himself was quickly aware of the disadvantages of straight multidisciplinarity.[9] The differentiated sub-disciplines were increasingly losing touch with each other, their intercourse largely confined to mutual critique – often based on semi-informed stereotyping. Sociologists of education swiped at philosophers and philosophers at sociologists, and everyone swiped at psychologists. Students were often initiated separately into each sub-discipline and left to make their own integrations. Partly because of the fragmentation, the concrete problems of educational policy and practice tended to go unheeded by educationists. Or else they received an attention that was after the event and, again, mainly critical. What was missing was a sense of theory as a positive guide, a creative and realistic instrument in the reconstruction of practice. Instead of addressing practice these sub-disciplines were functioning more as entrées to the fascinations of the parent 'pure' disciplines.[10]

(3) From the late 1960s onwards, these discontents have led to the establishment of *practice-orientated fields of study* in such areas as curriculum, policy and administration, multiculturalism and gender, alongside the existing sub-disciplines. But the logical status of these new fields was for a while ambiguous. Was the assumption still that educational theory was to be imported from philosophy, history and the human

sciences, only now the network that would carry it all the way to practice was more developed and coordinated than before? This interpretation of the new fields, as principally for providing a complementary *interdisciplinarity* to the previous straight *multidisciplinarity*, was dominant at first.[11] It is still quite common among those who work in the older sub-disciplines.[12] But in the new fields themselves interdisciplinarity now represents to most a largely outgrown phase in their institutionalization rather than anything ultimate in their logic. (Properly dialogical relationships with other major disciplines are a different matter, however, and forever crucial.)

(4) It was as these studies became implicated with practice, actively participating in policy and evaluation, actually developing curriculum and promoting practitioner reflectiveness, employing and developing action research and case study, that another interpretation of them rapidly gained ground[13] – involving, it might even be said, a whole new paradigm of educational theory. This interpretation turns on the perception that *deliberated, thoughtful, practice is not just the target, but is itself a major source (perhaps the specifying source) of educational theory*. There is now a growing confidence within these newer fields that their kind of theorizing, relating closely and dialectically with practice, is actually the core of educational studies, and not just the endpoint of a system for adapting and delivering outside theories. And in this reconceptualization the erstwhile 'foundation' sub-disciplines get recast as 'contextual' (where they are not altogether marginalized). They are seen as relating to the wider context of educational practice and enquiry, and as providing channels of communication between education proper and other branches of human knowledge. It may seem as though the wheel has come full circle then: from the holistic, to the multiply differentiated, to the multiple accompanied and offset by the integrated, to the reaffirmation of a central holism of theory. But, by comparison with the first, this last phase is hugely developed on the empirical side and it remains better equipped for dialogue with history, philosophy and the human sciences. Perhaps, too, the practice with which it interacts is more alive and self-critical.

TWO THEORISTS

Starting out from two of its leading British theorists, let us try to evaluate this new balancing of educational studies. The question to face is whether the leading role being ascribed to deliberated practice puts the depth and breadth of theory at risk. Our eventual answer will be that the risk is minimized if we keep in mind that the practice in question is education, and we are careful to take the full measure of that practice. Expressed in another way, if the question is about what 'reflective practitioners' need to know, it makes a great difference of scope that it is *educators* whom we have in mind.

John Elliott, out of a long experience of action research in curriculum and teacher development, describes what he takes to be *properly* educational research.[14] It stays within the framework of the researcher's commitment to educational values and is essentially a more sustained, methodical and wide-ranging form of the *practical deliberation* that is embodied in intelligent practice. It will occur as a dialogue with practitioners, and a dialogue as between people engaged on a shared task. It may be conducted with more or with less objectivity, of which it has its own canons, e.g. steadily to distinguish the wish from the fact and to check statements against behavioural evidence and the statements of others. Its outcome is not value-free knowledge but practical knowledge about what teachers and other actors in education ought to do. Elliott sometimes contrasts this attractive conception with a misbegotten, and rather easily dismissed, form of research. This, in the name of a poorly understood scientific objectivity, would bypass the practitioner and concentrate on 'techniques', which it would conceive as measurable inputs to be correlated with measurable learning outcomes.[15]

What is understressed in Elliott's account, however, is the variety of legitimate kinds of discourse and research in education. To anticipate an identification of four mutually supporting kinds of discourse in the next chapter: there is *deliberation* in the strict sense of weighing alternatives and prescribing action in some concrete here and now; there is *evaluation*, also concrete, and at once closely related to deliberation and semi-independent of it; there are then two further discourses that involve a methodical abstraction from the particularities of situations, one being *science*, which has a much less direct relationship to practice, and the other, which I shall call *utopian*, being that form of discourse in which ideal visions and abstract principles are formulated and argued over. Now it is unlikely that Elliott would really wish to deny the title 'properly educational' to all but the first of these. He might be interpreted, rather, as setting general conditions for them all, but with the result that their differences are rather glossed over.[16] Thus dialogue with practitioners may be an important desideratum in all four (I shall argue indeed that it is) – but they will be different kinds of dialogue, we should immediately add, and they may be collaborative in different degrees.[17] Again, we shall see that even educational science properly involves a resonance with educational values, but if this is 'commitment' of a kind it is different both from what we owe to our considered ideals and from the determination we owe to the job in hand.

Paul Hirst is another recently to emphasize the intelligence that is acquired and exercised in educational practice, and the continuity with this of well-conceived educational theory.[18] His account is sensitive to the range of specialisms in educational studies but misleading, I shall argue, in the particular coordination of these that it proposes.

Much earlier, Hirst had already argued that educational theory was primarily practical, and that its different sub-disciplines would find unity only in their common bearing on the task of achieving a set of principles for the guidance of practice. But at that time he had conceived these sub-disciplines as adequate for justifying, and perhaps even for generating, such principles.[19] Now he sees that as quite mistaken. They are rather to be generated from, and tested in, practice. How? I offer a fairly free interpretation of Hirst's account of this.

The account stresses that the great bulk of the knowledge and belief with which practice is instinct is unarticulated, tacit. The practice is not necessarily any the worse for this, premeditation being no universally necessary condition of rational action. But explicitness can help the critique and development of practice, and also the initiation into practice. The first task of theory, then, is to *make some of the body of tacit 'theory' explicit*, perhaps in association with case studies of particular practitioners in action. (However, since any explicit account will be partial and will connect with stuff that is still tacit, these accounts will have to be composed, and will be best understood, by those who share the tacit knowledge, i.e. by those with an inside knowledge of practice. It remains a family affair.) As the explicit accounts come in, the *critique stage* of theory-building can get going. Several jumping-off points may be envisaged. One is the criticism that is part of practice itself, also often tacit but now made (more) explicit in the accounts: the teacher's own doubts and self-judgements, perhaps stimulated by student feedback or peer comment, the concomitant and formative course evaluations and mid-course corrections, the summative judgements implicit in disappointment, frustration, satisfaction, and so on. Another starter is the comparison of the different operational theories exposed in case studies of different practices. A third is the formulation of alternative practices and the deliberate testing of these in action research. Over time such exercises should throw up principles, formulated in 'operationally effective practical discourse', that have stood up well to practical test. Hirst adds that these should come to constitute 'a consistent set'.

On the one hand, then, theory is to be a critical guide for practice, while on the other hand it is methodologically and epistemologically dependent on practice![20] Hirst offsets an impression of incest and the closed shop in this, however, with the role he goes on to ascribe to philosophy and the human sciences. Beliefs and values that are the business of these disciplines are incorporated in the concepts and principles of practice and of the descriptive and critical discourses arising from practice. Engagement with them is therefore necessary to the rationality of practical principles (though not sufficient – the principles must also be shown to work in practice). These disciplines may also *suggest* forms of practice, he says, though such suggestions would have to be filtered through the experience of practitioners to stand any chance of yielding defensible principles. Now these points would have permitted us to regard philosophy and the human sciences as *further sources*, operating in tandem with practice, of educational theory (which would not preclude their drawing in their turn on educational theory). Hirst rather shies away from this conclusion, however. He tends to play down their role by presenting it as 'indirect' and related to 'context'. This seems grudging in relation to items such as philosophical enquiry into the aims of education, or the inspirational power of a Plato's or a Rousseau's educational visions. Anyway, the line between a practice and its context can be no absolute one, and this is likely to be particularly true in the case of education, a practice we might think in some way unbounded.

Actually, these disciplines are *more* than sources. Where they bear on education they may also be thought of as *components* of educational theory in their own right. The reason, one which Hirst should appreciate, is that they are exercised already in well-developed educational practice. It is not a matter only that they influence that practice *ab extra* in many overt and covert ways, but that some of their argument is carried on within practice and the internal discourses of practice, and even within teacher–pupil dialogue. So they do not merely influence the rules, they are players in the game. This in turn bears on the *way* in which they are to be present to those descriptive and prescriptive stages of theory-building identified by Hirst. There are also implications for the conduct of the disciplines themselves on the one hand, and for teacher-education on the other. All this Hirst leaves unanalysed. In the end, and for all its considerable interest, his account of the theory–practice logic is a rather general one which neglects special features of this practice that add up to a highly distinctive profile as compared with law, social work, medicine, etc.

That neglect is indeed a striking feature of the better-known literature generally in the 'emergent theory' paradigm. Thus, as well as Elliott and Hirst, Carr and Kemmis are guilty of it, in one place even promising to address '*educational*' practice' before proceeding to emphasize 'practice' rather than 'educational'.[21] There is irony here: the paradigm enjoins attention to the particular nature of the practice, which is then overlooked! One likely cause of the neglect is that most of the concepts central to the new paradigm ('action research', 'extended professionalism', 'reflective practitioner' and 'practice' itself) are of quite general application, and the more seminal discussions of them[22] are not focused on education specifically. Another factor may be the inadequacies that we have discussed in the legacy of analytic philosophy: endless replays of 'the concept of education' in single keys have perhaps tired us of it. A third and deeper cause may be certain cultural obstacles to squaring up to what, as we shall see, is the main challenge of the concept, i.e. seeking a view of life as a whole, obstacles that include the fragmented state of our intellectual culture as well as our more obvious ideological pluralism.

Whatever has made us forget 'education', it is now time to remember it again. We are for one thing threatened with a reconceptualization of teacher-education as teacher-training (the British Secretary of State's 1992 address to the North of England Conference mentioned 'teacher education' once and that was to translate the acronym CATE; at all other times he spoke of 'teacher training') and if that domino is allowed to fall the idea of a general education itself may be next. Of more immediate relevance here, however, is the need to counteract the tendency in academic literature to over-simplify and to narrow the concept of educational theory. I will seek to demonstrate that the specific nature of this practice obliges its theory at once to a peculiar breadth and to a peculiar coherence.

A SPECIAL PRACTICE, A PHILOSOPHICAL PRACTICE

Education as practice is marked by talkativeness, extraordinary time-intensiveness, a characteristic (though not exclusive) orientation to children and young people, tension between professional ownership and public interest, deep complicity with other practices, and variability to context balanced by an aspiration to a view of life as a whole. Perhaps none of these is entirely specific to education, unless in degree, but in combination they compose a highly distinctive profile. Let us consider their implications for the conduct of educational theory.

On any account this is among the most relentlessly *articulate* of practices, a fact not to be obscured by our new awareness of its tacit underside. By nature it is passionate about making things clear and distinct, devoted to explanation and justification, committed to the language development of its clients, and at pains to provide them also with a taste of the theoretical impulse in, for example, science education. Second, on most accounts education is also committed to *self-possession*. The professional ideal of teachers 'owning' their own practice, individually and communally, is acknowledged and seen as a measure of a system's maturity. Also prized is the development of a critical self-knowledge and autonomy in students – of which one aspect would be their progressive assumption of control over their own education (hence, for example, the tolerance of children's groans at unpopular topics and exercises in junior school, the gradually increased space for guided student choice, the requirement of theory of knowledge in the International Baccalaureate, experiments in student participation in school government as a dimension of moral education, and so on). So far, and taking these two features together, we have an outline case for locating a good deal of theoretical reflection on education within the practice of education itself. Education is a particularly sweet example, indeed, of an area in which the theory is to be sought in the practice and the ideals of the practice to a significant extent – but this is something that is better gathered from the nature of the practice than assumed *a priori*.

Next, this practice is as *public* as any, and more so than most. It is responsive, more or less depending on the particular account of it, to the ideal picture of a truly education-minded society: generated by teachers, students, parents, local communities and government, via mechanisms of joint deliberation and action and of mutual account-ability; in which all are educated; in which many besides teachers, themselves a numerous lot, are recognized as educators; in which all have an intelligent interest in education founded, first, on having participated in it over long years at the receiving end (just about everyone has some of what it takes to be 'an educationist') and, second, on that particular feeling we have both for our children and for our own childhood; in which, then, democracy of educational comment flourishes and public opinion matters to theorists as well as practitioners. This public quality of education qualifies (but does not contradict) its commitment to self-possession. For example, it suggests that schools need to be open and culturally alert places – which is, perhaps, at once a condition and a likely fruit of a good partnership between them and higher education.

So far, then, we have a practice that should be *concomitantly* and *publicly* interested and active in its own theory. We move on now to features of the practice that particularly affect the *shape* and *composition* of this concomitant theorizing.

As a function of its scope, education is a practice of *great variability to context*. Think of the differences between nursery and further education, mathematics and art teaching, a class of 30 nine-year-olds in the UK and one of 100 in Malawi, the teacher conceived as an agent of a predetermined curriculum and the teacher conceived as a professional. It is not at all unnatural, indeed, to think of these plurally, as different practices, and there has to be a corresponding plurality in the theory of education.[23] Of course, basic questions recur from context to context. Who is to be educated? To what ends? In what? For how long and to what standard? Against what odds and with what resources? In what sequences and at what ages? But answers obviously have to be many and diverse to the extent that they address the specificity of situations and types of situation: the infant school, the mathematics class, the developing country, the UK since the Education Reform Act, etc. A plethora of practice-orientated theories relating to particular ages, curriculum areas, evolutionary stages, and national and historical contexts is the result. Though by no means insulated from each other, these constitute something altogether more sprawling than Hirst's ideal of 'a consistent set of principles' – a simplicity also missing from, say, medical and legal theory. (Note, too, that even the enquiries arising from single situations may resist theoretical combination, e.g. how to make the best of existing resources in some interim, and how to acquire better resources – reduce class sizes, get new materials, and so on – and thus move the goal-posts for the first enquiry. This indeed is typical of deliberative enquiry.[24])

It is obvious that some level of this specific kind of theorizing occurs *within* the corresponding area of practice. And it is obvious that at some level such theorizing begins to engage with philosophy, history and the human sciences. What we have still to clarify is how much these two levels overlap. How much philosophy of mathematics does the mathematics teacher use, or how up-to-date does the infant teacher's grasp of child development theory have to be? Again, it is obvious that a more abstract address of questions like those listed above – that is to say, a theory of education *in general* – involves a fairly immediate engagement with these disciplines. How otherwise could one begin to consider matters like the general aims of education, the shape of the whole curriculum, or the availability of education across classes, genders and races? But the question still remains of whether, and how much, the practitioner in his particular context would need to attend to such more general theory.

Now it is tempting to suppose that theory becomes 'external' to practice, and disconnected from the tacit knowledge and concomitant theorizing of practice, in the measure that it addresses either the more ultimate or the more general and veers towards its utopian or scientific modes. In different ways this is tempting for both theorist and practitioner. But both should resist it. For it would overlook another feature of this practice, i.e. its *consciousness of its own unity* – which is as integral to the will to educate as anything we have noticed so far and which allows us to regard the multiple practices referred to earlier as so many manifestations of a single practice, education.

The unity of education has a particular character. First, it is no mere abstraction based on the similarities among diverse practices, but something more like an obligation that is laid upon those practices. Second, this obligation requires not only planning and coordination from on high but a common consciousness among practitioners – the whole soul of education is present in every good educational practice, in the way (it has long been said) the souls of persons are present in every part of their bodies. Thus the primary teacher will keep in view the whole school career, and beyond, of her children. Teachers adapting to particular children of particular cultures will still see in each of them the universal human child. The science teacher will stir her consciousness of her subject's relationships with other curriculum areas and of the distinctive ways in which it realizes general educational values. And so on. To undertake a particular practice *as education* is precisely to inform it with something of this holistic spirit. Third, the unity sought is, so to speak, an open rather than a self-contained unity. It relates in some integral way to the ideal (a difficult one for our culture) of a coherent view of life as a whole – in which education bears some similarity with religion. So the consciousness needed within practice is a philosophical consciousness. To quote Louis Arnold Reid: 'if we are to educate sensibly . . . we must above all things do it with a sense of direction and proportion, and to have this is to have a philosophy'.[25]

Another route to this conclusion starts from education being complicit, indeed foundationally complicit, with a great range of other practices: scholarship and the arts, working life, citizenship and politics, personal relationships and reaching for maturity, and the life of the spirit. This requires breadth of it, and indeed many of the qualities of those other practices. But education has, furthermore, some responsibility to get those practices into coherent relationship with each other, and thus to support the overarching practice of 'the good life'. And, again, this requires it to embody and communicate a philosophy, as a context for the other things it embodies and communicates.

The commitments mentioned earlier will keep this concomitant philosophy open to discussion among teachers and students. If educational practice is to be its articulate, self-possessed and democratic 'best self' it will be a matter as much of philosophizing as of an agreed philosophy. In pluralist societies, in particular, it is likely to be something between an agreed compromise, an invitation to a communal enquiry and a space for a personal quest. Again, its sophistication should not be underestimated, considering, for example, that older and abler students are to be included in the discussion, and that 'practice' includes the processes of review and development. (In making his persuasive case for a pivotal role for schools in curriculum review and development, Malcolm Skilbeck acknowledges that it would oblige the school community, including even its students, to develop a high degree of cultural alertness and informedness.[26] This may seem a lot to ask of schools, but can 'education' hold out any lesser ideal?)

This is 'philosophy' in a broad and generous sense. Unlike current academic philosophy in the Anglo-Saxon world, it is not ruthlessly distinguished from theology, history and human science. So a school's, or a teacher's, or a project's 'philosophy' may well be informed by some religious principles and discussion, and/or pictures of human development that draw deeply on contemporary psychology, and/or a sharp historical and sociological sense of 'the challenges of our times' (e.g. to be girl-friendly, to begin to be environmentally conscious, to develop a curricular expression of a proper egalitarianism).

There are at least three vital consequences for *non-concomitant* educational theory, that is for educational theory as a practice in its own right, and for that part of teacher-education, initial or continuing, that is more than just learning on the job. First, 'philosophizing', and the kinds of knowledge and awareness it feeds on, should be no less integral to them. Far from being 'clutter', this kind of deep and unparochial reflection is absolutely necessary within, and across, the study of particular phases and areas of practice, if such study is to serve a practice that is truly educational. Thus it is not obviously paranoiac to read some current attacks on educational theory as directed towards the eventual narrowing of what goes in classrooms, and, via them, of social life.[27]

Second, the point of the non-concomitant approach to both theory and teacher-education must include the achievement of higher levels of explicitness, rigour and reflectiveness, and though this is likely to include some differentiation of the contributions of different disciplines, it is a more fundamental observation that it provides an opportunity to explore connections between the disciplines. While respecting real differences of logic and conceptual framework, educational theory needs to engage simultaneously with these several disciplines, hold their relevant outcomes together in the mind in order to bring them all to bear on this or that issue, and this undoubtedly has the effect of testing (often rather easy) assumptions regarding the inviolability of disciplinary frontiers. (I would estimate that the current intellectual climate is relaxed about frontiers – the writings of Habermas and Foucault, for example, continually flout those between social philosophy, social theory, psychology and history – and that educational studies has contributed to this relaxation.)

Our third consequence caps the previous two. That philosophy and human science are in some part intrinsic to educational theory, as in the first place to educational practice, suggests that these disciplines may get as good as they give in the way of ideas and inspiration from their engagement with education. If educational theory needs to be responsive to developments in them, it can also be *critical* of these, and it may indeed *generate* developments of its own in them. Dewey argued both these points strongly for philosophy. He saw education as a laboratory for testing the human, as opposed to the merely technical, significance of philosophical theories and distinctions, and also as a privileged vantage point from which to engage in philosophizing (evincing in this a self-confidence less obvious in recent philosophy of education). Indeed, he suggested rather controversially that European philosophy owed its very origins to the direct pressure of Athenian educational questions, and he continued:

> the fact that the stream of European philosophical thought arose as a theory of educational procedure remains an eloquent witness to the intimate connection of philosophy and education. 'Philosophy of education' is not an external application of ready-made ideas to a system of practice having a radically different origin and purpose: it is only an explicit formulation of the problems of the formation of right mental and moral habitudes in respect to the difficulties of contemporary social life. The most penetrating definition of philosophy which can be given is, then, that it is the theory of education in its most general phases.[28]

Even if this overstates philosophy's debt to education, it remains that education's central concerns are one profound stimulus to basic questions in philosophy. And analogous claims can be made about education's contribution to the human sciences.[29] In sum, education's proper relationship with philosophy and the human sciences is not a client relationship, but a seriously mutual affair.

NOTES

1. Or at least the 'ingredients' of this understanding are necessary, we should say, if we are to include the pre-educational society. See pp. 17–18 above.
2. Dewey (1916, 1938), Barnes (1976), etc.
3. Young (1971), Young and Whitty (1976, 1977), Apple (1982), Giroux (1983) etc. Whitty (1985) is a good survey. But critiques of culture, education and particular disciplines in relation to the interests they serve were pursued earlier, and from different philosophical standpoints, by Husserl, Heidegger and Weil, for example. Thus Simone Weil used a mainly Platonic epistemology and ethic for her very radical critiques (Weil, 1949, 1968, especially 'Classical science and after').
4. Polemical pieces include Dennis O'Keefe's article in the *Times Educational Supplement* (18 September 1987), Stuart Sexton's 'No nationalized curriculum' (*Times*, 9 May 1988), and the Centre for Policy Studies pamphlet, *Correct Core: Simple Curricula for English, Maths and Science* (March 1988). Bosanquet (1983) and Ball (1990) are critical discussions. This 'free market' emphasis represents the 'neo-liberal' strand in New Right philosophy, and it is in some tension with its 'neo-conservative' strand emphasizing the need for a strong state above all else, which is associated especially with the Hillgate group of Roger Scruton *et al*. Quicke (1988) and Chitty (1989, Chapter 8) discuss this tension.
5. Stenhouse (1975), Elliott (1980), Schon (1983) – who coined the phrase 'reflective practitioner' – Skilbeck (1984) and Van Manen (1991) – a beautifully nuanced analysis. It is a perception, however, that seems not to be entirely shared by governments.
6. Simons (1987).
7. Elliott (1985), Carr and Kemmis (1986).
8. Pring (1976) is a philosophical work that blends, critically and persuasively, borrowings from progressivism and the sociology of knowledge with a regard for a wide range of disciplines as curricular resources.
9. A 1972 paper, republished in Peters (1977b, Chapter 9). It refers to most of the following disadvantages. Jonathan (1985) picks out some of these failings in the particular case of philosophy of education.
10. Giving teachers the opportunity, in some cases, to move on to lecturing jobs in a higher education that was then expanding! One should not overstate this, however. Many came through these disciplines to view their practice in a broader light, though they may have had to make the connections for themselves.
11. Peters, in advocating the new forms of study, used Freudian imagery to express this view.

Educationists would still have their centres of gravity, their 'egos', in the educational aspect of their specialized discipline – in philosophy of education, say. They would in addition be careful to keep in touch with the voice of the father-discipline, their 'super-ego'. But the new factor would be involvement with the 'id', a venturing forth to explore problems with alien others in 'a world simmering with repressed aggression and with the anxieties of an unstructured situation'. From this would come a *collective* identity as workers in educational theory, and even – in time – somewhat less bounded and circumscribed individual 'egos'. He goes on to imply, in fact, that *properly* educational theory emerges only from such venturing. But he does not here envisage or recommend what has since happened, that there might be workers whose individual 'egos' would be primarily identified with these fields as parts, simply, of the discipline education (Peters, 1977b).

12. Wilson (1989) is a recent restatement of this view by a philosopher of education.
13. In the UK most quickly, and influentially, at the Centre for Applied Research in Education (CARE), University of East Anglia. This was connected with the Centre's close involvement with the curriculum development movement, in all its phases.
14. In many of his papers. See in particular Elliott (1975, 1980, 1988a, 1989).
15. Elliott argues that it misconceives both education and teacher development as forms of instrumental, rather than of communicative, action. This contrast may not, however, be sufficiently exact. It leads Elliott (1980, p. 314) into a paradoxical distinction between causal and other effectivity.
16. I came across Elliott (1989) only after writing this section. It does have persuasive and quite developed things to say about the (subordinate) relationship of 'the disciplines' (philosophy, psychology, sociology and history of education) to educational theory. I remain convinced, however, that it is more illuminating to analyse this theory in terms of 'discourses'.
17. Thus scientific discourse requires (at least indirect) communication between researcher and subjects who are often teachers. But in many instances this communication will be taken as, in Elliott's words, 'between people engaged on a shared task' *only* if the task is being conceived in very general terms, e.g. to make some contribution to the promotion of good education.
18. Hirst (1983).
19. Hirst (1966).
20. '[O]nly principles generated in relation to practical experience and that are operationally tested can begin to do justice to the necessarily complex tacit elements within practice' (Hirst, 1983, pp. 18–19).
21. Carr and Kemmis (1986, pp. 106ff.).
22. Lewin (1952), MacIntyre (1981), Schon (1983).
23. I am indebted to Malcolm Skilbeck for this reminder.
24. On this, and other aspects of practical reasoning and theory in education, Schwab's papers on 'The practical' (1970, 1971, 1973, 1983) were seminal.
25. Reid (1962), quoted in Carr and Kemmis (1986).
26. Skilbeck (1984).
27. See J. Elliott (1988b).
28. Dewey (1916, p. 329).
29. Walkerdine (1984) exemplifies one perspective on the two-way relationship between psychology and education.

Chapter 4

The Different Discourses of Theory

We have seen that the view of educational theory in recent decades has swung from the multidisciplinary – in which its unity was not apparent other than in the eventual 'applicability' of the disciplines to practice[1] – to regarding theory as emergent in practice and forming a single complex with practice. Case-study workers and action researchers now meet reflective practitioners on their own ground (if they are not actually the same people) and work together with them at making the operative theories of their practices explicit, subjecting those theories to critique, and experimenting with modified and novel practices. The new partnership is also reflected in the much larger role of schools and 'teacher-mentors' in forward-looking teacher education. While expressing a general agreement with this paradigm, we criticized a tendency in the supporting literature to oversimplify and to narrow the concept of educational theory. A theory that is adequate to *this* practice, we argued, is required to be seriously 'philosophical' – notably broad and notably coherent – as well as practical. Let us now be bold and attempt to articulate that requirement quite fully and formally.

A CLUSTER OF DISCOURSES

This attempt will involve distinguishing and relating different voices in the theory that is emergent in good practice, insisting at the same time on their equal necessity.[2] These voices, however, are not those of established disciplines. It is rare for a discipline to be tidily univocal in a logical sense. Usually, it will be home to several logical forms, some of which will recur in other disciplines (the appropriate explanation of which may be historical in many cases, for example, an insulation from other disciplines that has forced a discipline to maintain or develop its own surrogates of logical forms available elsewhere). Therefore, a return to a multidisciplinary model, even if we were to emphasize the links of each discipline severally with practice in a way that was not done formerly, would only serve to obscure the logical structure, and the complex logical coherence, of educational theory. I propose the notion of 'a discourse' as a more exact unit of analysis.

I define a *discourse*, in straightforward terms, as 'a sustained and disciplined form of enquiry, discussion and exposition that is logically unique in some significant way'. Logically unique is not the same as logically isolated, however, and I next define a *cluster of discourses* as 'any complete set of logically symbiotic discourses'. To explain, in their 'surface grammars' cluster discourses will be largely autonomous so that when they borrow ideas from each other they will tend to 'adapt' them in the process; but in their 'deep grammars', where it is a question of their basic point and terms of reference, they will be thoroughly interdependent, calling each other forth, and each making sense only alongside (at least embryonic) forms of the others.

I may now propose the thesis, intimated earlier: *educational theory is a cluster of four discourses relating to educational practice, namely (1) utopian, (2) deliberative, (3) evaluative and (4) scientific discourses*. Each of these discourses stands in a unique relationship to value and, therefore, to practice. But the stance of each presupposes and supports the stances of the other three. Over and above the fact of having a common subject matter, i.e. educational practice – and *all* of them lock with the experiential intelligence of practice – these four discourses will be seen to offer profoundly complementary perspectives on that subject matter. I shall offer sketches of the discourses that will suggest their main formal properties, evoke their distinctive recognizability to workers in the field, list the many ways in which they are nevertheless interdependent, and show their integrality to educational theory. Later I shall approach the question of the basis of their correlativity.

Utopian discourse

Utopian discourse has two defining characteristics. One, which it shares with deliberative discourse, is that it is directly committed to the flourishing of education (as an aspect of a wider human flourishing). The other, in which it is analogous to scientific discourse, may be expressed positively or negatively. Positively, it pushes to the limit; its focus is not just any good, but the ideal. Negatively, it excludes considerations of feasibility; it is 'purely theoretical' in the slightly pejorative sense. Not that it is concerned with the unattainable as such, any more than the attainable. An ideal can become an aim if one decides it is feasible, or at any rate worth trying, but that decision will take one beyond utopian reflection. This discourse simply *eschews* the question of attainability.

Among the established disciplines, it is not only philosophy that may engage in this discourse. So, and quite overtly, do some kinds of historical work (e.g. by Marxist historians), some areas of psychology (e.g. theorizing moral development) and that layer of social science which Habermas partly identifies and partly proposes under the title of 'critical theory'.[3]

Practices like medicine, law and social work also have their ideal scenarios and therefore their utopian discourses. But education's integral aspiration to a view of life as a whole implies that its utopian discourse has to be particularly broad and complete in its scope – in that sense particularly utopian. It embraces as a matter of course discussions of educational values in relation to general life values, analyses of cultural capital in general and theories of many aspects of human development. More than that, it is committed to seeking some coherence across these discussions and theories. Its quest is for an ordering of educational values, an analysis of cultural capital that will be related to this ordering, and a set of pictures of human development that will cohere with each other and relate to both the former. Carr and Kemmis remark that Dewey was perhaps the last of the 'grand theorists' in the English-speaking world and that more recent thinkers have tended to focus on narrower problems.[4] They remark this without murmuring against it, but to the extent that it is accurate it implies some abdication of theoretical responsibility. A 'consciousness of the need to place education as a process of "coming to know" in the context of a general theory of society on the one hand and a theory of the child on the other'[5] is no mere optional fashion but an obligatory element in educational theory, as in the first place in educational practice.

Nevertheless, it would be wrong to suppose that utopian discourse is *always* full-blown and visionary – not to mention dogmatic and atemporal. Admittedly, the word tends to conjure up the committed, completed and forever powerful portraits of education of the likes of Plato and Rousseau. But this discourse also includes the fragmentary (e.g. the abstract consideration of an individual principle or value like equality or friendship), the minutely argued and counter-argued (e.g. the question of the tensions in education between the values of equality, freedom and quality) and the tentative and exploratory as well as the passionately certain. It may also envisage in a general way some definite socio-historical context, as do, for example, Marx's revolutionary vision and Freire's ideal of 'conscientization', while still abstracting from everyday constraints.

Popper has famously criticized 'utopianism' as an inherently impractical project with a profoundly totalitarian tendency.[6] But to engage in utopian discourse does not amount to utopianism in Popper's sense. First, it is not inherently authoritarian; we may build into it, for instance, something like Habermas's conditions of ideal speech.[7] Second, we may aspire to build broad and stable highways between the various dimensions of a unified view of life, but in our fragmented culture we are unlikely to achieve more than unsteady rope bridges. What the nature of education obliges us to is a *quest* for coherence rather than the final achievement of coherence. Third, utopian discourse is conceived here as just one of a cluster of discourses constituting educational theory. In particular it is tied to a partnership with the 'piecemeal engineering' approach of deliberative discourse – to which we now turn.

Deliberative discourse

Deliberative discourse in education at once articulates and directs the art of achieving the best that is possible in a given situation of practice and development. (Not that it is intrinsically conservative. Radical courses of action have to be considered along with others, and one of them may be the best that is possible. But that would imply that it was compatible with a sufficient number of other goods, acceptable in its side effects, feasible, timely, and so forth – in addition to being good in itself.) There is no mystery about the general interdependence of this discourse with the utopian. They are patently the two sides of an intelligent devotion to good education. On the one hand, deliberative discourse cannot identify the best that is possible without utopian discourse. By itself, it would lack considered ideals and perhaps any ideals, and would be too intuitive, or too conservative, or tack gutlessly with every wind. On the other hand, utopian discourse on its own would be literally useless. Its willingness to weigh anchor eventually in deliberative discourse is a test of whether it is really committed to the good, and not just to the pleasures of speculation.

In general, deliberative discourse involves a step or two back from, the better then to focus upon, some given teaching–learning situation, and it relies on consultation, simulation and action research as principal research modes. Two sub-categories can be broadly distinguished. One is the discourse of *policy and policy-making*. This includes consultations, discussion papers, advocacy and directives – products of a kind now flooding British schools in the wake of the Education Reform Act. It emanates from authorities, pressure groups and interested parties at all levels of an educational system, and busies itself with units as large as the whole system and as small as the learning of a single student. It is as obliged as any discourse to support itself by argument and research, and it may co-opt academics to assist it in this, but its main exponents are those with *responsibility* in, and for, practice. The second broad category of deliberative discourse gives academics rather more to do, though still in close collaboration with practitioners. It is that form of *practical theorizing* we discussed earlier, when we reviewed, and in some ways qualified, Hirst's account of its genesis from practice. It involves, we saw, subjecting the articulated wisdoms of particular areas and contexts of practice to criticism, revision, amplification and further testing in action, and then re-presenting the results to those areas and contexts – all, as far as may be, in the task-orientated language of practice itself.[8] It is an essential resource in any practically minded teacher education. It also contributes to policy-making, not least by engaging in what Schwab called 'the anticipatory generation of alternatives', which increases the stock of possibilities that are available to deliberation and is particularly valuable when it comes to identifying and dealing with novel situations.[9]

Deliberative discourse must also 'take account' of theories in the narrower sense – theories of society, culture, personality, learning, knowledge, motivation, development and many other things – borrowing them mostly from scientific discourse. It employs such theories on its own terms, so to speak. In relation to their abstract nature, it uses various practical arts both to span the distance to untidy reality and to maintain a healthy sense of that distance. In relation to the multiplicity and diversity of such theories (so very many areas of theory with a claim to relevance, and usually so many 'schools' within each area), it practises a sophisticated eclecticism, defined by Schwab as 'the arts by which unsystematic, uneasy, but usable focus on a body of problems is effected among diverse theories, each relevant to the problems in a different way'.[10] This requires not just outline knowledge of the theories, but enough understanding of their controlling conceptions to be able to sense which practical courses they will run well on, and which not. A good example would be Richard Peters's pragmatic plea for a pluralist approach when using psychology in planning moral education: that we should look broadly to cognitive interactionism in relation to the development of a properly generalized sense of justice, to depth psychology in relation to 'natural' virtues like compassion, and to behaviourism in relation to 'executive' virtues like courage.[11] (We remarked earlier that such eclectic activity can have a spin-off for theory, too, by beginning to test assumptions regarding the incommensurability of disciplines and schools.)

Evaluative discourse

Evaluative discourse describes, analyses and judges educational practices and contexts with a view to their maintenance and development, and educational proposals with a view to their adoption. Considered as a discourse in its own right, it has grown apace with the curriculum development movement and the advent of professional evaluators in recent decades, and it has been quite exercised with questions of its own direction and logic.[12] Some of this ongoing discussion is reflected in the remarks that follow.

Since it has maintenance, development and adoption 'in view'[13] (the phrase is meant to suggest both distance and relationship) this discourse has an obvious 'deep grammar' connection with deliberative discourse. In Chapter 2 we demonstrated that the descriptive use of 'education' presupposed the normative use while being in its turn needed, as far as its employment in evaluation goes, as the complement of the normative use. The felt importance of education dictated descriptive and normative uses together, we said. Here we can extend that point in reference to the symbiosis between the developed discourse of evaluation, and the developed discourse of deliberation, in each of its two forms. Project evaluation reports, analyses of political contexts and 'pluralistic' policy papers may choose to refrain from recommendation, and even from judgement. But they still need to be imbued with so lively a sense of the concerns, constraints and possibilities of a particular situation that they are ready-made for insertion into the deliberative process relating to that situation. Thus evaluative discourse achieves much of its sophistication in relation to the complex particularity of policy contexts. In the other direction, it may be said that sophistication in policy and planning, including the moral sophistication implicit in democratic consultation, depends on developing this sustainedly impartial, sometimes even non-judgemental, kind of clarification. Equally, what we called practical theorizing above at once presupposes and gives a point to articulating the operational theories of existing practice.

As 'particularistic', like the previous one, this discourse's focus is the identified single unit, large or small, even when it uses comparisons with other units to illuminate this unit. Thus its natural form of enquiry is the case study, understood broadly to include the system-wide survey – where 'the case' is the whole of an education system, or of some sector of it, e.g. primary schools – as well as the naturalistic enquiry into the 'pond-life' of an individual school or classroom. Such a study will be primarily significant for those connected with the case itself. It will be secondarily significant for the many others whose own different cases it illuminates, challenges or casts into relief – and this wider interest will in part derive from its very particularity.

The subject matter of this discourse is all aspects of practice, not just new proposals and developments, though it was in association with them that it first achieved a formal prominence. In principle it serves maintenance and protection of the worthwhile old as well as development of the new. Indeed, in a properly rational service of development itself an evaluation of existing practice might be thought necessary to establish the need for development and to suggest some initial specification of it. Would not that evaluation, even, be temporally and logically prior to the evaluation of the innovation? Although this last may be too linear a representation,[14] it remains that evaluation of the status quo must deserve an at least equal attention. This is a point often made in the (now large) literature on unsuccessful curriculum change and, of course, one strand of the more recent 'school self-evaluation' movement.

This discourse includes both the judgemental and, as intimated above, the methodically non-judgemental. The latter is a sub-discourse that aims to facilitate judgement while itself eschewing it. Its rationale connects, on the one hand, with the ordinary requirement of prudence and fairness that we should discipline ourselves against hastiness of judgement, and, on the other hand, with the perception of educational evaluation as a highly political business.[15] But evaluative discourse also includes the moment of judgement – whether separated from reflection in the way just noticed or proceeding more or less seamlessly from reflection as in the exercise of curriculum 'connoisseurship'[16] – when its dependence on utopian ideal becomes evident; when, too, it easily crosses over into remedial recommendation and, therefore, the second discourse.

Finally, formal evaluation is increasingly recognized as political: having real effects on the distribution of power and the advancement of particular interests, and, therefore, obliged to be democratic in the range of interests it causes to be considered, the range of participants it will admit and the range of audiences it is prepared to address.[17] It is obliged, we might say, to facilitate that wide democracy of comment on which we remarked earlier. To this end, formal evaluation properly engages with the informal evaluations of many others, most obviously of teachers. Again, a narrow professional protectionism is eschewed and the new skills are appropriately taught to teachers and others that they may more effectively monitor their own and their colleagues' practice. (This is to define some of the specialist evaluator's roles rather than to do away with her.)

Scientific discourse

Scientific discourse of itself seeks only to understand and explain education. It does not seek also to direct it and it lacks, too, evaluation's indirect orientation to deliberation and action. It views education, one might almost say, contemplatively, as a quasi-phenomenon worthy of being understood in itself and in its relationships with other human and social constants and near constants. At the same time we would expect it to be more intimately caught up in values than natural science is. Isn't it ethically required, in fact, that its detachment, though it be radical and sustained in comparison with most inter-human discourse, should still be contained within a sense of common humanity and common human concerns?

That the very idea of 'human science' seems problematic nowadays is, I believe, due less to this complication in itself than to epistemological confusions that have made it seem more intractable than it really is. Positivism,[18] already inadequate as an account of the natural sciences, not only was even less adequate as an account of the human sciences but exercised a baleful influence over much of their development. Its association of 'objectivity' with a particular interpretation of neutrality and value-freedom and its pursuit of generalizations that would be law-like in character contributed to a voyeuristic depersonalization, equally of the relation between researcher and subject and of the subject. The phenomenological reaction to positivism, on the other hand, was much too quick to abandon detachment and objectivity in any really tough sense – as though these were not particularly important in a great range of human intercourse – as well as being often too pessimistic about the possibility of *any* form of illuminating cross-cultural generalization. These criticisms in effect suggest the hypothesis of a discourse which is value conditioned in its definition of field, respectful and empathic in its conduct of research, radically objective in aspiration and distinguishable from other discourses in being concerned just to understand and explain. There is enough good science that is relatively untainted by positivism – or rises above its positivism in practice – on the one hand, and is passionate about objective understanding – or rises above its subjectivism in practice – on the other hand, to encourage belief in the compossibility of these conditions.

If the hypothesis – which we shall shortly be elaborating much more fully – is granted for the moment, the scientific *differs* from the evaluative in the following interconnected ways: it lacks an immediate relationship to deliberation and action; it is often focused on the general rather than the particular, though its theories cannot aspire to the degree of universality available in natural science; and it values understanding for its own sake. On the other hand, the scientific *supports* the evaluative, not only by making a store of theories available to it (as to deliberative discourse), but by standing behind its more provisional detachment with its own special brand of fascination.

On this hypothesis, too, scientific discourse differs fundamentally from utopian. For all its value-conditionedness, its concern is what is rather than what ought to be. On the other hand, there is an elusive relationship between these discourses. One aspect of this is that they combine in that 'philosophical' involvement, which, we argued, is a condition of education. In progressivism, for example, an ideal picture of human development and a programme of educational action may draw on an empirical theory of stages of development; in social reconstructionist approaches the ideal picture and the programme will draw on some broad empirical analysis of existing society and culture. It is in its broad theories that science gets taken up in this way – again, and if for no other reason, because of education's particular stake in a broad and coherent view of life.[19]

THE UNITY OF EDUCATIONAL THEORY

I have referred repeatedly to interrelationships among the discourses. Deliberation gives point to evaluation and feeds off it. Both draw on considered broad ideals and models that may in their turn have absorbed, as well as influenced, broad scientific perspectives. Ideals are approximately achieved, and sometimes corrected, through deliberation and evaluation in particular situations. Deliberation and evaluation make eclectic use of more particular scientific theories, and evaluation mimics scientific detachment to a degree. We might add that discussion and writing about education switch easily and coherently from one discourse to another.[20] Are there, however, underneath these many surface interactions relationships of a more systematic and structural kind? Intuitively, we must feel there are – why else, for instance, would the order in which we discussed the discourses above seem natural rather than random? But they are not easy to articulate.

The first step is plain enough, perhaps. We would distinguish between the first two discourses as prescriptive or normative discourses that extend the action-directing side of experiential intelligence, and the third and fourth as descriptive discourses which extend the observing and appraising side of experiential intelligence and give the first pair a purchase on reality. (To repeat an earlier warning, this is *not* the fact/value distinction as commonly understood and rightly criticized. Logical symbiosis, rather than a logical gulf, is what is envisaged.[21])

Beyond that first step there are two possibilities. We might add a further distinction, cutting across the first one, between the utopian and the scientific as general or context-free, and the deliberative and the evaluative as particular or context-specific. That would give us a double-axis model as follows:

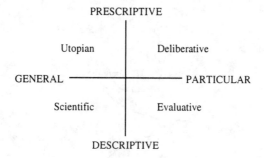

Figure 4.1

But it is a weighty objection to this scheme that it would fail to provide appropriate accommodation for some forms of educational enquiry – history certainly, and probably also the more 'anthropological' forms of classroom research – in which the particular is pursued for its own sake and with little or no interest in generalization but, at the same time, without the orientation to action of the deliberative and evaluative discourses. Scientific discourse, if it is to accommodate these forms of enquiry, must be characterized primarily in terms rather of the 'contemplative' nature of its understanding than of any concern for generalization.

The other – and better – possibility leads us to refine the prescriptive/normative distinction more than we have so far had to. On reflection, the initial classification of discourses into prescriptive and descriptive is crude. For evaluative and scientific discourses describe *in different ways*, in one case with, and in the other without, an orientation to action, and similarly the utopian and deliberative discourses prescribe *in different ways*, in one case for ideal, and in the other case for actual, situations. Evaluation and science do not seem 'equally' descriptive; rather science seems more 'purely' so. Similarly, utopian discourse seems more 'purely' normative than deliberative discourse. Following through with that reflection, it is more illuminating, I suggest, to represent the discourses as occupying four different points on a single prescriptive/descriptive axis, and to represent their relationship in the following quasi-genetic way.

All the discourses have to do with the sustained methodical process of education. Now sustained methodical action involves the twin thoughts of where one is starting from and the better place one is trying to reach, and at a more formal level the concepts of 'review' and 'plan', the bases, respectively, of the evaluative and deliberative discourses. We may then proceed further to distil from those concepts the more abstract notions of descriptivity and normativity and push each to its limit. At one extreme, beyond the idea of understanding how things actually are as a condition of effective action, we get to understanding as a value in its own right. At the other extreme, beyond the idea of the realizable good, we reach that of the ideal. At one extreme is a discourse at two removes (but not therefore altogether divorced) from how we would wish things to be, and at the other extreme a discourse at two removes (but also not divorced) from how things actually are.[22]

In this representation the deliberative and evaluative discourses emerge from, and attend closely upon, action, and this much seems unproblematic. These discourses then become platforms for the other two. By processes that would repay further analysis but that seem to involve abstraction and pushing to the limit, utopian discourse emerges from deliberative and scientific from evaluative.

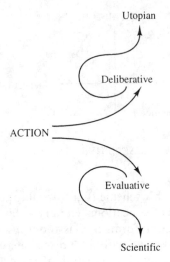

Figure 4.2

CONCLUSION

The main points in the position built up over two chapters can be rendered visually as:

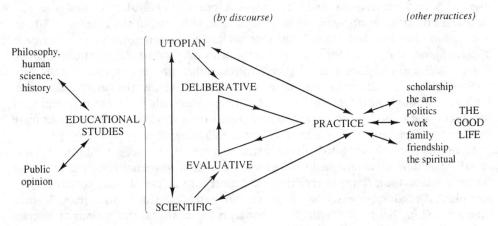

(arrows indicate the direction of marked or crucial *influence)*

Figure 4.3 Theory and practice in education.

Working from the left, the diagram represents:

- the *two-way* relationships between educational theory and some other major disciplines;
- the similar relationship that should hold between theory and public opinion in this key area of democratic life;
- the thesis that educational theory comprises four discourses in a cluster;
- the mutual presence to each other of practice in its particularity and the evaluative and deliberative discourses, and the general direction of the movement of ideas in this inner triangle;

- the containment of that triangle in a larger triangle which indicates the inter-dependence of this practice, in its holistic aspiration, with utopian and scientific discourses in combination;
- closely connected to the last, the strategic role of this practice in relation to other practices and to the good life.

NOTES

1. Hirst (1966).
2. This contrasts with a search for distinctions between core and contextual (implied in Hirst, 1983), or between properly and improperly called (Carr and Kemmis, 1986; J. Elliott, 1989), types of educational theory.
3. Habermas (1971/2).
4. Carr and Kemmis (1986, p. 11).
5. *Ibid*.
6. Popper (1945/66).
7. Habermas (1972).
8. Hirst (1983).
9. Schwab (1970). Schwab's series of papers on the 'Practical' remain the most penetrating and assured discussion that I know of deliberative discourse in education.
10. *Ibid*. Again: 'A curriculum grounded in but one or a few sub-subjects of the social sciences is indefensible; contributions from all are required. There is no foreseeable hope of a unified theory in the immediate or middle future, nor of a metatheory which will tell us how to put those sub-subjects together or order them in a fixed hierarchy of importance to the problems of curriculum. What remains as a viable alternative is the unsystematic, uneasy, pragmatic, and uncertain unions and connections which can be affected in an eclectic. And I must add . . . that *changing* connections and *differing* orderings at different times of these separate theories, will characterize a sound eclectic.' Schwab (1971) discusses these eclectic arts in detail.
11. 'Moral development: a plea for pluralism', reprinted in Peters (1974).
12. See House (1977, 1980), MacDonald (1974), Hamilton *et al.* (1977), Eisner (1984), Simons (1987).
13. Its further *educative* function, its particular contribution to the enlightenment of various categories of practitioner, depends on it retaining that primary intention.
14. A school asks itself if it should invest in Ginn Mathematics. Here the availability of the programme (and the school will assume it has undergone evaluation trials in its development) stimulates an evaluation by the school of its current practice, of the Ginn programme, and of the two in relation.
15. There is also some carry-over from the idea of the disinterested social scientist. This is a delicate matter about which the most important things to observe are that it is open to a non-positivistic interpretation, as we shall see in Chapter 5, and that there remains some difference between evaluative and scientific discourses in the kinds of detachment that are appropriate. Cronbach *et al.* (1980) speak of a 'multi-partisan' spirit, and House, somewhat similarly, prefers to speak of 'impartiality' rather than of 'objectivity' or 'dis-interestedness', since the point is not 'to deal with interests by excluding them', but 'by including and balancing them' (House, 1980, p. 224). It will become clear in Chapter 6, however, that I would be reluctant thus to cede the terms 'objective' and 'disinterested' to their positivisitic abusers.
16. Eisner (1984), and elsewhere in his works.
17. MacDonald (1974) has become the *locus classicus*. Simons (1987, Chapters 1 and 2) is a fine review of the issues and the literature in the UK and the USA.
18. *Positivism* might be said (disparagingly) to be the reduction of all knowledge to the model of scientific knowledge, of all scientific knowledge to the model of physical science, and

of physical science to a device for recording events and predicting their future courses. Auguste Compte gave it its classic expression in the 1830s in his six-volume *Cours de philosophie positive*. It was taken up by Emile Durkheim in his very influential (1895) *The Rules of Sociological Method*, which proposed that a properly scientific approach to the social world depended on treating social phenomena like things, 'social facts' like the facts of the natural sciences and human beings as natural objects (contrast Giddens, 1976). Thence it became an essential ingredient of functionalism, the dominant orthodoxy in social science – at any rate until recently. Fortunately, beginning with Durkheim's own classic studies of religion, suicide and the division of labour, functionalist social scientists have managed to avoid being too tediously consistent in their positivism. Positivism also influenced, though less markedly, Marx and Marxism – perhaps the main rival perspective in the history of modern social science. American pragmatism, though emphasizing the unity of science (e.g. Dewey, 1910), was less inclined to interpret this 'reductively'. But the real antithesis of positivism is the *verstehen* or 'interpretive' tradition, with roots in the nineteenth-century German philosopher William Dilthey, which was a marked influence on Weber, and of which the phenomenological and ethnomethodological approaches to social enquiry flowing from Alfred Schutz are more recent expressions, as is the hermeneutic approach of Gadamer (1975). More recently, Jürgen Habermas, with the aid of a theory of 'knowledge-constitutive interests' (1968), has embarked on the mighty project of 'overcoming' the division between positivist and *verstehen* traditions, indeed of drawing on *all* the traditions above to create a 'critical' (and therefore normative) kind of social theory. See the highly praised study of Habermas by McCarthy (1978).

19. Different from this *overt* kind of 'taking up', perhaps, is the kind of case in which it is 'with invisible ink' that the utopian viewpoint is written into a theory in social science, metaphysics or theology, so that special interpretive skills are needed to decode it (less a matter, incidentally, of utopian discourse masquerading as scientific, than of the 'deep grammar' relationship between the two discourses). For example, Val Walkerdine (1984) persuasively analyses Piaget's theories of development in this way. We might note, too, the debate among some Christian theologians as to the religious function of theology, with some claiming that theology fails to the extent that it does not make God live for its participants, while others maintain that it is no more in the business of making people holy than is thermodynamics in the business of making them warm.

20. In more or less pure examples of a discourse (of which there are many for each discourse) we often find *borrowings* from other discourses which fail to compromise 'purity' because of the way they are adapted and assimilated to the host-discourse.

   By contrast, properly *mixed* discourse (of which there are innumerable examples, including books that range over all four of the discourses), involves a measure of commitment to the distinctive grammar of each discourse in the mix. It is particularly it, and the coherence with which it can be pulled off, that suggests the underlying complementarity of the discourses.

   Apparently *borderline* discourse, e.g. an election manifesto that is half-way to the utopian, a heavily theorized case study that seems semi-scientific, an inspector's report that glides effortlessly between evaluation and practical prescription, poses a different question. Are the discourses distinguishable in a fully adequate way, so that what looks like borderline discourse would in fact be subtly mixed discourse with all its elements ultimately assignable to one side or the other? Or does each pair of neighbouring discourses constitute a spectrum, with utopian shading gradually into deliberative, deliberative into evaluative, evaluative into scientific, and perhaps scientific back into utopian? Our accounts of the discourses imply (assume?) the first view, i.e. that the discourses are fully distinguishable. But it is not clear whether or not this issue is of any real importance.

21. See pp. 20–1 above.

22. I owe the germ, at least, of this idea to David Jenkins.

Chapter 5

Science?

If humanistic science may be said to have any goals beyond sheer fascination with the human mystery and enjoyment of it, these would be to release the person from external control and to make him less predictable to the observer . . .

(Abraham Maslow, *The Psychology of Science*[1])

In this chapter we shall – tentatively and quite gently – explore further the idea of a scientific discourse that is at once distinct from the other discourses of educational theory and yet falls *within* educational theory by virtue of the closeness of its relationships with those other discourses. We shall consider whether, and how, even austere science maintains a connection with the normative and practical sides of educational discourse.

Now, certainly, science seems to involve a more thoroughgoing 'descriptivism'[2] or detachment than evaluation. The economist attends to rival conceptions of education – vocational preparation versus liberal development of mind, say – not to judge between them, nor yet (primarily anyway) to facilitate others in judging between them, but simply as a variable to be understood in its relationships with such other variables as rates of economic growth and wealth distribution patterns within complex social equations. The detached comparativist takes care not to let his 'personal view' intrude anywhere on his meticulous analysis of ideological training in China. And so on. Clearly this is the more radical kind of detachment, extending beyond the efficacy of instruments[3] to educational aims and conceptions, which, as we noticed earlier, is *already* a vital moment in the open society's evaluations. But here it would seem to be sustained in a way that it is not sustained in critical evaluation. There, one describes detachedly so that one may then pronounce more objectively; description is put directly at the service of value judgement (the evaluator's or someone else's), and indeed the judgement itself remains part of the description (until it passes over to recommendation). But the case seems different with the human sciences. Such services as they render to value judgement and, beyond that, to the improvement of practice are less direct, longer postponed and rather more (which is not the same thing as 'totally') extrinsic to the discourse itself. But does this warrant thinking of these sciences as 'value free and easy'?

And, on the other hand, if there are such services in the end, can the difference in question be more than one of degree?

If any science, natural or human, seeks understanding essentially for its own sake, does that mean that any 'utility' its discoveries may turn out to possess is quite irrelevant to its quality as science? Even more strongly, does science's commitment to a critically objective understanding actually *preclude* it from all 'contamination' by (other!) values? An implication of that would be that not much sense could be made of the ideal, canvassed earlier, of a critically objective evaluation – since it clearly requires that matters of value be not irredeemably subjective. Indeed, we have been implying, and will shortly be arguing, that a tough objectivity is an ideal of educational theory *generally*, and therefore of all four of our discourses. Again, we might take exception to a too easy lumping together here of the natural and the human sciences. There are (ought to be?), surely, quite profound differences between these, including some that may bear on the *range* of values they connect and disconnect to and the *kind* of detachment that is appropriate in each. For instance, the anthropologist should worry about what, morally speaking, distinguishes his trade from the voyeur's, while the geologist need not. What we want, it seems, is an account of the human sciences that is alert to *both the similarities and the differences* between them and the natural sciences in such respects as:

- the nature of the understanding yielded;
- the detachment with which it is appropriately sought;
- methodology;
- the relationships of research to values and value deliberations;
- the distinction, and the relationship, between 'pure' and 'applied'.

This is too tall an order here, of course.[4] But we can hope to open up these areas a little before leaving them. We shall start out from a fairly simple extended example.

A DOUBLE INVOLVEMENT WITH VALUE

Suppose a discussion on the relevance of education to economic growth. M_1 asserts a relevance – and appeals to a study of a large number of countries which purports to show a correlation between increases in educational provision and later increases in national wealth. N_1 denies a relevance – on the grounds that true education, like true virtue, is its own reward. Education is corrupted when pursued as an economic investment. Indeed one of its main tasks is to counteract the materialism of the age and of humankind. As for the purported correlation, it is hardly to be presumed that the researcher in question could identify true education!

(1) We surely suspect here a confusion of two issues, as opposed to just two views on the same issue. M_1 seems concerned with what is intended and offered as education (with education in the descriptive sense) and with what we may realistically expect from it. N_1 is concerned with education in the ideal sense and with what it permits and does not permit. So it may be doubted whether their claims really come to grips with each other. Consider, by contrast, the kinds of counter to either claim that *would* move unambiguously on the same plane. In response to M_1, N_2 queries, instead, whether the correlation demonstrates the supposed cause–effect link. It may be that educational expansion is a standard part of the kinds of planned investment that yield economic

growth because it is generally *thought* to be an essential part of the package, but that it is *actually* a non-contributing part. In fact – to quibble further – that it regularly precedes growth does not of itself entail even that it is generally thought of as an agent of growth. It may more commonly be undertaken, say, as an advance withdrawal on confidently anticipated growth. In any case, even supposing there is some causal connection, the correlation is too coarse to help us identify it with any specificity. It suggests, but is no help with, such further questions as: Does the expansion of primary and secondary education pay a better dividend than the expansion of elite third-level institutions? Do differences on this score correlate with differences in the extent to which the new wealth is shared around? How much depends on whether curricula are given a deliberately vocational orientation? Are the answers to these questions the same for industrialized and developing countries, and for socialist and capitalist ones?

The whole exchange is now firmly located within the economics of education and its furtherance clearly depends on more information and research in that area. On the other hand we can also imagine the debate settling down on the other plane. In response to N_1's original puritanism, M_2 retorts that economic growth is one perfectly legitimate goal of education and a legitimate priority in poor countries and that any ideal of education which denies this is unbearably precious, quite certainly elitist in practice and almost sure to be self-deluding, indeed a paradigm example of 'false consciousness'. Clearly, the conflict is now mainly about values.

So we have here our distinction between a discourse that is normative and utopian, and another which is detachedly empirical and, at some level of sustained sophistication, starts to count as scientific. This distinction N_1 may have failed to observe.

(2) Yet on the evidence before us we cannot be entirely sure that N_1 did fail in this way, did misinterpret M_1. For M's claim that educational expansion generally led to economic growth might not have been intended as a purely factual observation. It might have been advanced as *also* a general reason or motive for educational expansion – just as 'you have a wasp on your ear' functions as simultaneously statement and warning. In that case the N_1 response, whatever else we think of it, would have been a genuine counter-claim. Now, that a statement can thus simultaneously belong to our two modes of discourse would suggest that, even at their more formal and disciplined levels, they are not so distinct as to have no bearings on each other (which would also explain how they can be confused).

Two such bearings emerge from the questions in economics posed by N_2. First, recall those distinctions between intended and unintended consequences, presumed and actual consequentiality, investment and consumption of anticipated income. They remind us, if we need reminding, that the economics of education is necessarily involved with the perceptions, intentions and values that inform educational policy and practice as with *an aspect of its subject matter*. For it, these are crucial 'phenomena'. Second, and at another level, those empirical questions and investigations would take much of their point from our attachment to values like material progress, breadth of culture and equality. Largely at least, it is because there is a practical interest in bringing about and maintaining (or, perhaps, in preventing) material well-being, enlightenment, equality, etc. that these questions first arise and become significant. Max Weber gave classic, and robustly absolute, expression to this point in reference to what he called 'cultural sciences' generally:

> We have designated as 'cultural sciences' those disciplines which analyze the phenomena of life in terms of their cultural significance. . . . The concept of culture is a *value-concept*. Empirical reality becomes 'culture' to us because and insofar as we relate it to value ideas. It includes those segments and only those segments of reality which have become significant to us because of this value-relevance. Only a small portion of existing concrete reality is colored by our value-conditioned interest and it alone is significant to us. . . . We cannot discover, however, what is meaningful to us by means of a 'presuppositionless' investigation of empirical data. Rather perception of its meaningfulness to us is the presupposition of its becoming an *object* of investigation.[5]

Values, then, are *a crucial determinant of the questions posed* in economics, as in other human sciences. So it is not just a matter that the findings of pure economics can later be 'applied' in policy-making. 'Pure' economics is *already* shaped by the kind of deep values that also remotely direct policy – which indeed makes its eventual applicability seem less fortuitous. (This is compatible, we can say, with these values being in some way suspended or 'bracketed' during the actual conduct of research and investigation. But Weber himself translated this 'bracketing' as a 'value freedom' similar to research and investigation in the natural sciences – hence his well-known adage that the cultural sciences were at once 'value-relevant and value-free' – and this is distinctly problematic. Are we really to level the psychologist's research relationship with children, say, to the geologist's relationship with rocks?[6])

Do these two value involvements of sciences like economics not begin to open a gap between them and the natural sciences? It might seem that the second, at least, does nothing of the sort. For in the natural sciences, too, theoretical research can be motivated by practical interests, from the development of weapon systems to the cure of disease. True, much natural science (including some that later turns out to be technologically potent) seems precisely not to be practically orientated in this way. But then are there not areas in the human sciences as well, much of anthropology for instance, where research is pursued from a desire, simply, to know and understand how things are (Maslow's 'sheer fascination with the human mystery')? These parallels are broad, however, and one suspects they conceal important differences. In the end, surely, value relevance must condition the human sciences *in some more intimate way* than it does the physical sciences. Now this would be precisely because human sciences deal with the human. So such a more intimate species of value relevance would link up with the feature we noticed first in them, that they include values and value-related aspects of life among their 'phenomena'. Let us explore this clue, in effect the linkage between the two value involvements of human science, between the values that lie behind enquiries giving them 'relevance', and the subjects' values being enquired into.

COMMUNICATIVE SCIENCE

The understanding that the economist, say, seeks is of a phenomenon which already has some understanding of itself. Furthermore, since that self-understanding goes into making the phenomenon what it is – an investment rather than a consumer purchase, a gift as opposed to a loan, etc. – the economist *must* take account of it. Her understanding must start from the phenomenon's, although it is not bound simply to replicate it. In the same vein, we noticed previously that the descriptive user of 'education' accepted the self-identification, though not the self-endorsement, of the normative user, and that an anthropologist might diffidently speak of 'education' in a tribe that did not speak so of itself, only if it did speak of itself in related terms like 'rearing', 'maturing' and 'learning'. Now what this implies, in a word, is *communication*.[7] The researcher may be face to face with the researched, or she may choose to rely instead on intermediaries like pollsters or do 'keyhole' research with one-way mirrors and such. The latter strategies may risk a lower yield in understanding and probability, but, in any case, it remains crucial in them that the researcher has access to *what her subjects say, and say about themselves*. It is not only a matter (important though this is, and the basis of all else) that the researcher shares human being with the researched and, therefore, can draw on her ordinary understanding of herself and her own circles (itself in large part based upon communication) in understanding them. Beyond that, she must either share a language with them or rely on interpreters, if her understanding is to rise above the rudimentary. It is, then, a minimal condition of human science that the researcher and the researched *belong to a common communicative network*, and an optimal condition – for at least some human sciences and other things being equal – that they communicate directly. Clearly this is a different relationship between scientist and phenomenon from that which obtains in the physical sciences. Or, we may rather say, it is *only* in the human sciences (though ethology might fall in the middle here) that there is really a question of a 'relationship' with the phenomenon – and now the term 'phenomenon' seems inappropriately detached!

That this difference between human and natural science is fundamental is shown by the number of other differences that are easily represented as flowing from it.

Physical phenomena cannot query the researcher's motives and rights, refuse their cooperation, bargain over the dissemination of findings, set out to deceive, be deceived about themselves, or in their turn research the researcher.

In the other direction, the human scientist can change what she studies by her study of it, and this not just by some lack of refinement in her instruments but by virtue of the ineradicably communicative basis of her work. So, it may be that her very questions will promote in her subjects a more distinct self-understanding and a more explicit commitment to their existing practices; or, on the other hand, her 'why?' may provoke them to a 'why indeed?' and to some change in their practices. True, the chemist too will manipulate, change, even destroy, materials as he investigates their structure. But the changes at issue here are rather those which occur in, or near, the area of precisely that which is to be understood about the subject under investigation – the nature and incidence of certain social practices, for instance. True, again, some interventions in the physical sciences also change precisely that which is to be understood or measured. A thermometer measures heat by first absorbing heat, thus altering slightly the ambient temperature. But this can be calculated and allowed for. The changes of this kind which the human scientist risks are, crucially, much less predictable. Often she cannot be sure whether the effect of her research process on her subjects will be nil, negligible, substantial or massive.

Beyond that effect, and often just as unpredictable, there is the possible effect on her subjects should they come to learn her results – and for this there seems no analogue at all in the physical sciences. 'Atoms cannot get to know what scientists say about them, or change their behaviour in the light of that knowledge. Human beings can do so.'[8]

Another corollary of communication dependence leads us back to value relevance and detachment. The subjects of research may seek to involve the social scientist in *their* cares and values, or she may come of her own accord to sympathize with these or to react to them in some other way. This means that there is a question of the researcher extending her methodological detachment from her own initial values to cover those of her subjects as well. On the other hand, there is also a question of coming to redefine the research so that it will be relevant to their cares as well as to her own initial ones – or, since this may be anticipated, of (one reason for) delaying the precise specification of the research until after a period of getting acquainted with the subjects.

Communicating with subjects with values of their own does not just broaden the scope of value relevance and detachment. It makes for that more intimate kind of value relevance we had expected, and for a (slightly) paradoxical intimacy in the practice of detachment itself. The crux, as we foresaw, is *an engagement at some level between the values that lie behind an enquiry, giving it its significance, and the values being confronted directly in the enquiry*. In the natural sciences, even when the practical applications of enquiry are up front from the beginning, the enquiry is not into the conceptions and values that make those applications desirable. There is nothing in the abstracted phenomena themselves that can either mirror or challenge those conceptions and values. Thus in biochemical cancer research the images, hatreds and hopes which give the research poignant significance are not themselves under investigation. It would be another kind of enquiry, no longer biochemical, that focused on people's feelings and beliefs regarding 'pointless' pain and disablement, 'premature' death, the 'malignant' incubus that ambushes and consumes from within, and so on. Now of that enquiry we might say that it had considerable *human interest*. This is precisely to say that the attitudes it revealed in the particular subjects being researched would tend to engage with the attitudes to cancer of those of the general public who followed or read of the research, as, in the very first place, of the researchers themselves. An additional point relates to certain groups, like hospice workers, health monitors and drug companies, who could be expected to have a *special* interest in this social research. Would these special interests bring into play their owners' own attitudes to cancer? I should be inclined to say that they would fail to do this to the extent, only, that they were exploitative; that is, saw people precisely not as fellow humans, but as things to be manipulated.

To be sure, there must be a place for detachment as well as engagement in the human sciences. The Western anthropologist studying traditional patterns of rearing and instruction in an African society, say, will guard against foisting her own normative conceptions of education on their system, whether by 'reading them in' (underestimating the possible differences), or by judging the system against them. She will place a disciplined check on her natural inclinations to compare, challenge or feel threatened, and will seek to understand them 'in their own terms', as opposed to her Western terms. But this disqualification of her own educational values will be neither total nor final. These, as Weber would remark, will already have been instrumental in her choice of education as an area of life that is of common significance, significant not just to them and to some envisaged audience of her work, but to her herself. Second, the contrast between 'their terms' and 'her terms' cannot be made absolute. She aspires eventually to understand their education as they do, but for initial reference must surely use conceptions of education she already understands, including the one she herself tends to espouse. Her first gropings, even if they eschew explicit comparisons, will tend to highlight the similarities and dissimilarities with these. More important, perhaps, for *her* eventually to achieve an understanding of them in their own terms is for their terms in some way to be brought into relationship with hers, to enlarge hers as they become hers. Third, after detached understanding has been attained and articulated, she (or others) may use it as a basis for explicit comparison, and indeed for comparison and enquiry that lead to value judgement – whether at the general utopian level, or at the level of evaluation and deliberation relating to this particular context. Questions as to what is true and false, just and unjust, better and worse, good and evil, may then be let off the leash. (Not, however, relieved of all discipline. That she might consider this changed enterprise no longer 'strictly scientific' would not preclude her tackling it too in ways that were non-ethnocentric, open-minded, nuanced, methodical and critical.)

In short, *detachment and human interest might be said to interpret and to limit each other dialectically in the human sciences.* We have arrived at a view of human science as involving a form of layered communication (but perhaps no more layered than any reasonably subtle conversation) in which a detachment that is radical and sustained on the scientist's side – more sustained than it can, or need, be in critical evaluation with its fairly immediate responsibilities to action – is to be contained within a respectful solidarity, a sense of a common humanity and shared human concerns.

Our argument, however, has been of the 'in principle' kind. The way in which the human sciences have *actually* developed is another complicated story. Suffice it to say that the influence of positivism has inhibited normative interest to the point that much human science does not lend itself easily to the further step of critical normative enquiry. It is – as I should have to say, having in effect argued that some normative interest is a condition of profound understanding in human science – too shallow for that. What this tainted work has seemed to lend itself to is 'social engineering'.[9] This would be not too surprising. The point here is not the frequent indifference of scientists, both natural and human, to how their science might be applied, but something deeper which bears fully only on the human scientist. This is that the positivistic project, by the finality with which it shuts the door on a normative exchange with the subject, or by the distance which it puts between itself and any such exchange, must tend to a depersonalization of the communication between scientist and subject and, thereby, to a depersonalized view of the subject. In this the positivistic pure scientist and the engineer, the voyeur and the manipulator, are brothers and sisters under the skin.

NOTES

1. Quoted in MacDonald (1977).
2. 'Descriptive' here, as all along, contrasts with 'prescriptive' and 'normative' – not, of course, with 'analytic', 'explanatory', 'speculative' or 'theoretical'.
3. In fact these sciences have traditionally included evaluations of instruments too, but by reference only to the norms of the system for which they were designed, norms towards which the scientist maintains a methodological neutrality.
4. Winch (1958) remains an important work. It was seminal to a boom in the philosophy of social science in the Anglo-Saxon tradition, of which the three anthologies Emmet and MacIntyre (1970), Wilson (1970) and the more recent Hollis and Lukes (1982) are very useful expressions. Of course, the philosophy of the physical sciences did not conveniently stand still during these reappraisals of the social sciences. On the contrary, it was revolutionized in such works as Polanyi (1958), Popper (1963) among others of his works, Kuhn (1962) and Lakatos and Musgrave (1970).

5.   ' "Objectivity" in social science', first published 1904, translated in Weber (1949, p. 76).

6.   Weber (1949). Myrdal (1970) is one work that challenges the possibility of value freedom during investigation. Lessnoff (1974, Chapter 6) is a clear survey of this and related matters from a Weberian standpoint (emphasizing, and concurring with, Weber's fundamentally relativist position on values, however, from which I would dissent).

7.   The work of Habermas, of course, brilliantly exploits the involvement of the human sciences with communication (some of this being his legacy from the hermeneutic tradition). It acknowledges both that the communication of people with each other is a central focus of human science, and that the community of human scientists itself belongs to the same broader communicative network as its subjects. To my knowledge, however, Habermas does not discuss, as I do here, the effects of this communication dependence on the scientist–subject relationship.

8.   Giddens (1982, pp. 14–15).

9.   Rose (1985) has recently made a strong case for viewing much psychology in this way. Walkerdine (1984) presents a similar view of specifically developmental psychology in its relationship with pedagogy. Foucault is a principal inspiration of these two works (e.g. Foucault, 1975). But the connection between 'social physics' and 'social control' was both explicit and unashamed in Compte, with his slogan *prévoir pour pouvoir*.

Chapter 6

Objectivity?

For merely looking at an object cannot be of any use to us. All looking goes over into an observing, all observing into a reflecting, all reflecting into a connecting, and so one can say with every attentive look we cast into the world we are already theorising.

(Goethe[1])

In discussing the dialectic of open/loaded uses of 'education' in Chapter 2 we noticed that debate over general conceptions of education is tacitly premised on the assumption that there is some true (right, proper) substantive sense of 'education'. Now people are apt to become fidgety with solemn talk about 'truth', associating it with rigidity and intolerance. And, anyway, might not that objectivist anticipation of debate be unrealizable, illusory? The hard subjectivist believes that indeed it is totally unrealizable. He either avoids debate, or engages in it without hope of profit and only because he cannot help himself. The soft subjectivist believes it is unrealizable in the last analysis, but that in the shorter term, and with just these people, there may be something (exactly what may be difficult to say) to be gained from debate.

A significant point about both these positions is that they are more or less consciously disillusioned and unhappy. That suggests the question of what then drives people to them. The answer, I believe, is not primarily 'arguments' like the classical sceptical ones, but certain values and beliefs from the interface of intellectual and ethical life which are seen as at once incompatible with objectivism, and compensating in some measure for the sacrifice of objectivism. These include

- an awareness of our fallibility and of the fragility of our certitudes;
- a distrust of abstract generalization;
- a sense that some of the best of our thinking evades 'logical' expression;
- a belief in a large freedom as a condition of human thriving;
- a sense that certain perennial issues are for different generations and individuals to face and to answer for themselves.

Defending objectivism is, to a large extent, a matter of showing that these values and beliefs can be accommodated within it, thus too displaying the distance between it and the fanatical and fundamentalist. It is a matter, we might say, of revealing the human face of objectivism. (I shall use the terms 'objectivist' and 'objectivism' simply as a short-hand reference to the view that objectivity is possible and desirable, in a sense of 'objectivity' that connects it intrinsically with 'truth', via notions like 'respecting the truth' and 'seeking the truth'.[2])

The series of exercises that follows eventually requires us to venture beyond educational theory, in particular into philosophy of science since that is where the discussion of these matters has been most advanced.

SOCIO-HISTORICAL RELATIVITY

There may or may not be one loaded use of 'education', conveying one ordering of educational priorities, that is right for every time and place. But any such use would certainly be insufficient. In some, if not all, particular situations it would need supplementing by uses responsive to just those kinds of situation and expressive of the right priorities for just them. You may think 'conscientization', political consciousness-raising up-front as the condition of all else, is right (i.e. *truly* what is needed) for the adult oppressed of 'cultures of silence' in Latin America and elsewhere.[3] You don't then have to think it equally appropriate for infant schools in Western-type democracies. Assuming you don't, you may seek a thinner but still useful interpretation of it to apply to both contexts. But even if you find this you will still need the more substantial interpretation for the adult oppressed.

In other words, 'truth', even 'general truth' or 'principle', and 'local circumstance' are not incompatible objects of acknowledgement. At least one tradition in Western philosophy, the Aristotelian, has always recognized this. For it practical reasoning, like all reasoning, has an inherently general character. But its job is to direct action, which is always particular, and usually under real, rather than laboratory, conditions. Hence its principles have a rough-hewn character. Unlike scientific laws, typically (perhaps not universally) they include an 'other things being equal' clause in which the 'other things' cannot be fully specified in advance. They can clash with each other in particular situations while remaining generally consistent and even mutually supportive. And exceptions do not necessarily disprove the rule.[4] *This kind of 'relativism' is perfectly consistent with objectivism.* Truth (in as absolute a sense as you like) remains crucial in it – with regard to what is really best in such and such particular circumstances, or the actual degree of generalizability of some order of priorities, or the validity of some individual value consideration. In these matters, it allows, people are right and wrong, more and less right and wrong, and, of course, really disagree, i.e. hold views that really do, more or less, exclude each other.

A PROPER FREEDOM

An 'objectivist' ethic does not have to prescribe *everything*. The instinct is strong, indeed, to regard freedom as the oxygen of real education. Much of education, surely, including much that is most formative in it, is a matter of interest, bent and legitimate free choice. But this is compatible with much else in it being 'essential', a matter of objective requirement. Of course, the line here can be hard to draw and is the subject of much disagreement. The same is true in sexual matters, where we have example after example of one person's question of inclination being another's question of morality. Similarly with situations in which different cultures meet and mingle: when should one redescribe one's 'moral distaste' as 'cultural prejudice'? and when should one not? Actually, in each of these (overlapping) areas of life the line between freedom and obligation is not only controversial, but is itself one of the more important things to get right. Again, matters of free choice and of obligation *relate* to each other in more or less complex ways. Real obligations arise constantly in situations which one was under no obligation to enter in the place. Thus in intellectual life – as in friendship, marriage and career – paths are commonly more freely entered than left, and this is as much an ethical as a psychological fact. And on the other hand, we are often free as to *how* we meet our obligations. But these complications do not detract from – indeed they presuppose – the main distinction between the essential and the optional. For a given society, time or person, then, *there can be many combinations of learnings that would each constitute 'a true education'*, as well as very many others that would not.

FALLIBILITY AND UNCERTAINTY

Truth as an ideal and truth as attainment are quite different things. The worthwhileness of the quest relies on no particular estimate of the extent of actual or possible attainment. Whether it rules out some estimates, and what these may be, are large questions in epistemology. But, historically, it has even been thought compatible with some kinds of scepticism and agnosticism. This was so in the best of medieval natural theology, as is attested in this striking remark of Aquinas:

> It is therefore said of us that when we come to the end of our knowledge, we acknowledge God as the Unknown, because the mind has made most progress in understanding when it recognizes that God's essence lies beyond anything that the mind in its state of being-on-the-way can comprehend.[5]

A better-known example nowadays is Karl Popper's 'dynamic scepticism', which involves the following claims: (1) Of their logical nature theories cannot be verified, only falsified. Any theory can be false, though it fits or explains all the known relevant facts, including improbable facts that have been checked out purposely to test it and that would not otherwise be known. For, as the history of science abundantly illustrates, yet-to-be-discovered facts may contradict and falsify it, and thereby challenge us to find a better theory. So it is as much falsifications (which should therefore be deliberately sought) as successful predictions that advance our knowledge. (2) Observation statements (purported facts) can be mistaken, if only because what we call facts are themselves impregnated with lower-level theory.[6] Thus even our falsifications of theories, since they depend on such observations, are fallible. (3) The pursuit of truth is not therefore pointless. We may know (fallibly) Newton's physics to be false, absolutely speaking. But the vast range of what it could explain and correctly predict legitimates our thinking of it as 'having much truth in it'. If Einstein's relativity theory accounts for all that plus other things, including the observations that contradicted Newton, then we are entitled to think of it as getting us still 'nearer the truth' – though it is unlikely to have got us all the way, and even if it had, we could never be sure that it had. In short, for Popper, the idea that truth is 'manifest' – if only we had eyes to see it, could rid ourselves of prejudices etc. – is a mistake, but *it remains that truth is laboriously 'approachable'.*[7]

Education is a practical business. Its theories are more concerned with the truth (rightness, appropriateness) of action, than the truth of fact and explanation. They are certainly no less fallible for that – the extent to which they vie with each other makes that clear. The logic of this fallibility seems similar in some respects and dissimilar in others to what we have just noticed. Thus here too openness to experience and its corrections is commended, but so may be steadfastness in the face of contradiction and, as we have mentioned, exceptions do not necessarily falsify the general rule. The point remains that *fallibility provides no more excuse here than in science for abandoning the quest.* If Popper is right, even radical unverifiability would not excuse this.

INCOMMENSURABILITY, VISION AND THE LIMITS OF ARGUMENT

At the end of Chapter 2 we were critical of the view that 'education' is an *essentially* contested concept inasmuch as 'essential contestability' left itself open to interpretation as 'rational irresolvability'. But why suppose irresolvability? The most significant answer to this question in the wider philosophical literature is that such contests are irresolvable because the rival views are incommensurable. This presents a trickier challenge. For one thing, as we shall see, it seems to make falsification not just fallible but quite as uncertain as verification.

Does rational resolution require commensurability? Is discerning the relative 'truthfulness' of rival possibilities and views fundamentally a matter of 'calibration' – parallel listings of pros and cons and step-by-step comparisons against some neutral standards? On the one hand this is expected. The discovery of its absence in key areas has caused dismay – in proportion to the previous reputation of the area for objectivity – and promoted both rather desperate reaffirmation and subjectivism.[8] On the other hand this expectation may be no more than a prejudice about how we do and should think. *This kind of comparability may not be necessary for an objective discernment and choice.* Perhaps it is not even a condition of everything that could properly be called 'proof' here. I shall consider three cases: irrational numbers (the original incommensurables), scientific progress (again) and (at some length) revolutions in general.

(1) Is there a number which multiplied by itself gives 2? Does $\sqrt{2}$ exist, in whatever way mathematicals do exist? Arithmetically, though progressively approachable, it is not finally articulable – which suggests a negative answer. Yet it must exist, for it is the exact ratio between the diagonal and the side of a square – it must be as real as they are. This had an importance for the Greeks that is hard for us to recover,[9] but it retains an obvious value as a parable: that which cannot be fully articulated can yet be exhibited; demonstration can go beyond articulation; the incompletely articulable can be perfectly intelligible ('rational' after all). And this emerges in mathematics, the spiritual home of exhaustive articulation.

(2) To return to science, we already have it from Popper that science grows not by simple accumulation – adding new theories, laws and facts to the old – but by displacement of the falsified old with the new. We should now add, going beyond Popper and

following Thomas Kuhn,[10] that *these displacements have the character of revolutions.* This is to say the following.

(a) They are relatively infrequent events, a fraction only of the total activity in any particular area of science. So there is a contrast with 'normal' science. Normal science is characterized by a fine tuning of existing theory, law and fact – as opposed to a search for major novelty – and by sustained attempts to resolve known anomalies *within* existing theory. These attempts involve high degrees of mathematical, conceptual and instrumentational innovation, and are in most cases completely successful.

(b) Displacements of theory occur as parts of wider displacements of whole orders of things. An order of things (paradigm, disciplinary matrix, theory in the widest sense) for a particular area of science embraces versions of its key definitions, permitted metaphors and analogies, interpretations in practice of general scientific values including standards of proof, the recognition of certain notable achievements as exemplars, a view as to what the main unsolved problems are, criteria of membership of the community – all these as well as integrated sets of formal hypotheses. Shifts in the last are tied to shifts in all the other dimensions of the order. A very partial example is given by the definitional changes required by relativity theory:

> What had previously been meant by space was necessarily flat, homogeneous, isotropic, and unaffected by the presence of matter. If it had not been, Newtonian physics would not have worked. To make the transition to Einstein's universe, the whole conceptual web whose strands are space, time, matter, force, and so on, had to be shifted and laid down again on nature whole.[11]

Taking on such a multidimensional change, though not to be accomplished in an instant, is in the end an all-or-nothing affair.

(c) It cannot be *proved* that the change is right – not, that is, in that common sense of 'proof' that looks to mathematics for its standard – as is attested by the usual resistance of a section of the scientific community.

> If there were but one set of scientific problems, one world within which to work on them, and one set of standards for their solution, paradigm competition might be settled more or less routinely by some process like counting the number of problems solved by each. But, in fact, these conditions are never met completely. The proponents of competing paradigms are always at least slightly at cross-purposes. Neither side will grant all the non-empirical assumptions that the other needs in order to make its case. . . . Though each may hope to convert the other to his way of seeing his science and its problems, neither may hope to prove his case. The competition between paradigms is not the sort of battle that can be resolved by proofs.[12]

Proof here includes disproof, falsification. From Popper one might take the impression that science likes nothing so much as a falsification, and strikes out the relevant theory at the first whiff of one. But this would be very much too simple. Indeed its refutation is implicit in Popper's own view that observation statements, 'facts', are already impregnated with theory. This implies that the same phenomenon may be read differently – thus, as falsifying or as not falsifying. The 'problems' of a theory in a normal phase of science could *as logically* be read as 'falsifications'.[13] Those that are not resolved in the meantime probably will be so read in the next revolutionary phase – while the unconverted will read the problems of the new theory as critical objections to it. We should not expect, then, 'knock-down' kinds of falsification.

(d) Finally, what does positively effect and legitimate the change is a certain interplay between argumentation, critical of the old and supportive of the new, and a *vision* of new promise – to which we shall shortly return.

The picture of scientific development in (a) to (d) is lucidly and persuasively supported in *The Structure of Scientific Revolutions* by a wealth of illustration from the history of science. It seems to me essentially correct. However, Kuhn is led by it to dispute that science progresses towards the truth; although he maintains that this should not count as a failure for science. For the real task of science is puzzle-solving, something with no particular connection with truth, and at this it does progress. Now this is deeply uncomfortable. If 'puzzle-solving' is not immediately to reintroduce truth, as in criminal detection, say, the model has to be the artificial puzzle, like the Rubik cube or the chess problem. Then science would be no more 'about' the world than these are. There would be no connection between science and reality sufficient to explain even the technological success of science. Kuhn offers some not very thought through reasons for his view of this.[14] But behind them, almost certainly, lurks the assumption that a sequence of incommensurable theories can hardly be a route to truth. We may note the at least equal plausibility of the converse proposition that if even *science* proceeds incommensurably then incommensurability can be no very final barrier to objectivity.[15] We remarked in Popper the intuitively attractive ideas that false theories can have truth in them, that theories like Newton's owed their immense success at predicting the improbable to a high 'truth content', and that basically objective procedures contribute to progressive increases in the 'truth content' of scientific theories. Are these ideas really precluded by the incommensurability of theories?

(3) To take this further we need to dwell on the *positive* correlate of incommensurability: that is, *the interplay of argument with intuition and vision* that takes the place of 'commensuration' when incommensurables are deliberated over. But first we shall move to a more general context than just science.

Consider, then, the more general form of 'the revolution', and let us begin by distinguishing it from other kinds of departure from the usual. One of these kinds appeals only to *exceptional* circumstances. By so doing, it reintegrates itself into the establishment, though perhaps teaching it a degree more flexibility. Another kind presents itself as just *modernization*, keeping up with the times. Again we are reassured that no fundamental challenge is intended, though for some the idea that the system itself evolves will be challenge enough. In a third kind, the *renewal*, the dissenter appeals to one part of the established order as fundamental, authentic and original against another part. So, disappointed socialists of the Stalinist era appealed to Lenin against the Soviet state, Kierkegaard and a long line of Christian reformers to Christ against Christianity, Jesus himself (though he belongs much more to our next group) to the Old Testament against its lawyer guardians and interpreters, and the early deschoolers to the idea of education against schools. A way of life or a central institution is challenged, but by reference to the very ideals that gave it birth and by which it still professes to identify itself. Such challenges essentially look backwards, then, to shared first principles if not to a golden age, and their plea is for repentance and purification. They are directed at individuals (to recall the ideals of their youth, or their family tradition), and small groups (a couple is to recollect the spirit of their first love and honeymoon), as well as whole societies. Last, there is the *genuine revolution* where something new is being brought to birth *out of, and at the expense of*, the old. In addition to the standard political cases, the histories of art and science afford numerous examples and in the religious-moral sphere we have, for instance, Jesus' 'It was said to you of old. . . . But I say to you . . .'.[16] Arguably, the transformations that Piaget and the 'cognitivist' school see in ordinary mental and moral development would also qualify – if they exist – and education's involvement with them would make it a revolutionary activity. Historical developments in educational theory and practice that might qualify include Rousseau's *Emile*, the introduction of mass schooling and the transitions, first to meritocratic, and then to comprehensive, ideals and practices.

'Revolution' entails some incommensurability. For how is the revolution to justify itself?[17] Not simply, *ex hypothesi*, by an appeal to new or exceptional circumstances – and any such appeal may seek to redraw the boundaries between the 'normal' and the 'exceptional', and indeed the 'essential' and the 'circumstantial', thus serving only to restate what has to be justified. Nor can appeals to the past or to accepted principles suffice, and in any case these too will tend to involve reinterpretations that seem to the sceptical to beg the question. In the Piagetian model those at some higher stage cannot simply explain its superiority to those less advanced. There is no *proving* the moral relevance of intention, for example, to one who does not yet see it. So, more generally, the revolutionary has no straightforward way of justifying her cause to the guardians of the established order, the accepted premises and criteria of justification (for the given area) being themselves part of what she is challenging. Indeed, to begin with, for all her blazing conviction, she lacks the means of articulating arguments that satisfy even herself, since the concepts she has are almost all from the old store. Her intuition, she herself recognizes, runs ahead of her discursive argumentation. In time, language and argument will catch up and consolidate, but even then they will not be such as *logically to compel* the assent of the old guard, who will have as much trouble with the new premises as the revolutionaries had with the old order's. This, then, is the incommensurability of pre-and post-revolutionary situations – and the reason why revolutions succeed in part by having youth on their side and outliving their opponents.

Revolutions are not, as a rule, mindless affairs, however. Consider, now, how much *positive* thought is involved in coming by the vision, gaining adherents, and building the future.

(a) To start with, a radical critique of the old order. This will display not just compromise and inconsistency in the accretions of the ages, but inadequacy in the sources themselves. For that, it probably has to be already informed by some vision, as yet incipient and inarticulate, of a new order.

(b) That vision develops in stages. This or that item is seen in a new way – first fitfully, then more steadily. A series of such pictures builds up. At first they have in common just that they cannot be accommodated in the current general view. Then the outline of the new vision is called forth in them, and embraces them. And the pioneers will try to repeat these steps in potential adherents – realistically those already 'drawn' towards the vision (not, we hope, by the lure of novelty alone, still less of violence) – getting them first to see this, then that, in a new way, and so on.

(c) Now discursive reason reasserts itself. The old guard's counter-attacks, a wider audience, intellectual conscience (one hopes!) – all these will force developments in argumentation. Prominent among these developments, the critique of the old order will now be transmuted into point-by-point comparisons between the two orders. Incommensurability allows that much. But it rules out the possibility of these being decisive by themselves (the old guard will be producing its own counter-calculations), which is, perhaps, to say two things. First, the force of these point-by-point comparisons is not purely additive. Rather, they interact with more general arguments and comparisons, drawing from these as well as contributing to them. Second, the vision cannot now be dispensed with, for it continues to contain tacitly more than the arguments (particular and general) do discursively. But – a final important twist to this tale – while the vision remains a source and a touchstone for the arguments, these are in turn a crucial test for the vision, and not merely rationalization and propaganda. Weakness of argument at first makes only for redoubled efforts, but if it persists it starts to tell against the vision, even for the committed. It threatens not so much to disprove it as to dispel it: in the end, just an illusion! (And visual metaphors stay apt to the end.) *Arguments, then, are never sufficient but good ones do become necessary.*

(Of course, for many kinds of revolution this would be a severely disembodied account. One would want to add that the dialectic between vision and argument is set into a larger dialectic between life and thought. Actions, sufferings, the very lives of the revolutionaries – we might think of the crucifixion of Jesus – are charged with symbolic value and become part of the revolution's thought, part of its process of envisioning and arguing. And it is this larger whole that wins and loses people to the revolution. But this correction is beside the point here, I think.)

Is rationality saved, then? Needless to say, the process described is not infallible. But can it be objective? Does it make sense to speak of objectivity in connection with it, to aim at objectivity in it? Intuitively, more than the act of revolution is at stake here. A negative answer would imply that no revolution could be justified before and in the event, but also that none could be justified afterwards. The revolutionary was not right to trust instincts and vision ahead of the argument, even if they later 'turned out all right', and, in any case, it could never be known objectively that the revolution had turned out all right, that the new order did improve on the old. Furthermore, objectivity could strike no deep root in settled situations since a settled situation is the product of the last revolution and the material for the next one. So, if objectivity is impossible (as opposed to just difficult) in the practice of revolutions then it may be out more generally – at least in any radical sense. This consequence the subjectivist will accept, while the objectivist may see it (as in the narrower case of science) as a *reductio ad absurdem* of the premise. The question is whether our positive attention to the dialectic of vision and argument can break the impasse between the objectivist and the subjectivist.

We can see how it might. The crucial realization is that this dialectic is not confined to full-blown revolutions. Argument leading to insight and vision, then vision nurturing argument (partly fixing the meanings of its terms, saving the interaction between general and particular considerations from straight circularity, and so on), before being in turn judged by it – all this seems quite familiar. Are these not also the ingredients of more modest innovations – indeed, one wants to ask, of all thought except perhaps the most mechanical? Their balance would vary, of course, but could we not take the overt incommensurability of revolutionary disagreements to illuminate the frustration of everyday disagreement, and the prominence of vision in revolutionary thought to remind ourselves of its more unobtrusive presence in other kinds of thought? That prominence may even suggest the idea that vision is present in all thought, no doubt often imperceptibly – as the dramatic radioactivity of some elements suggests to physicists the theoretical radioactivity of all elements. After all, even the 'mechanical' actions of counting and measuring involve moments of interpretation and judgement – regarding margins of error, the degree of accuracy required, what counts as a unit or a boundary, and so forth. Even here do we not think rather more than we can articulate?

So, we reach again the conclusion that if there is no objectivity in revolutions then there may be none anywhere. But the effect of coming to it from this direction is to spotlight that which all along is creating the difficulty, namely the overforcing of 'mensuration' as a metaphor of objective thinking. It is being assumed that objective thinking is just like measuring and that measuring is just its mechanical components; that objectivity requires *everything* 'out in the open', not only a readiness to argue the case and an openness to criticism but that the case be articulated or 'objectified' in a sense that – so one might say – empties it of thought, obviates the need ever to think about it again, and turns it into a computer program. *Without these assumptions our problem would disappear*. And just to state them is to become aware of their implausibility. A norm of objectivity in thought which can be approximated only in the measure that thought vanishes into the mechanical and automatic seems fundamentally misconceived. At the very least the burden of proof is on those who would propose it.

So, that certain basic and lucid mathematical ideas are incompletely articulable, that scientific advances are to a degree 'immeasurable', and, most important of all, that in just about all our thinking vision, or something like it, precedes, informs and transcends our articulations of it adds up to a strong case against taking 'measuring' too seriously as a metaphor for objective thinking. We may well wonder how it gained its dominance and, in any case, why we should any longer be troubled by it.[18]

PERVERSITY AND CONVERSION

Science, we have seen, does progress, if by a logic more complex than had been supposed. In it, consensus may be lost but is soon found again. Much less tractable, however, are educational differences and contests, along with the ethical and cultural ones in which they are rooted. Here revolutions do not carry all before them, even in the long run, and they can be reversed. So, for example, the ethical points of view expressed by the participants in Plato's dialogues, or those surveyed in Book 1 of Aristotle's *Nicomachean Ethics*, have a kind of interest for us, a contemporaneity, that the biological disputes of that time lack. They are still with us, broadly, and still competing. This suggests there is more than logical incommensurability at work here.

Of course, some differences are of judgement on what is to be done in complex or novel situations, and coexist with agreement on the principles involved. These are not the significant ones. They are paralleled, indeed, by differences of scientific judgement once science leaves the laboratory and its control of the variables, as in ecology for example. What matters here is, rather, the differences of fundamental principle and of broad value orientation. Note, too, that what matters about these deep value differences is that they survive mutual exposure and critique. Exoticism of practice in very isolated societies, though often trotted out in this context, is less to the point. Like exoticism of cosmology in the same societies, it might be attributable just to an insufficiency of questioning. But the evidence of pluralist societies and cultures, ancient and modern, is that even after traditions have met, argued and diluted each other's purely inertial forces, ethical differences continue to flourish. Thus it seems precisely not the case that deep differences will disappear in some coming 'global village' of rational humanity.

There is, however, a way of accounting for many, perhaps most, of these persistent differences that does not land us in subjectivism. It refers to the familiar logic of human perversity and conversion. The element of will, and therefore of freedom, in value judgements can be taken as pointing, not to some subjectivist construct like 'the criterionless choice', but to this logic. We may indicate some of its features.

We are creatures often drawn in conflicting directions, free in our choice of an actual direction, but subject to ethical judgements, in particular our own, which include half-hearted, uncertain and half-glimpsed ones. Differences between these judgements and our patterns of choice and lifestyle will be more or less painful. The resolution of such conflicts will be our natural desire, if not by changing our lives, then by moderating or blocking our judgements – in which we risk self-deception. All this applies to classes, communities and societies, as well as to individuals (an only slightly less familiar thought, though one that raises some difficult questions[19]). Rationalization and self-deception, then, are probabilities rooted in the very basic ethical realities of choice and obligation. So too, therefore, is ethical disagreement. It transpires then that, so far from being embarrassed by it, any half-sophisticated objectivism that recognizes human freedom will actually *predict* more or less radical ethical disagreement.

Another part of this picture is our understanding that moral enlightenment (an objectivist idea) depends not just on understanding and imagination, but also on good will. We may even have to start by actually living differently if we are ever to figure our way round the next moral corner. So the 'dialectic' that we saw in paradigm conversion in science becomes, in the case of moral conversion, a 'trialectic' involving our deeds, as well as our arguments and our vision. Again, consider our responses to bad faith. Satire, irony, good example, some forms of correction, and the sublime 'overcoming evil by good' – these *combine* a clearly objectivist assumption of a moral truth that is being evaded with an assumption that getting this truth acknowledged is going to involve the touching of hearts as much as of minds.

Implicit in fairly ordinary moral consciousness, then, is a quite sophisticated objectivism (the sophistication may get lost in translations into explicit theory) which is far removed from a faith in the sufficiency of argument, yet holds fast to the aspiration for truth. And it easily accommodates deep ethical disagreements – which include some deep educational disagreements. Nor, incidentally, is it a recipe for intolerance. It directs us at least as much towards our own self-deceptions as to anyone else's. It is open to the realization that these matters are often impossibly difficult to judge in the concrete. And, of itself, it leaves open the question of how we should confront bad faith where we may identify or suspect it.

CONCLUSION

We have been defending the objectivist anticipations of educational debate (and debate generally). We have argued that the objectivist attitude is perfectly hospitable to a series of values: sensitivity to the local and the circumstantial, freedom to follow one's bent, a decent humility considering our fallibility, an acknowledgement of the tacit, intuitive and visionary, and a sense of the inevitability of value disagreement. In specific relation to education, we have been arguing that aspiring to the true meaning of 'education' is compatible with recognizing 'education' as an idea that is flexible, permissive, uncertain, vision-dependent to the extent of being incommensurable in its variants, and, even, an idea for each of us to make up his or her own mind about.

NOTES

1. Quoted in M. Armstrong, 'Thinking about children's learning', *Forum*, 29, 1 Autumn 1986.
2. I do not refer, therefore, to the doctrine that there is a small set of basic truths which are foundational to all other truths, nor to the doctrine that there is a certain kind of highly articulated 'objectification', mathematical and/or scientific in character, which is a norm of objectivity generally. The latter doctrine, in fact, I criticize below – even as a proposal for mathematics and science! In this general connection, see Bernstein (1983). The 'objectivism' he seeks to transcend is, I think, much closer to the one I criticize than to the one I defend. I came to this work after I had written this section. In some respects our approaches overlap, especially in our discussions of Kuhn, though he does much more than me in the way of situating the issues in relation to the history of philosophy and, more particularly, to the work of some important contemporary philosophers. (Still later – at the point of going to press, in fact – I read MacIntyre (1990). This remarkable work 'overcomes' incommensurability among the three views it discusses in a way with which, it seems to me, what I propose in this section is consistent. His account is, however, much more developed.)
3. Freire (1970, 1972).
4. This was well recognized, for instance, by Aquinas, *Summa Theologica*, I, IIae, q. 94 a. 4.
5. In *Libro Boethii de Trinitatis Expositio*, 1,2 ad 1.
6. A point beautifully made in Goethe's aphoristic remark, quoted at the head of Part 2.
7. Popper likes to string together some fragments from the pre-Socratic Xenophanes in a way which suggests a remarkable anticipation of his views:

> The gods did not reveal, from the beginning,
> All things to us; but in the course of time,
> Through seeking we may learn, and know things better. . . .
> These things are, we conjecture, like the truth.
> But as for certain truth, no man has known it,
> Nor will he know it; neither of the gods,
> Nor yet of all the things of which I speak.
> And even if by chance he were to utter
> The final truth, he would himself not know it:
> For all is but a woven web of guesses.

He returns repeatedly (Popper, 1959, 1963, 1972) to the main points of this outline. As examples: the non-verifiability of theory in the first essay of 1972; the theory dependence and the fallibility of basic observation statements in sections 25–30 of 1959 and in Addendum 1 of 1963; the ideas of a theory's 'truth content' (its 'having truth in it'), its relative nearness to truth, and the related idea of 'verisimilitude', in the tenth essay (section 3) of 1963 and the second essay (sections 7–11) of 1972. Section 32 of the last-mentioned essay discusses 'dynamic scepticism'. The idea of the truth as 'manifest' and its dominance in Western thought, at least since Bacon and Descartes, are discussed and criticized in the first essay of 1963.
8. On the subjectivist side Kuhn (1962), discussed below, and, among the slightly desperate – in my view – Scheffler (1967), though this remains a useful corrective to a too *sweeping* denial of commensurability.
9. They held that proportion was the guarantee and the key of a rational universe and were therefore disturbed to find that the geometric mean between a number (n) and, for instance, its double (i.e. $n\sqrt{2}$) was finally inarticulable. Simone Weil (1965, letters 37–9) suggests, however, that our usual view of this Greek crisis may be upside down. Pythagoras proved that the ratio of the diagonal of a square to its side was exactly $\sqrt{2}$ (and that in a rectangle [$\sqrt{2} \times 1$] of that diagonal times a line equal to the sides of the original square, the ratio of *its* diagonal to its shorter side would be exactly $\sqrt{3}$, and so on). Now what is usually said

is that this sparked off a search for the numerical values of $\sqrt{2}$, $\sqrt{3}$, etc., leading to the discovery that they were not 'rational', i.e. exact. But suppose the Greeks made their arithmetical discovery first. Then the geometrical one could well have seemed the *resolution* of the difficulty, showing that the proportions which could not be exactly articulated could be *exhibited* as exact. The evidence for putting the matter this way up – apart from the point that it seems intrinsically more reasonable – includes, she says, the fact that the study of numbers began long before the study of lines, the likelihood of Babylonian knowledge of arithmetic incommensurability and of the Greeks having learnt it from them, and the generally pleased and positive air of references to Pythagoras's theorem in Plato and other Greeks.

10. Kuhn (1962).

11. *Ibid.*, p. 149.

12. *Ibid.*, pp. 147–8.

13. 'Excepting those that are exclusively instrumental, every problem that normal science sees as a puzzle can be seen, from another viewpoint, as a counterinstance and thus as a source of crisis. Copernicus saw as counterinstances what most of Ptolemy's other successors had seen as puzzles in the match between observation and theory. Lavoisier saw as a counterinstance what Priestley had seen as a successfully solved puzzle in the articulation of phlogiston theory. And Einstein saw as counterinstances what Lorentz, Fitzgerald, and others had seen as puzzles in the articulation of Newton's and Maxwell's theories. . . . There are, I think, only two alternatives: either no scientific theory ever confronts a counterinstance, or all such theories confront counterinstances at all times.' (ibid., pp. 79–80).

14. (1) Kuhn: *normal science is commonly more a matter of finding ways to outcomes already confidently anticipated in detail than of adding to the known detail* (p. 36). Perhaps! But it remains, presumably, that to anticipate results is to assume that certain things will turn out to be true about nature. Truth remains a rule of this puzzle-solving game.

   (2) Kuhn: '*Does it really help to imagine that there is some one full, objective, true account of nature and that the proper measure of scientific achievement is the extent to which it brings us closer to that ultimate goal?*' (p. 171). But this ('one', 'full') is too quickly to identify the (modest) 'truths about somethings' with 'the Truth about the Universe'.

   (3) Kuhn: '*There is, I think, no theory-independent way to reconstruct phrases like "really there"; the notion of a match between the ontology of a theory and its "real" counterpart in nature now seems to me illusive in principle*' (p. 206). But this seems no more than to refer to the obvious paradox implicit in the very idea of truth, rather than to anything specific to science.

   (4) Kuhn: *The ontology of a theory (i.e. the entities with which it populates nature) often bears some resemblance to a much earlier theory that it does not bear to its immediate predecessor.* Thus '*in some important respects, though by no means in all, Einstein's general theory of relativity is closer to Aristotle's than either of them is to Newton's*' (p. 207). The idea this suggests is that progress towards the truth may often be a matter of 'two steps forwards and one backwards' – that scientific revolutions may involve losses as well as gains.

15. This is to use Kuhn against himself. Successfully to import 'revolution' and 'paradigm' from art and politics into science was to bring them nearer to each other. But where Kuhn saw this as tending to 'relativize' science, we may do better to see it as allowing us to 'absolutize' art and politics a little.

16. The Christian may indeed go further to argue, with Kierkegaard (*Philosophical Fragments*), that Jesus was a revolutionary in a class all his own.

17. Overheated rhetoric aside, it is not good simply by definition – the contemporary gamut runs from the Sandinistas, whom perhaps mainly the sinister thought sinister, to the unspeakable 'year zero' of the Khmer Rouge – and indeed suspicion may be as much owing to knowing how atrociously revolutions can turn out as to any attachment to the given order.

18. On this whole topic see Polanyi (1958), a book that was years ahead out of its time. See also, and especially on the historical side, Bernstein (1983).

19. Here, of course, we overlap with Marxist notions of ideology as distortion and false consciousness. But for a more general, and unusual, discussion see Lonergan (1957, pp. 217–44).

Part 3

Education and Meaning

Chapter 7

Is Education Possible?

Every education teaches a philosophy; if not by dogma then by suggestion, by implication, by atmosphere. Every part of that education has a connection with every other part. If it does not all combine to convey some general view of life, it's not education at all.
(G.K. Chesterton, *The Common Man*)

At the end of our analysis of the formal and the wide senses of 'education' we came upon the challenge to justify the assumption, shared by nearly all sides in educational debate, that there is *some* conception of education under which it is worth pursuing as a matter of conscious and deliberate policy. It is now time to address that challenge directly.

RETURN TO THE PRIMITIVE: A LIFE WITHOUT EDUCATION?

Usually we assume that we are better off for having developed an explicitly educational perspective on childhood and growing up, and furthermore that – short of bombing ourselves back into the stone age – this adoption is irreversible. But perhaps both these assumptions are wrong. In this connection it will be instructive to begin by attending to what was an interesting development in the deschooling literature, i.e. a move from abjuring school in the name of education to abjuring education itself. We shall find here two explicit objections to education, and we shall argue that, though certainly radical and directed at a quite wide range of conceptions and practices, they need not be construed as the objections to the *very idea* of education that they present themselves as. In discussing them, however, we shall come upon a third objection lurking in the background, which *is* directed at that very idea, and which will prove rather less tractable.

In 1970 Illich was claiming that the educational process would unquestionably gain from the deschooling of society. This would sound to many schoolmen like treason to the enlightenment, but 'it is enlightenment itself that is now being snuffed out in schools'.[1] Illich, however, was not advocating that education should henceforth be left to happen as it may, that we should learn to rely again simply on the family and the 'university of life'. He argued, indeed, for large developments in the informal educational power of a wide range of industrial, cultural and political institutions. But he also pleaded for a new kind of *formal* education and for agencies which, though quite different from schools, would be specifically educational, what he called learning networks or 'webs'. These should be voluntary rather than compulsory; provide access to resources rather than 'pre-packaged' curricula; and be of three or four kinds according to the nature of the resource – educational object, peer-learner, model, 'elder' or educator-at-large. Our concern with all this is just to note that Illich's new society would still be education-minded. (Both the wide and the formal uses of 'education' would survive in it, though both would be overhauled.)

Within a few years, however, two works had appeared which envisaged and advocated a society which would not be education-minded. Their titles were already suggestive of this: Carl Bereiter's (1973) *Must We Educate*? and John Holt's (1976) *Instead of Education: Ways to Help People Do Things Better*. Both were severely antipathetic to *any* kind of public institution or provision of a deliberately educational nature. They advocated resource centres for children and youths (ones that might well use present school premises), but on the condition that they would not think of themselves as educational; rather they were to be places for the enrichment of the *present* lives of those who attended them – voluntarily, of course. Bereiter envisaged, in addition, provision for formal skill-learning, even compulsory learning as regards literacy skills. But this was to be conceived, also in deliberately non-educational fashion, as narrowly task-specific training. And neither author presented his total ban on formal education as for the sake of education in a wider and informal sense. Rather, Holt observed:

> In such a society no one would worry about 'education'. People would be busy *doing interesting things that mattered*. Doing them, they would grow more informed, competent and wise. They would learn about the world from living in it, working in it, and changing it, and from knowing a wide variety of people who were doing the same.[2]

True, *we* might say of such a society, as of a primitive one, that education was going on informally in it, and even (some might add) that it was going on the less impededly for the absence of formal education. But it would be unnecessary for *them* to think in this way, and – if our earlier argument for a tie-up between formal and general uses is correct – it is unlikely that they would. They would be too 'busy doing important things that mattered' to attend reflexively to their own resultant growth in knowledge and wisdom. (Presumably, most uses of the word 'education' would eventually die away with them, weakened no doubt by direct assaults of the kind we are familiar with in regard to sexist usages.)

Why do these authors have it in for education as self-conscious perspective and formal system? Two lines of objection may be distinguished. The more explicit one is that the central business of such deliberate education is always a determination of people's beliefs, values and attitudes, what Holt calls 'people-shaping' and Bereiter 'making people over'. Education is, then, an irredeemably tyrannical, indeed totalitarian, enterprise. Thus Holt again:

> Next to the right to life itself, the most fundamental of all human rights is the right to control our own minds and thoughts. . . . Whoever takes that right away from us, by trying to 'educate' us, attacks the very centre of our being and does us a most profound and lasting injury. . . . Education, with its supporting system of compulsory and competitive schooling, all its carrots and sticks, its grades, diplomas, and credentials, now seems to me perhaps the most authoritarian and dangerous of all the social inventions of mankind.[3]

The other objection is that the educational perspective is one within which the present is viewed simply as raw material for the future and, in particular, the child is sacrificed to the adult she is to become. There is no respect in it for what the child actually is and actually can do. In fact in this mental-set she is scarcely even *seen* as one who is and does, but only as one who learns and becomes. This objection is, in particular, part of Holt's critique of the big deal he claims we make of distinguishing 'learning' and 'doing' – a distinction he regards as almost wholly artificial.

Can the idea of education be saved from these objections? Let us try out the reply to each of them in turn that it may tell against this or that educational system or conception of education but is miscast as an objection to education as such, because deliberate education is *not necessarily* conceived in either of the objectionable ways.

A TYRANNY?

Does this charge not neglect the distinction, laboriously evolved in more or less free and pluralist societies and now of fairly wide currency in them, between *education* and *indoctrination* – a putatively sharp distinction indeed, so that whatever counts as indoctrination to that extent *cannot* count as education? Of course this is now a more demanding or loaded concept of education than, say, the one we earlier envisaged coming to birth in a primitive society. And even after developing it we ourselves continue to employ the less differentiated one to embrace systems we take to be indoctrinatory, say those of ancient Sparta and modern North Korea. But our purposes in this are likely now to be only those of noncommittal reference and description. It is not education in a sense still undistinguished from indoctrination that most of us would seek to defend. Of course, too, we are often hypocritical in our use of this distinction: we may be sensitive to the indoctrinatory features of systems that purvey beliefs and values we dislike but oblivious to them in the transmission of beliefs and values we cherish. But we can attend to this beam in our own eye without having to ditch the whole idea of education.

It is a characteristic of any system of schooling that it is to some degree common – a common initiation into a common heritage. But this does not have to be construed as 'moulding' educands to some pattern. On the contrary, we find it again *wired into* many of our specific conceptions that education must attend to the aptitudes and interests of the individual student, and not merely attend to these (effective 'moulding' would require that much), but protect and promote them. For instance, we find education being deliberately conceived as a dialogue or negotiation between the individual and the common heritage, and this latter itself conceived not rigidly as 'curriculum-packages' but flexibly as *'a conversation' of many voices and layers*. Thus Oakeshott (no radical) writes:

> Education I will take to be the process of learning, in circumstances of direction and restraint, how to recognise and make something of ourselves. Unavoidably it is a two-fold process in which we enjoy an initiation into what for want of a better word I will call a 'civilization', and in doing so discover our own talents and aptitudes in relation to that civilization and begin to cultivate and to use them. Learning to make something of ourselves in no context in particular is an impossibility; and the context appears not only in what is learned but also in the conditions of direction and restraint that belong to any

education. . . . If, then, we recognise education as an initiation into a civilization, we may regard it as beginning to learn our way about a material, emotional, moral and intellectual inheritance, and as a learning to recognise the varieties of human utterance and to participate in the conversation they compose.[4]

True, here too our practice (and indeed our theory, the hardline behaviourist versions of the 'objectives' curriculum model, for example) might often belie our ideal. But, again, the jolting of complacency does not require an assault on the very idea of education. In fact it could as well be achieved by an appeal to a widely held, if fairly loaded, version of that idea! Thus Stenhouse in his well-known critique of the behavioural objectives model takes it almost for granted that education must be liberating to deserve the name. 'Education as induction into knowledge is successful to the extent that it makes the behavioural outcomes of the students unpredictable.'[5]

It might be said that all this is too easy a way out of the first objection. For it leaves us still presuming that there are *some* legitimate ways of exhorting, persuading and generally influencing others, and especially the young, at rather profound levels – basically those ways that promote and appeal to their reason. Again, while we have problems with forcing convictions on others we remain happy to force a curriculum on them. We hope not to be predetermining their opinions, but go on compelling their 'conversation'!

Here we need to be carefully judicious. On the one hand, though it seems true that in anything we would be inclined to call a system of education there would be restraint and direction of some kind and degree, including some that was externally imposed, this in itself could not be a sufficient objection to it. For it is impossible to envisage any form of human life in which no restraint or direction whatever would be imposed (whether in the name of 'education' or some other name), nor indeed one in which restraint and direction would not be quite general practices as regards the young. An extreme libertarian position – such as Holt seems to flirt with – according to which the only discipline ever justifiable is self-discipline, incorporates a quite unreal view of the individual, and especially of the young individual, in relation to her social environment. This kind of unreality is sometimes described as a neglect of 'original sin'. But it might more appositely be conveyed by reference to another item in classical theology: the angel. The angel is said to have no youth and no young. It is a being sprung into existence without parentage or nurture, already fully formed and spiritually self-possessed, master of an innate stock of ideas and knowledge, standing or falling entirely by its own autonomous decision, each one in fact a species to itself.[6] For such a being external direction or restraint would indeed be an indignity, if not an impossibility. But we humans fall some way short of angels, and especially in our beginnings. Whatever is to be said about being 'originally flawed',[7] it is certainly true that we come into the world weak, ignorant, vulnerable and thoroughly dependent – and the glory we may trail will have to be detected in and through these humble circumstances. That is one side of the picture.

On the other hand, we should beware of concluding too much from these very general observations about the human condition. In themselves, for example, they come nowhere near overriding all the scruples we might sometimes reasonably feel about a system of compulsory schooling from 5 to 16. In more sophisticated terms, they would not do much to soothe a Foucault-inspired dread of education, with its attendant human science, as just one more modern system of normalization and surveillance. But then it is not our present intention to defend the standard system, nor to pre-empt the power of imagination to envisage radical alternatives to it. The idea was only to defend the continued use of 'education' as the flag under which imagination might sail.

A SACRIFICE OF THE PRESENT?

What of the other objection, that education sacrifices the child to the future adult?[8] It too calls for a general remark on the human condition. A form of life in which thought was never taken for tomorrow would hardly be recognizable as human, and nor would one in which some did not sometimes exercise foresight on behalf of others and in particular of the young. To be sure, we can readily admit that a life lived always 'ahead of itself', with little or no room for resting in the present moment (no worship, no art, no play . . . no leisure) is a poor and desperate thing. On just about any calculation it is also deeply irrational.[9] To see and to shape the lives of others in this pattern would be still more objectionable. But, intuitively, just as earlier the real problem might have been said to be striking some appropriate balance between freedom and constraint, so here it would seem to be finding a balance between, or a higher synthesis of, living in the present and living towards the future. So, education cannot be dismissed *simply* because it is future-orientated. One point here is that even if that were its whole story we might have been able to compensate for it in our other perspectives on childhood. For example, even educators who divorce education and play have been known to give play its own time – not all have been Gradgrinds! And if it is said that no compensation could be adequate here, considering the huge proportion of a child's time that our society gives over to education, this would still be to object to the exaggeration of a value, not the value itself.

We must also attend to the possibility of redressing the balance *within* the educational perspective. Thus, surely, play is in fact educationally significant as well as immediately absorbing, and these two aspects of it are not entirely independent – at least in part, it is futurally significant *because* it is presently absorbing. More generally, education need not be conceived exclusively as preparation for adulthood and the future, nor its immediate and future impacts as things quite unconnected. And here again we find the point at issue actually written into several of our more loaded conceptions of education. The most obvious example is the 'child-centred' view, according to which the curriculum is principally to be dictated by a pupil's *present* interests. But there is also a requirement of significance in the present, somewhat differently conceived, in the classical ideal of 'a liberal education'. For in it the curriculum is to be made up chiefly of activities that are worthwhile in themselves – and therefore worthwhile *from the beginning*. Educands are not mere 'learners' of things that in the future they might 'do' – history, science, music etc. They already do these worthwhile things in some real sense, and learn by their doing. Consider, for example, 'learning physics' and 'doing physics'. The learner already is (or should be) one who attends to the phenomena under study, enquires about them, entertains hypotheses in their regard, manipulates them, marvels at them, in ways and to degrees with which the enquiries, manipulations etc. of the physicist are recognizably continuous. This is not altered by the fact that the learner is by his doing one who catches up, as opposed to one who expands, on existing knowledge.[10]

These are not just starry-eyed ideals with no effect on practice. For governments, indeed, the word 'education' triggers solemn pronouncements on the needs of future citizens. For those who have to work with children, like parents and teachers, the matter is usually more complex. Long-term considerations matter, but the day-to-day measure of success is just as likely to be the extent to which children are interested and fulfilled *now* by what they are doing. When demands made in the name of future needs are judged to be too strident or insistent (not to mention too narrowly conceived) teachers will sometimes interpose themselves as buffers – against over-anxious governments and parents, against proposals to lengthen still further the shadow of examinations, against their own impatience to get on with the syllabus – and they will act thus precisely *in the name of education*. None of this is to say that we have currently got a proper balance of present and future, nor even that we are moving towards it (in the UK the quite new deliberateness about the marking of progress in 'key stages' and subject 'levels' worries many), only that we are not entirely uninfluenced by this ideal and that the term 'education' itself can remind us of it.

Is this a sufficient reply to the objection? It might still be said, and with some intuitive force, that its future orientation is more basic to 'education' than any association with present value and fulfilment, that the term always projects us forward more than it directs our attention to the present. But if this is true, the question it raises is whether it is enough, granted their time-intensiveness, to think of schools and curricula in educational terms. Might we not need other terms *as well*? Perhaps we do need to offset, deliberately and as often as we speak of these things, the discourse of 'learning', 'becoming' and 'school' with a discourse of 'doing', 'being' and 'activity centre'. Among other things that would shore up the requirement of present-significance we noticed in some uses of 'education'. It would be modest compared to Holt's proposal to abolish education-mindedness and education-speak, but still far-reaching – and at once more just to education and less likely to be dismissed out of hand.

Finally, recall that we can think of education, especially education in the widest sense, as a lifelong process. True, it may be only in some kinds of society that this thought is likely to be entertained, and even in them there is perhaps a rider to the effect that the precisely educational dimension of living and doing is more to the fore in early life. It remains that this is a further way in which we undermine a too rigid distinction between a learning phase of life and a doing phase – tunnelling now from the other side of the wall.

There are, then, versions of 'education' that require us to conceive adult life as continued development and schooldays as days already of experience and doing.

REVIEW – AND A THIRD OBJECTION

We have been attending to two objections to education-mindedness. We found *against them* that, to the extent they do not simply neglect some basic facts about human life, they seriously underestimate the flexibility of the educational perspective. What is reasonable and important in them can be accommodated within the discourse of education, and sometimes is. We found *for them* that they force on our attention concerns that are reasonable and important. The first makes us think about the relationship of the (more or less) common curriculum of formal education to the individual with her own experience, talents, interests, ideas, ideals – perhaps, too, her own sub-culture and language or dialect.[11] Some might see this as deciding when and how to iron out, and when and how to tolerate, differences. But in proportion as a society values the liberty of individuals to make their own way it will be conceived in more complex ways: how to educate without indoctrinating, against indoctrination even; and how to promote a common civilization that will assist, not hamper, the individual as she makes something of herself. The second objection makes us think about the bearing of education, a protracted and time-intensive enterprise with an inherent reference to the future, on the present lives of children and youth. There is the general requirement to tailor curricula and pedagogies to the developmental stage of the educand, in taxing children not to overtax them. This might be so interpreted, however, that childhood is acknowledged only as a complicated passage to the prize of a successful adulthood. To go on actually to prize childhood, we must conceive of education as directed at the enrichment of the present as much as of the future. We may even need to reinforce this by the further step of supplementing education-speak with action-speak, a discourse that starts with the future even if it comes to include the present, supplemented with one that actually starts with the present even if goes on to include the future.

It might now be wondered why we have been defending the idea of education with such obstinate ingenuity. Why build into it so many 'epicycles'? A deschooler might acknowledge the innocence of some of its variants, yet still think it compromised as a whole by its association with the standard educational practice to which he objects. It is more prudent, in starting anew, to abandon it altogether in favour of less ambiguous notions like 'doing', 'learning' and 'training'. Why, he may want to know, should we insist on the idea even in advance of a verdict on current practice? What, *positively*, does 'education' import that could make it worth clinging to?

What it particularly imports over and above those other notions is, of course, the pursuit of a view of life as a whole. The near tautologies that education 'is for life' and 'is of the whole person' relate to this, and it is this, indeed, that gave some initial plausibility to complaints about 'people-shaping' (Holt) and 'making people over' (Bereiter). We are becoming very familiar with this idea, having invoked it, or presumed on it, in noticing that schooling is challenged by the idea of education, most explicitly by 'education (in the widest sense)', to justify itself by reference to some wide 'scheme of things', again in imagining the genesis in a primitive society of the ideas of teaching and learning 'for life' out of a combination of nurture and training ideas, and again in discussing and articulating the exceptional obligation that is laid on educational theory to be broad and coherent.

We have also sometimes hinted at the problematic nature of this ideal of a unified view of life. Contemporary Western culture, secular and fragmented as it is, makes us sensitive to this (though we rarely appreciate that the idea of education is among the things at stake). Is the pursuit of a unified view of life possible without the artifices of indoctrination and/or self-deception? What particular obstacles to – and perhaps opportunities for – this pursuit are there in contemporary culture and contemporary educational practice?

A VIEW OF LIFE AS A WHOLE: RUMINATIONS

We may recall Chesterton's particularly forceful statement of this aspiration quoted at the head of this chapter: an education, as such, is imbued with a philosophy which it tends to convey, whether indirectly or directly, and hence, too, it is itself a unity and much more than just the sum of its parts. In short, if it does not all combine to convey some general view of life, it's not education at all.

Against this we might set a satirical scene from the end of Monty Python's *The Meaning of Life*. After the caption 'The End', the camera returns to John Cleese, who says 'That is the end of the film. Here is the meaning of life.' In the style of an announcer of an Oscar award, he takes a card from a sealed envelope and continues:

> Nothing very special really! Be kind, avoid eating too much fat, read a good book now and then, get in some walking – oh, and live in peace and harmony with people of all nations, races and creeds'.[12]

The question posed by this juxtaposition is why it is thought right and important to have (consciously), and to hand on (deliberately), a view of life as a whole. Certainly a multitude of religions, ideologies, philosophical systems and therapies are at one in assuming a hunger for some unifying, pervading, overarching meaning to life. They assume this hunger in the act of offering themselves as its true fulfilment. Even some of those who have denied the possibility of fulfilment have borne witness to the demand. Thus Sartre saw human being as a passion for God, but 'a useless passion' because God was non-existent and impossible. A moving passage:

> The being of human reality is suffering because it rises in being as perpetually haunted by a totality which it is without being able to be it, precisely because it could not attain the in-itself without losing itself as for-itself. Human reality therefore is by nature an unhappy consciousness with no possibility of surpassing its unhappy state.[13]

On the other hand, the Cleese-like resistance to these traditions and to an education in them – what the traditions will identify as worldliness, cynicism, indifference, apathy, philistinism – might be read as evidence that the demand is less than universally spontaneous. And where it exists it has often seemed a whipped up thing, a case of advertisement creating the need. It is also important soberly to remember the shadow side of ideology and religion, the fundamentalism, fanaticism or just plain simple-mindedness, that goes with the closure of thought into total systems, and, in other contexts, the quietism that results from some kinds of belief in divine, or evolutionary, or historical, process. But – to switch back to the other side (which I believe to be right in the last analysis) – these things may be seen as aberrant or deformed expressions of the desire for unity, integrations of human life that are premature, or of the wrong degree, or located in the wrong dimension. Sometimes that is how some of them are seen within the traditions themselves – thus superstition was in the first instance a *sin*. Counted as deformations they would not discredit the aspiration to unity itself.

Richard Peters remarked in an early work that 'education' implied the transmission of what is of *ultimate* value.[14] Commenting on this later, John Wilson wrote, 'it might be thought to imply that, until we actually know "what is of ultimate value", we cannot know what is education and what is not.'[15] He seemed to intend this as a *reductio ad absurdum*. But is it not reasonable to maintain that uncertainty about ultimate values would entail some uncertainty about what to do in education and what to count as good education, and in that sense about what is, and is not, education? Education seems indeed a prime example (morality is another) of those things that are affected by uncertainty over ultimate values. Of course, up to a point education can live with uncertainty, even thrive upon it. A *cut-and-dried* conception of ultimate values is not necessary to it. Thus a better statement than Peters's (and more in keeping with his own general position) might be that education implies the equipping and supporting of people in an ongoing quest for what is of ultimate value – by those who do not know all the answers but who are more experienced and advanced in this quest. But an uncertainty that is not just over the best ordering of values and the relative merits of various schemes for ordering values, but over whether there can be any valid ordering of them, may reasonably be thought to create difficulty for the very *concept* of education. To the extent that ideals like 'seeing life whole', 'a scheme of things', 'the quest for meaning and coherence' and 'ultimate values' lose their appeal, then, the idea of education – not just some particular loaded versions of it, but the basic structure of the idea – is weakened.

Might there be in the ideal of 'breadth' a modern and sufficient substitute for these grander aspirations?[16] Arguably, this substitution is already under way. But if it is, a weight is being placed on 'breadth' that it cannot sustain. It is one thing to cultivate it as the essential complement of 'coherence', our insurance against too simple and monolithic a unity, but quite another to ask it to stand on its own. For (like its companion 'balance') it presumes a background of what have been called 'prior value commitments' – it is across the range of *independently valued* activities and discourses that breadth is to be sought – and, directly to the point, it is necessarily accompanied by some notion of a due or just proportion among these,[17] which refers us right back to something like 'a scheme of things'.

Let us begin to anchor these general ruminations. In education there are two main arenas in which the issue is joined between the requirement of unity and the doubt concerning it, as there are two kinds of pluralism against which the aspiration to coherence is tested. One arena is the common school of the pluralist society. Of its nature (by contrast with, say, the church school) it involves serious ideological compromise, and therefore a diminution of the aspiration to coherence in one dimension. As against that, at its best it works in another dimension to an egalitarian, fraternal and democratic vision of its own, partially captured in the image of 'the melting pot'. This vision might be described further and it might be asked if it could be sufficient in itself, and to what extent the tension between it and visions of the first dimension is inevitable, indefinitely sustainable, resolvable at some higher level, and so on.[18] In fact we shall confine our attention to the second arena, which is the standard curriculum. The contest here is between, on the one hand, the ideal of curriculum coherence and, on the other hand, the plurality of subjects, practices and skills that have to be covered and, at longer range, that explosive fragmentation of intellectual labour that is a feature of contemporary culture. This is as much, or not much less, an issue for the church school as for the common school. It, and the questions it opens up, will occupy us for several further sections. But our reflections on it may not be conclusive between hope and doubt regarding the prospects for coherence. There may be wisdom in keeping both hope and doubt alive.

CURRICULUM CONNECTIONS

Curriculum, used in the singular to cover the varied activities of teaching and learning in an institution, already suggests some organization and unity. (The science curriculum, the mathematics curriculum, the humanities curriculum, etc. add up, not to 'curricula', but to 'curriculum'!) The idea of a *core curriculum* is stronger in this respect.

At least in the hands of those who know its history (which seems not to include governmental ministries) it implies much more than a loose assemblage of basic skills and subjects. As the metaphor of 'core' suggests, it is that part of the curriculum which is to hold the whole curriculum together. Indeed it is to be an instrument of unity and wholeness, of progressive organization and reorganization, in relation to the student's life experience generally. Furthermore, as *common* core, it is charged with articulating and enabling our common social life and citizenship, indeed our common humanity. This then is an idea that passes Chesterton's test for an education, the 'reconstructionist' philosophy or vision that it conveys or 'teaches' being that of actively 'whole' people in the open and participatory democracy.[19] But the idea of an *integrated curriculum* is in some respects stronger still. It interprets Chesterton's requirement that 'every part . . . has a connection with every other part' in the direction of every part having to be explicitly taught and learnt in its connections with every other part.

How much of all this is possible, in some desirable form, in a complex and fragmented culture? *What kind of unity may the curriculum of today have*? We shall assemble a patient answer to that question. It will distinguish the partial from the overarching, and contrast the common perception of many particular connections and the correlative enthusiasm for some integrations and some cross-curriculum themes with the lack of confidence regarding the overall coherence of the whole curriculum. It is not too difficult to evoke a sense of the curriculum as a veritable manifold, indeed, of connections. But the questions will be: What kind of connections? Who has to make them? And do they add up to anything?

One could begin from almost anywhere, but let us take the familiar business of teaching children to write in a primary school. From copy-shaping individual letters, this quite quickly becomes a many-faceted affair. Pupils' work is soon being judged against a formidable checklist of skills and qualities: the 'basics' of handwriting, spelling, grammar, syntax, speed; and more 'literary' items like clarity, style, descriptive power, creativity, expressiveness, authenticity. But, despite there being times and exercises specifically devoted to this or that skill or quality, it is not the case that these can be considered and taught for in splendid isolation from each other. Let us leave aside for the present overlaps and connections of a conceptual nature (e.g. the bearing of syntax on clarity) and consider them only as distinct. There remain – on any reasonable account – two purposes for which these items must be brought into relationship, namely to settle *issues of priority* between them and to check on the *compatibility of methods* relating to them.

Under the first heading we would find that old chestnut of how 'the basics' as a bunch are to be weighted, in terms of time, attention and resources, against literary qualities – both in general and at this or that stage of schooling and development. We would also find the more delicate issues of weighting these latter intangibles against each other, honesty as against imaginativeness, expressiveness as against polish, and so on. Note that we are unlikely to get far with this ordering without some reference to different uses of writing (e.g. expressive, transactional, poetic) and to different genres of text (story, letter, diary, etc.), and without some estimate of *their* degrees of importance – and what could that not lead us on to? All this is to do with settling priorities. Second, the mature act of writing requires the *simultaneous* deployment of clusters of these skills and qualities, so they must be imparted with an eye to their fit with each other. An insistence on copperplate might cripple expressiveness, now and later. There will be advantages, in addition to those of straight economy, in techniques that impart some of them together, for instance, in methods of teaching spelling or grammar which associate them with some literary virtues even if they are not the most supremely effective methods in their own terms. In general, approaches and resources are to be scrutinized for, and judged by, their full range of effects and side-effects.

It will be risky, then, to proceed with teaching any facet of writing except against some kind of considered view of all facets together. On a wider front such a considered view will have to mesh, for the same two reasons, with perspectives on other parts of the curriculum. In one direction writing will be considered in relation to reading, in another as it develops oral expression, and in a third as it is required by and promotes a series of particular subject matters. An ordered set of these and further deliberated perspectives will begin to look like a coherent language policy. This, in its turn, could hardly avoid reference to other kinds of development, such as the emotional and the aesthetic, and to other cross-curriculum matters, like race and gender.

TRAFFIC FLOW OR ASSEMBLY LINE?

What *kind* of coordination is being implied here? Is it just a matter of 'traffic regulation', of rules and lanes for a large number of separate items that jostle for the same space and compete for the same time, occasionally travelling together but mostly not? If so, then 'curriculum' would name an aggregate after all, though of elements that had been adjusted to each other (and the ideal might be as in the classical liberal picture of the state: each element to enjoy as much freedom, including the freedom to enter into cooperative arrangements, as would not interfere with the equal freedom of other elements). Checking for compatibility, the second of our imperatives, of itself would imply only this much unity.[20] But our first imperative, the settling of priorities, suggests another kind of coordination, more convergent, like the assembly line, than divergent, like the traffic flow. For if elements are to be weighed and balanced against each other then they must be broadly commensurable. The picture lurking here is of a scheme of things, some composite of criteria of relative value and maps of knowledge and skill, in which each element has 'its proper place'. If we are also to move away from managerialism, i.e. from a coordination in which those coordinated play no part, we should add that this scheme is itself to be communicated to students, not just in the interests of productivity – as perhaps with Volvo's well-known attempt to humanize the assembly line – but as a principal focus of learning in its own right. And if there were, as we should expect, some uncertainty about the scheme and some openness as to its interpretation, then these features too could be communicated to students and they too could work at resolving or exploiting them.

This is still to leave the question of how it is that the elements are broadly comparable. It is also, so far, short of what a core curriculum or an integrated curriculum intend. It omits, or omits to make explicit, the idea of the tailoring of parts to each other, and of this as something for students to be active in on their own behalf, to do and to learn to do for themselves. To get further, or even just to explain how we have got so far, we should begin by reinstating *conceptual relationships* as a consideration.

FLEXIBLE CURRICULUM BRICKS?

Returning to our two checklists of writing qualities, the basic and the literary, let us dwell on the conceptual relationships between these qualities individually and the practice of writing itself. Non-controversially, let us say that writing is a *visual form and record of expression and communication*. (a) Of the 'basics', some relate to the specifying idea of a visual form and record, others to the more generic linguistic ideas of expression and communication. Legibility is of the first kind. It is a quality of *nothing but* written records, and without it nothing *succeeds* as a written record and the practice of writing becomes pointless. The same is true of approximately correct spelling. Approximately correct grammar and syntax, on the other hand, have a kind of mutually conditioning relationship with linguistic expression and communication generically, and are conditions of writing as a particular form of these. (b) The case with the more literary qualities is slightly more complicated. Clarity, expressiveness, elegance, accuracy, authenticity – all these can characterize other things besides language. They can characterize music, painting, architecture and body language, and some of them can characterize human deeds and natural objects. But as attributed to speech and writing, one wants to say, they have a meaning that is to some extent specific to that context. At any rate, qualities like clarity and elegance can only be identified in speech and writing from the inside, by the use of the tacit knowledge of these arts that speakers and writers possess. They are not 'stuck on' and independently recognizable, like the redness of an old pillar box. In the other direction, expression and communication either require or are facilitated by these qualities, depending on the context.

What is the significance of these conceptual connections? It is that any impression we may have got that those checklist items were basic 'units' of curriculum currency, or building bricks available for just about any curriculum construction, would be quite wrong. It is not the comparative weighing and the mutual adjusting that first bring these items into relationship. They are *already* parts of the same system. Yet their relative positioning is not so fixed as to leave no need or free play for the weighing and the adjusting. Rather, the system makes weighing and adjusting possible by supplying relevant criteria for these operations. We ask 'how legible must the writing be?', 'how explicit should be the knowledge of grammar?', 'how important is style?', etc., and these connections refer us, quasi-automatically, to the nature and purposes of writing as to a somewhat wider scheme of things.

Is writing as a whole, then, the sort of thing that could count as a basic unit? As the common bearer of those qualities it would make a better candidate than any of them. But it is not an infinitely flexible building brick. Most obviously, and despite attempts in the nineteenth century to teach reading without it, it has a relationship to reading that is as close and as mutual as anything we have seen. What, then, about *literacy as a whole*? Though it is large for a brick, are not its uses legion? But consider for a moment its 'sideways on' relationship with school subjects (those other curriculum 'bricks'). It is more than a convenience to them. It is, in fact, *essential* to the kind of sustained concentration of thought that disciplines like science and history evince, an internal condition of their development. (This needs some argument – to be supplied in one of the concluding case studies – which is consistent, however, with regarding it as at least partially a conceptual point.[21]) In reverse, literacy achieves much of its most valuable potential in its use in such disciplines. The conclusion seems overdue that *nothing* quite fits the bill of 'flexible curriculum brick'.

We have many times referred to education as 'a practice' in the singular, and one that is foundational to other practices. We have before also referred to it as a complex of different practices, the level and degree of whose interrelatedness is the point presently at issue. Alisdair MacIntyre, in an acclaimed book, presents a practice as any complex, coherent, established and cooperative activity that meets the following conditions:

(a) it has internal goods, i.e. satisfactions that have to be lived to be understood;
(b) it has standards of excellence that partially define it;
(c) it tends to the progressive development of our understanding of both the goods and the standards, though without ruling out the danger of decline – thus it genuinely has a history and prospects of its own;
(d) these features imply another, i.e. that it provides a setting for the practice of virtues like courage, patience and friendship.[22]

Examples are said to include farming (but not planting turnips), football (but not taking corners), chess, the making and sustaining of family life, politics (as classically understood, at any rate), science, history, portrait painting – and arts generally. Now writing would seem to meet the clauses of this definition just as well as the examples quoted. (We had already ascribed to it (a) and (b) above, and it would not be difficult to make a case for (c) and (d).) But if writing is a practice, then *practices do not have to be too strictly bounded*. For equally good cases could be made for the larger unit of literacy, and, again, for a rather particular kind of writing and reading: literature. To the same effect we might consider portrait painting in relation to painting, or physics in relation to science. 'Practice' is indeed an appropriate and useful concept in relation to curriculum. Its condition of 'internal goods' offers some partial and provisional response to the demand for justification; it implies just the kind of patient, sustained, initiation that is associated with the idea of 'curriculum'; it suggests useful queries about what curricula typically omit, e.g. farming (even in rural areas); and it would be a bulwark against the tendency to 'atomize' everything into lists of skills, qualities, criteria or objectives. But it seems – like 'plant', which covers both 'tree' and 'grass' – to be a concept of something that does not have to be strongly individuated (even if in particular cases, e.g. chess, it is).

CURRICULUM AND CULTURAL DISUNITY

To the extent that the practices and sub-practices of curriculum are individuated and autonomous they give the lie to the slightly silly[23] image of 'the seamless garment of knowledge'. To the extent that their individuality and autonomy are limited we can still hope for something more unified than a patchwork quilt. But we have so far referred only to the common dependence of many major curriculum practices on literacy. This does indeed confer a certain unity on the curriculum – the unity of the academic. But what now of the relationships of these major practices with each other? Oakeshott, we saw, suggested that education is 'learning to recognize the varieties of human utterance and to participate in the conversation they compose'.[24] We may feel like asking: what conversation?

It does seem obvious that in our culture such a conversation is more fond dream than reality. There are sub-conversations, sometimes struggling to start up or to keep going, within each of the broad areas of the humanities, the sciences, the arts and technologies. But there is little 'lived' contact between these larger blocs, and little enough between them and the work and practices of everyday life. In the nineteenth century, for instance, Bakunin looked to science 'becoming fused with the real and immediate life of every individual', and Marx, famously, to the overcoming of 'the degrading division of labour into intellectual and manual labour' – but how much nearer are we to achieving these things? Somehow, circuitously, each sphere may connect with every other, but it seems precisely *not* the case that, as Chesterton would have wanted it, 'all combine to convey some general view of life'.

NO ARCHETYPAL IDEAS

What we especially lack is much by way of archetypal images and ideas running through these areas, creating analogies and resonances between them. In the ancient Greek world – so Simone Weil argues[25] – 'form', 'proportion' and 'equilibrium' were a family of ideas at the very heart, at once, of their mathematics and science, their ethics and politics, their art and literature, and their spirituality. This comes across marvellously in a passage of Plato's, in the dialogue *Gorgias*, where he is considering the charge that morality is just a system of conventions by which the weak attempt to rein in the strong. Socrates, defending morality against Callicles, who has advanced the proto-fascist position, argues that the excellence of anything – implement, physical body, soul, organism – springs from its having a 'certain ordered beauty' appropriate to it. He continues as follows:

> The man who adopts the course (of allowing all his appetites to go unchecked) will win the love neither of God nor of his fellow-men; he is incapable of social life, and without social life there can be no love. We are told on good authority [he means Pythagoras], Callicles, that heaven and earth and their respective inhabitants are held together by the bonds of society and love and order and discipline and righteousness, and that is why the universe is called an ordered whole or cosmos and not a state of disorder and licence. You, I think, for all your cleverness, have failed to grasp the truth; you have not observed how great a part geometric equality plays in heaven and earth, and because you neglect the study of geometry you preach the doctrine of unfair shares.[26]

We are not entirely without feeling for this kind of sweep in argument; it survives in pockets of our culture and corners of our minds. But in the mainstream the idea, for instance, that geometry and physics lie near the centre of moral education is likely to seem eccentric, of some 'poetic' force perhaps but hardly a serious proposition. Actually to take it seriously would involve us in radically rethinking our science education, and – almost certainly – our science itself.[27]

NO UNITY OF METHOD

Another, but flatter, idea was that unity could be found in *method*, in the principles of well-conducted enquiry whatever the subject matter. It has surfaced from time to time in Western culture, and never more strongly than in the seventeenth- and eighteenth-century school of rationalist philosophy stemming from Descartes.[28] Having himself discovered coordinate geometry by a unification of algebra and classical geometry, and like Galileo attributing the recent triumphs in science to a new unification of mathematics and natural science, Descartes went on to conceive of a distillation of mathematical method that could function universally. It would bring to all spheres of enquiry the kind of spectacular advances that were becoming the hallmark of physical science and would, indeed, bring all enquiries into one science.

> Those long chains of reasons, all quite simple and quite easy, which geometers are wont to employ in reaching their most difficult demonstrations, had given me occasion to imagine that all the possible objects of human knowledge were linked together in the same way and that, if we accepted none as true that was not so in fact, and kept to the right order in deducing one from the other, there was nothing so remote that it could not be reached, nothing so hidden that it could not be discovered.[29]

We have less to mourn in the passing of this idea, but are we in danger of being left with something flatter still as a basis for unity in our intellectual lives? In the place of analogies of content or a common method, what have we got to add to the bare fact that our forms of knowledge are all ours? Perhaps only the thought that they are all 'academic', i.e. literate and 'concentrated'.

CONCLUSION

That would be a situation of some peril for the idea of education. Let us take, as an example, the science teacher in a secondary school. She does not think that her identity as 'science teacher' should vanish into her role as educator, even in the best of all possible worlds. But she does consider herself an educator as well. On what basis? There will be, of course, her general relationship with her students, her pastoral work and so forth. But she wants to think of her science teaching as *itself* educational, perhaps even as her main contribution to her students' education. Now by this she means to imply both some significant *connection* between it and the work of her colleagues in other departments, and some *distinctiveness* in its contribution to their collaborative enterprise, without which science could be replaced on the curriculum without educational loss. We generally approve of her thinking in this way, being haunted by this thought indeed, but does our culture provide her with the means to realize her thought? Certainly the ideal of 'the academic' seems insufficient. The development of literate and concentrated thought is a cross-curricular goal, even an important one and the subject of a later case study. But it is only one of the goals that teachers would commonly subscribe to and, more immediately to the point, it seems altogether too thin to sustain the notion of *distinctive and complementary* contributions from different subjects. For that, surely, one needs to be able to refer subjects to different aspects of human being, e.g. cognitive, emotional and physical, and/or of the world around us, e.g. natural, social and spiritual, and then to see these aspects as constituting together ordered wholes. It is precisely this reference and this holistic view that are made difficult in a fragmented culture.

In the end truth is a still more important ideal than education. If we *knew* that unity was a chimera, or could be achieved only by artificial imposition, we should abandon 'education'. But of course we do not know this. We know only that there are some obstacles in the way of our quest. In the next chapter we shall address the question of overarching educational values, those values with a claim to span and to direct the whole curriculum, and we shall argue for a particular ordering of these. Carrying that position with us, we shall move in Chapter 9 to the questions of differentiation and complementarity in the use of our cultural 'capital'.

NOTES

1. Illich (1971, p. 19).
2. Holt (1976, p. 19).
3. *ibid.*, pp. 7–8.
4. 'The study of politics in a university', in Oakeshott (1962) (cf. 'Michael Oakeshott's philosophy of education', in Peters (1981), which cites this passage).
5. Stenhouse (1975, Chapter 6).
6. See, for example, Aquinas, *Summa Theologica*, First Part, Questions 50ff.
7. 'Original sin' and its consequences were not generally presented as an affliction peculiar to children. Thus it is probably the case that only as misunderstood could the doctrine have been thought to justify disciplinarianism in education. Rousseau in his reaction to this kind of education famously thought it essential to deny the doctrine. But his own project of removing the pupil from society could *just as well* have been presented as one of preventing the exposure of the child to the adult, institutionalized and 'full-blown' manifestations of original sin! The doctrine, it seems to me, is in fact neutral as between traditional and child-centred positions on education.
8. This objection overlaps but does not coincide with the first one. Even if education were always a matter of people shaping themselves, and this always a self-initiated project, one might still object that it involved a sacrifice of the present to the future.
9. One tack here – not unpersuasive – is a cost/benefit analysis of the policy of robbing the Peter of childhood to pay the Paul of adulthood. But it does not strike deeply enough, nor does it offer enough security to childhood. Once before I tried to express what I think is at stake in the terms of christian humanism. 'Each age of man [*sic*] has internal relations with the other ages. In the case of childhood it is true that, from this point of view, it has the character of a "preparation" for something else. But each age has also its own intrinsic validity and value. This, which is even true, up to a point, of animals, is particularly true of human beings. For if human beings have in some sense an absolute value, then so must the stages of their lives. Thus childhood has not only its great importance in relation to what follows. It has, additionally, not only a certain charm of its own, as also have gambolling lambs and frisking puppies. It has as well its own *dignity*. It already possesses the dignity of human-being, but in its own special way. And so it cannot be simply reduced to a means towards something beyond itself, even if the "something beyond" is its own future maturity. Human childhood already has the kind of absolute irreplaceability that is signified by "personhood" ' (Walsh, 1975, pp. 87–8). See also Karl Rahner (1971).
10. The same mistake, though in a quite different context, is made by Sealey (1979). He argues that education is, conceptually, a matter of reflection on experience and not an actual engagement in experience. It is not clear why he thinks it could not be both, or, indeed, how we are to reflect on what we have not in some way experienced. (I am inclined to say that if Sealey was right about education, then and only then would Holt be right to oppose it in principle; but Sealey is not right and, so, neither is Holt.)
11. Sub-cultures in this context face both ways. Like individuals they have problems with legitimacy and the right to be different. Like the wider society and its common curriculum they create those problems for some individuals, their own members.
12. The quotation is from memory and may not be word perfect.
13. Sartre (1943, p. 90). Actually, for Sartre in this work man desires *to be* God, that is to say, an impossible combination of the (for him) polar opposites of 'being-in-itself' and

consciousness ('being-for-itself'). God, for him, is the name for the projection outwards of that impossible thing which we cannot but desire to be.

14. Peters (1966, p. 29).
15. Wilson (1979, p. 50).
16. A question suggested to me by Brian Crittenden.
17. Dearden (1981).
18. See R. S. Peters, 'Democratic values and educational aims', in Peters (1981), and Crittenden (1982).
19. I have pieced together my account of core curriculum from Skilbeck (1984, Chapters 6 and 7), who also alludes briefly to its history, going back through generations of mainly American educators, to the nineteenth-century German thinker, Herbart, and to the wider theoretical underpinnings of the contemporary form of the idea in Cassirer, Dewey, Mannheim and others. On these points see also Lawton (1980) and Williams (1961). The latter, in a classic discussion of British education, argues that the organizing principle for a common curriculum should be 'what a member of an educated and participatory democracy needs'.
20. It adds, however, the explanation we have noted as to why the elements should cluster on the curriculum in the first place, i.e. that they cluster in life. Notice two kinds of concurrence in the operation of skills and qualities: the repetitive and predictible, like many of the combinations required in writing or in driving a car; and the unpredictible, like those required to act properly in the relatively unusual or infrequent combinations of circumstances that constitute a practical *problem*. Preparation for the latter must essentially include gaining experience of them – so practical problems on the curriculum! As often noted, this would have an integrating effect (of one kind), bringing together, *ad hoc*, forms of enquiry that are otherwise pursued apart.
21. I am sympathetic, however – as should be clear from some earlier sections – with the view that there is no absolute distinction between conceptual and empirical truths, rather a gradation from deeply embedded assumptions to claims widely acknowledged to be open and debatable (see Quine, 'Two dogmas of empiricism', in his 1953 work). Some conceptual points seem evident at a glance, like the connection between legibility and writing. Some seem more difficult, being built into more specialized concepts or uses of concepts. Some seem not to be conceptual at all, though they might be considered (better or worse supported) conceptual stipulations. All are in principle open to criticism as to their truth – definitions can be wrong and concepts (e.g. 'astrological influence') can lack application.
22. MacIntyre (1981, Chapters 14 and 15). His analysis is a strongly Aristotelian one. See also John White's (1973) 'category I' activities (any X where 'no understanding of X is possible without engaging in X').
23. Silly, if only because it neglects the obvious point that conceptual relationships – and the differentiations that are their 'flip' side – are of *many kinds*, differing, for example, in degrees of closeness, of necessity and of mutuality.
24. 'The study of politics in a university', in Oakeshott (1962).
25. See in particular, 'Classical science and after' in Weil (1968), and her letters to her brother, numbers 37–9, in Weil (1965).
26. *Gorgias*, 507–8.
27. Simone Weil consistently advocated just such a project. As well as the works cited above, see her *Oppression and Liberty*, and *The Need for Roots*. Husserl and Heidegger were other philosophers of this century to make this sort of critique of modern science.
28. Aristotle (*Posterior Analytic*) and, in this century, Dewey have also pursued this ideal.
29. *Discourse on Method* 2. One of the classic works generated by this rationalist ideal was Spinoza's *Ethics*. Its suggestive Latin title was *Ethica ordine geometrica demonstrata* (Ethics demonstrated in geometric progression).

Chapter 8

Basing Values on Love of the World

'That heavy greenness fostered by water'

.
.
.

Heaviness of being. And poetry
Sluggish in the doldrums of what happens.
Me waiting until I was nearly fifty
To credit marvels. Like the tree-clock of tin cans
The tinkers made. So long for air to brighten,
Time to be dazzled and the heart to lighten.
    Seamus Heaney, 'Fosterling', from *Seeing Things*, courtesy of Faber & Faber

The order of the world is the same as the beauty of the world.
    Simone Weil, *The Need for Roots*

FOUR KINDS OF VALUE

Suppose the question is raised as to why science should be on the curriculum. The answer might take any of the following forms, partly depending, no doubt, on who the respondent is and what his relationships are to science and to education.

One kind of answer will stress the *'pay-off'*: in societal terms, the contribution of science mediated by technology to national wealth and power, and, correspondingly, the need to educate for a scientifically literate community which will at once produce and support professional classes of scientists and technologists. This is the perspective of governments in particular, in both the developed and the developing worlds. It is also, surely, the answer that best expresses that prestige of science which makes the question itself an arresting one.

Another answer would proclaim the intrinsic *fecundity* of science (both pure and applied) and the opportunities it thereby provides for the development and stretching of minds, for intellectual challenge and adventure. It has a natural appeal for educators and educationists, at any rate those in the liberal and the progressive traditions.

A third answer will insist rather on the *rationality* of science; that is, certain ethical, or quasi-ethical, qualities which it embodies (not exclusively but paradigmatically) and which it therefore encourages in those who are exposed to it – precision of thought, objectivity, a commitment to truth, and perhaps international-mindedness (on the somewhat idealized view of science as knowing no frontiers). Such an answer would appeal to the sober, steadfast philosopher.

Finally, there is a romantic viewpoint according to which all the values so far mentioned are but incidental to, or perhaps consequent upon, a more fundamental value, namely the value that accrues to science from the *object* which it studies, that is to say from the order and the resources of the universe in general and in its parts. These invite attention and enquiry, and an education in this attention and enquiry, simply by being awesome, wonderful, marvellous, beautiful! Here is the young Einstein (and the scientist herself is a not unlikely respondent in these terms) on what he took to be the truly scientific spirit:

> A finely tempered nature longs to escape from his noisy cramped surroundings into the silence of the high mountains where the eye ranges freely through the still pure air and fondly traces out the restful contours apparently built for eternity. . . . The state of mind which enables a man [*sic*] to do work of this kind is akin to that of the religious worshipper or lover.[1]

On this view, an education in science should be a profoundly spiritual affair. An ecological dimension would also be more easily accommodated. In the 'green' movement, reverence for nature – a responsible reverence or, in Heidegger's terms, a shepherd's tendance – is even more basic than is the calculation of long-term, future-generational, utility.

Each of these four answers may be considered as valid in its own way – science education, we might say, is fortunate to have four important kinds of value going for it. But we could hardly just leave it at that. This is no mere matter of transferring a fixed body of knowledge and enquiry to the minds of schoolchildren. There are questions of which selections to make, how to present these, what kind of developmental sequence to give to the science curriculum – of, as one might put it in general, the *spirit* of science education. Thus a covert competition to isolate progressively the cadre of university scientists and technologists may work out as one thing and fostering the spirit of the lover or worshipper as something quite different. These values may be expected, indeed, to conflict often and deeply in practice. It follows that any serious address of the original question 'why science?' must attempt to *order* them.

This four-fold categorization can be generalized to refer to *education as a whole*, however, and it is in regard to their claims on it that I shall presently attempt to order what I shall call *possessive*, *experiential*, *ethical* and *ecstatic* values and viewpoints. (The last, 'ecstatic', is in the technical sense of the Greek root 'standing out of oneself' – the reference is not to unusual 'peak experiences' but to a, perhaps extraordinary, dimension of ordinary daily life. Think also of the metaphor 'being *absorbed* by a person, story, scene, etc.': the everyday is made remarkable in the image of the mind as water draining into the mind's object as sponge.) I shall discuss each category in turn and simultaneously develop an ongoing sketch of an argument for an ordering of them that gives priority to the last-named. This will endeavour so to expose each of the first three classes of values as ungrounded or incomplete that the next one is naturally elicited as its presupposition or corrective. Necessarily fairly abstract, this general sketch is complemented by the later case studies.

JUSTIFICATION AND A ROAD NOT TAKEN

As a preliminary, let us recall the burden of justification that education carries and consider strategies for dealing with this burden. In a mature system teachers, in particular, will be routinely challenged by government, parents, employers, journalists, colleagues in a team and, not least, students. Much is perceived to be at stake here, and, further-more, the matter is one not of what people are spontaneously interested in and inclined to value for themselves, but of what some people are to be allowed to encourage, cajole or compel other people to do and, ideally, to value in their turn. Again, if, as we have noticed, education as theory cannot avoid making value judgements in its normative modes and running up against them in its descriptive modes, this is because it is value-saturated as a *practice*. Like other objects of public debate and policy – housing, health, the economy, the environment, public order, defence, the arts, etc. – education both is a value in itself and involves more particular value choices in all its policy deliberations. Unlike them (except inasmuch as they too take on educational functions, as in com-munity health provision), it additionally involves a deliberate *communication* of values, as we saw (pp. 23–4): education consciously shapes values as well as being shaped by them. It follows that to some considerable extent the justification of curriculum decisions will be the justification of values and not just of prudential or technical judgements. This remains true of decisions that are *also* obviously prudential and/or technical, e.g. the choice of an approach for the teaching of reading.[2]

How, in general, might we prepare ourselves to accomplish this justification of values in the educational context? We assume here our earlier defence against a sceptical sub-jectivism that would preclude our ever starting out. Granted that, there are two strategies we might consider. The one we shall actually adopt, as indicated, will be to identify significant categories of value to which individual values like equality or the vocational might then be related, to consider the claims on education of each of these categories, and to consider whether, and how, the categories may be ordered. Alter-natively, we might have chosen to identify historically significant philosophies or ideologies (in one sense of those terms[3]), within which individual values might be situated, and then to compare the merits and demerits of these. We might have started by identifying *educational* ideologies like progressivism, classical humanism, recon-structionism and technocracy,[4] and later invoked some philosophy of *life as a whole*, like liberalism, Marxism, Christianity or Islam, to provide some more ultimate justifica-tion. The advantages of this approach are in terms of intellectual convenience and politics. It promises some intelligibility and some basis for consistent action that are ready made; and it promises identifiable allies and historical roots. Its disadvantages are three risks that it carries. There is a danger of historical and conceptual oversimplifica-tion: there are Marxist Christians, liberal Christians, Muslim socialists, non-elitist classical humanists, etc. A closely related second danger is of getting trapped into some too narrow and/or inflexible set of positions. The third danger is of a philosophically disappointing second-handedness. Of course, we might have guarded against these dangers by historical exactitude, a studied eclecticism and the treating of ideologies as starting points for our own enquiries.[5] But then we would have lost the easy system-atization, and to put order back into our enquiries we might have been forced, belatedly, to something like the first strategy anyway.

POSSESSIVE VALUES AND VOCATIONAL EDUCATION

Wealth, status and power, considered in relation to the individual, a class or a society, are values with which education has sat uncomfortably in Western culture, at least since

Plato and the Sophists were arguing over them. There has been, and there remains, controversy over their *actual* relationships with educational systems and, more markedly still, over the stance which education *ought* to assume towards them. And other material values have been drawn into this uncertainty, though they did not deserve to be, values like health, housing, making a living and creating (as opposed to accumulating) wealth.

What do these values have in common that they should be lumped together in the same penumbra? To begin with, they are interconnected in the sense that one tends to bring the others in its train. This is notoriously so for wealth, power and status. But if we concentrate for the moment on these we can, in addition, detect certain common features centring on the notion of possession. They are all three such that they can be possessed, in greater or lesser amount or degree, with more or less security, and their possession bears some relationship to the effort and contrivance of the possessor. Because of their perceived relationship to effort and contrivance they can become goals to be pursued. Because of the variations of quantity and of security they can become constant concerns and, even, overriding preoccupations. Now this much could also be said of health, and indeed, as I shall emphasize presently, of knowledge. But with regard to wealth, power and status we have to add both that possession of them is exclusive possession – shared, they are diminished – and that the generally available amount of each is limited (contingently in the case of wealth, necessarily in the case of the others). Because of these features strivings for wealth and for power have an intrinsically *competitive* aspect. These extra conditions do not apply to health or to knowledge *as such* – though they do apply to many of the *conditions* of these, hospital beds and university places for instance, which is the basis of much illuminating analysis of health and of knowledge as 'commodities'.

There are two main manifestations of a rampant possessive instinct in education: unqualified vocationalism and encyclopaedism. These are to be distinguished from measured concerns, situated within a larger value context, for the vocational and for the breadth and the retention of knowledge.

A *rampant vocationalism* both conceives education as a whole as instrumental to working life, *and* conceives working life as wholly instrumental to the securing of money, possessions, status and power. The first is a narrowness of attitude that would entail a narrowing of curriculum (though there would still be a question of 'generic' as well as of specific job skills, including, for example, the market value of an arts degree, and of work attitudes as well as skills). The second goes naturally with the first, for it would be inconsistent to value other aspects of work, like comradeship, service or intrinsic satisfaction, without valuing them in other contexts as well and then allowing those contexts their broadening influence on the curriculum. This kind of vocationalism is the natural educational expression of vulgar materialism, for which possession is the overriding value and passion. Obviously it can take, overtly and covertly, societal as well as individual forms.

The most immediately telling objection to it is the old one that it is irrational in the narrow sense of being inadequate in its own self-serving terms.[6] In general, possession, of its very nature, refers beyond itself to other values. Vastness and security of possession can rationally be valued only if what is vastly and securely possessed has a value for us that does not reside in the mere fact of possession. A secure title deed to a remote star would not be of much value to a rational person. More specifically, money and power have of themselves the character of being means to further ends, while survival, health and the extension of body space 'property' are all enabling conditions in the pursuit of further goals, and derive much of their real value from that fact. Among the further goals and values that could give point to possessions are many that education, under broader conceptions of it than the materialist's, seeks to promote.

Encyclopaedism is a subtler manifestation of the possessive instinct, and a kind of mental materialism. In it knowledge itself (and not merely the credits and diplomas in which it is given public acknowledgement) takes on the aspect of a possession, and the point becomes to amass and retain it rather than to use it and live through it. The crammer for an examination is a materialist of this sort, though his usual unconcern at forgetting what he has learnt after the crisis shows his commitment to have been provisional. But some may be more serious crammers. A person may build an empire in his mind, embarking on each new book or course of study as though it were new territory to be annexed. He may glory in his store of learning, and when he takes out and dusts off the odd item it is mainly to reassure himself that he still has it. The library walls may be the principal horizons of his life, spiritual as well as physical, the object being to transfer everything from the shelves on the wall to shelves in his head – like the 'autodidact' in Sartre's novel *La Nausée*. But the irony is that he does not make knowledge really 'his own'. In some sense he kills it in his attempts to possess it. 'Knowledge' for him has no connection with action, intimacy or contemplation, does not yield life experience or wisdom, is indeed altogether useless and hardly deserves to be called 'knowledge' at all.

On the other hand, there is nothing in these arguments to show that material values and breadth of knowledge should not be given place within a larger conception of value and of education. As it happens, *vocational education* is newly respectable in educational discussion and proposal. The proper response to this is a complex one,[7] as the following fairly standard observations indicate.

First, as Dewey remarks, 'education has been much more vocational in fact than in name'.[8] Arguably, education has *always* in practice had a vocational dimension, even when it pretended it had not, and we could hardly sustain an objection just to making this explicit. But, anyway, education and schooling are properly in the business of communicating knowledge and skills that relate to important human concerns and that need a protracted period for their acquisition. At least some material values, and the knowledge, skills, attitudes and virtues that bear on them, meet these conditions. In principle, then, education takes them up *legitimately*. The qualification is two-fold, as we shall see: education has both to take up other values as well, and to integrate material values with these others.

Second, a rational, balanced attitude to material values does not come easily to the human species. ('Money isn't everything, but who needs everything if you've got money,' goes the wry wisecrack.) Hence, among other things, there is a pressing need to consider the *distribution* of goods and services, and to cultivate and apply to this area the virtues of justice, equality and humanity. Vocational education, then, overlaps with moral education. (We refrained earlier from this ethical point because a solid materialism would seem to have no 'logical space' for it – and in practice a wiser self-interest may be a necessary stepping stone to the ethical for the dedicated materialist. Besides, a materialism tempered only by considerations of fairness and justice would still be irrational, would it not? For it must falter before the question of what use one's fair share of possessions is – other, that is, than for enlarging further the common stock, and so one's fair share, of possessions. This is to say, perhaps, that distributive justice is not the most fundamental virtue, even if sometimes it is much the most urgent one.)

Third, there is very much more to an education for work than 'accommodating' students to the labour market by training them in the skills and attitudes that make them easily employable. It needs also to include, for example, the development of a critical and informed interest in the organization of industry, in labour relations, and in the nature, destination, social effects and environmental effects of products. Thus vocational education also overlaps with economic and political education (traditionally much neglected) and becomes a part of education's 'transformative' mission in society.[9]

Fourth, 'employment', 'a job', 'a career' – most of all 'a vocation' – are all concepts that break the bounds of material values as defined earlier. Indeed they relate to all four categories of value. For is there not question in a job of fulfilment and satisfaction as well as of a wage or salary? Is there not also a relationship with such ethical notions as 'being of service' and 'playing one's part'? And is there not a matter of getting 'out of oneself', perhaps 'out and about' and, in many jobs, a hard, but salutary, contact with the world, with its sometimes pitiless necessity but at the same time its beauty and inexhaustibility? So, as everyone knows, unemployment is a tragedy not just at the level of one's purchasing power: as well as poor, it may leave one bored, 'useless' and withdrawn. The concept of 'a career' strikes an additional note of care for one's life as a whole, a concern not to waste it or throw it away. The still wider and deeper concept of 'a vocation' strikes this note too, among others:

> it is necessary to define the meaning of vocation with some fullness in order to avoid the impression that an education which centers about it is narrowly practical, if not merely pecuniary. A vocation means nothing but such a direction of life activities as renders them perceptibly significant to a person, because of the consequences they accomplish, and also useful to his associates. The opposite of a career is neither leisure nor culture, but aimlessness, capriciousness, the absence of cumulative achievement in experience, on the personal side, and idle display, parasitic dependence upon the others, on the social side.[10]

In this deliberately wide definition, Dewey omits to mention only the special connections which the word can still have with some caring professions in which the dedication can notably outstrip the remuneration, and, beyond that, with the idea of a calling by God.[11]

EXPERIENTIAL VALUES AND JOHN DEWEY

Now the emphasis passes from 'security of possession' to 'richness of experience'. Culture, education, the disciplines of learning and the wider curriculum are conceived and judged in reference to their potentially large contribution to the full, or the interesting, life (whether individually or socially considered, and whether future- or mainly present-orientated). There is a kind of vaunting of the life of the mind – we might also have called these values those of mental and intellectual 'vitality'. But the vaunting, note, is not in terms of pleasures alone, for this is more than a refined version of hedonism. As elsewhere, so in the intellectual field there is the hope that defies apparent failure, the rather grim satisfactions of endurance through trial, and the occasional experience of oneself as living powerfully in one dimension of oneself.[12] These are themes of much literature – Kazantzakis's *Zorba the Greek* and Hesse's *The Glass Bead Game* come to mind – of the popular film *Dead Poets Society* and, among philosophers, of Kierkegaard's *Either/Or*, vol. 1 and of Nietzsche *passim*. But in directly educational terms, it is Dewey's view of education as growth that is especially notable: 'the education process is a continuous process of growth, having as its aim at every stage an added capacity of growth.'[13] In another place,[14] he quotes Tennyson:

> . . . all experience is an arch wherethro'
> Gleams that untravell'd world, whose margin fades
> For ever and for ever when I move.

But if this is true of *all* experience, then how do we select curriculum experiences? Wouldn't any experiences do? Dewey's famous reply to this was that while any experience may promote some growth in some direction or other, the question is rather of whether it promotes or retards *growth in general*. We shall see that in giving this answer, and in making of 'experience' a sort of self-contained infinitude, Dewey seeks to avoid having to refer to the 'world-in-itself' as a source of value.

First, however, we should distinguish here too the rampant and the qualified: on the one hand, conceiving culture and life itself as essentially 'play' and making the pursuit of the interesting and challenging the cardinal value in a whole life-stance; on the other hand, a contextualized admission and pursuit of these values among others.

Now the former is not simply to be dismissed as a kind of frivolity. The serious scholar or scientist may conceive his work primarily in the spirit of the chase, and in that spirit choose to work at the limit of his powers and endurance rather than well within himself. 'Aesthetic Man', as Kierkegaard calls him,[15] can be patient and sensitive in his personal relationships, even generous in his concern that others too should enjoy fulfilment, such attitudes being seen as ones that enlarge his own life. Again, he may welcome anxiety and depression as novel and interesting experiences, choose the uncomfortable trek in preference to the comfort of a plane, and extract amazing benefits from his bereavements and griefs.

It is not frivolity that is his problem. It is futility. Smile he might at the materialist hoarder of things he never uses, but nemesis attends his own pursuit of experience inasmuch as – as he conceives it – it gravitates fatally towards that which it most shuns: boredom, and what the medievals called *acedia* or world-weariness. Indeed, just as there is a sense in which the encyclopaedist never actually possesses his knowledge, so there is a sense in which Aesthetic Man never quite succeeds in experiencing anything. He is 'into' experience but not properly 'in' his experiences, tending rather to the role of their detached observer and analyst. Thus in Kierkegaard's *Either/Or* the absurdly introspective seducer stands revealed in his diary as longing to be the simple 'force' that Mozart's Don Giovanni is while knowing that he, of all people, cannot be this.

This nemesis is to be explained, surely, as the natural outcome of taking parasitic values as host values, while allowing the real host values to languish in subordinate positions. The real host values are, particularly, the trio of truth, respect and justice, all so many basic acknowledgements of the independent value of objects of experience. Experiential values depend in the end on such acknowledgements. This claim has some immediate intuitive force, but philosophers might envisage an extended argument for it in the form of an analogue for affective and value-life of Kant's 'deduction' of the categories of cognitive experience.[16] Just as the possession of the concepts of 'experience' and of 'self' are shown by Kant to be inseparable from the possession of the concepts of 'things' and 'sorts of things' that exist in themselves with their own pasts and futures, so 'experience' can only be properly *valued*, it might be shown, in a context in which value is being attributed to things, and sorts of things, in their own right, as they exist in their own time-spans.

On the other hand, 'vital' values considered as one category of value among others are almost self-legitimating. Just as a person does not usually have to 'justify' going on with life (i.e. not committing suicide), so she shouldn't ordinarily be required to justify stretching herself and living at the top of her bent – assuming, that is, that no one else is being hurt and so on (though perhaps some conflict here would not be so extraordinary). We should add that the will to live, and have others live, largely and fruitfully, to empower oneself to make one's mark and to empower others similarly, can be taken up into a moral, and even a religious, perspective, as in the Christian parable of the talents, or in the injunction *carpe diem*, seize the day, which can have an ethical as well as a vital appeal. Indeed, in the lives of some individuals and cultures, experiential values may be so well integrated into the ethical and/or the religious that it would be difficult for them to analyse them out and conceive of a way of life focused primarily on them.

We must now return to Dewey, the philosopher *non pareil* of an education 'of, by and for' experience. He relied especially on the active or reconstructive aspect of experience to mount his truly formidable critique of traditional education for the mismatch of its methods and contents to student experience and to the processes by which that experience can grow to be progressively more sensitive, intelligent, empowered, coherent and absorbing. On the other hand, he deployed analyses of other aspects of experience – its continuity, the interaction in it of the subjective and objective, and again of the individual and social – to mount almost as severe a critique of the excesses of some progressive education. He is also the philosopher of democracy as the form of social organization that promotes the widest access to good human experience, so that there is a strongly ethical dimension to his work which coheres well with the rest of his philosophy of experience (but which, also, he thought to *derive* from that philosophy). All this is accomplished on the page with great humanity and a sense of the reality of classroom and student learning that should be the envy of other philosophers of education.[17] These qualities make Dewey still the educational philosopher most worth reading, and it seems therefore churlish, though it is necessary, to go on to tax him with a basic flaw in his approach.

This flaw was his rejection, in line with his 'pragmatic' theory of meaning and knowledge, of the proposition that the objects of experience can possess value in themselves.[18] He did indeed save himself from the worst consequence of this rejection. Though the reader may be occasionally struck by some lack of a wondering awareness before the givenness of the world and a too absolute insistence that 'objects' are the constructions and reconstructions of 'subjects', Dewey does incorporate – eloquently and originally – the *ethical* significance of education in his position. The question that arises, however, is whether he was logically entitled to this – whether it does not put more weight on a self-contained (though complex) 'experience' than this can take; whence, in particular, the principle of impartiality that is implicit in his support for democracy? Why should the individual care about the experience of others – unless only as a form of more enlightened self-interest? It is all very well to go on about the interdependence of individual and communal experience, as Dewey does, but the ethical issue is, importantly, what to do when my interests conflict with others' interests. Yielding to what we see as the superior claims of others is not always, as a matter of fact, in our own longer-term or wider interests. More important, even when in fact it is, this is not the ethically respectable reason for doing it. That, rather, would refer us to the needs, rights and, fundamentally, the independent 'reality' of other persons. But it is precisely that reference that a view of experience as self-contained seems logically to exclude.

There is an obvious historical explanation for Dewey's uneasiness about 'the given' in terms of a basic trend in philosophy over the past three hundred years. In the seventeenth century, Descartes drove a wedge between experience (what he called 'ideas') and the real world. At an early point in his famous *Meditations* he finds himself alone with his experience, uncertain for the moment whether it is anything more than a dream – and so he sets himself to prove that under certain conditions his experience could be relied upon to represent a world beyond experience. The impossibility of any project formulated in this way had as its two eighteenth-century heirs the idealism of Berkeley, in which experience and world were simply identified ('to be' *was* 'to be perceived'), and the intellectual scepticism of Hume. Kant's transcendental deduction, alluded to above, was the brilliant response to both of these. Unfortunately, however, its reaffirmation of the reality of objects was a severely relative affair. For Kant chose to contain objects within a 'phenomenal' realm that remained, in the last – and mysterious – analysis, distinct from 'the noumenal' realm or the world-in-itself. This then was Dewey's inheritance, as it is that of other philosophers. Certainly, he joined some other American philosophers in giving it a new 'pragmatic' twist: he emphasized, probably overemphasized, the interplay of knowledge with action in the 'construction' of experience. Also, as had by then become common in the tradition, he interpreted 'experience' in social as much as individual terms (which conveniently glosses over the likelihood that our knowledge of other persons commands no more status, of the relevant kind, than our knowledge of other kinds of object: why should they alone be 'noumenal' among the things we experience?). But he retained the by now traditional wedge between experience and the world-in-itself in the notion of knowledge as fundamentally a construction; and this is surely the root of his rejection of the doctrine of independent or intrinsic values.[19]

I believe this wedge to be a profoundly mischievous instrument. In general, the so-called 'problem of knowledge' is a misnomer. Knowledge is not 'a problem'. That is not to deny that, like existence, it is an appropriate object of great wonder. But it is this precisely under a certain aspect, namely as an 'assimilation' of the world that yet of itself leaves the world as it is. If that paradox is written out from the beginning knowledge ceases to be a wonder – and what it then becomes is not a problem but a surd. (Needless to say, all this is the merest outline. That might be thought a pity considering that a – direct or non-representational – realist position in epistemology is integral to the argument about values that I am currently developing. But even the philosopher must sometimes be content just to come clean about his presuppositions!)

ETHICAL AND ECSTATIC VALUES: AN EXPANSIVE INTERPRETATION

An account of education, Richard Peters's, that helped to shape a generation of British teachers runs as follows. Education in the widest sense is to be conceived primarily as the initiation into the wise, or at any rate the rational, life – what Socrates called 'the examined life', perhaps scaled down to the reach of the average person. Formal education is to be designed primarily to contribute to this strategy. Initiation into the disciplines of learning in general education is to be motivated and structured by the relevance which they can have to a rational approach to the concerns and predicaments that are inevitable, or probable, in life. A 'rational approach' is defined chiefly by a concern for truth and related virtues like authenticity and integrity, a respect for persons, justice and a care for the intrinsic features of activities and things.[20]

As so far outlined, this account suffers from a systematic ambiguity. It could be interpreted as follows: the issues and predicaments are those on which we inevitably take a position, rather than all those we inevitably encounter; non-interference is the main ingredient in respect; the paradigm exercises of a concern for truth are the constraining of actual prejudice, and the restraining of wishful thinking and of flights of fancy and speculation; and 'care' is more carefulness than love. In general, the rational values are to be seen as primarily a series of restraints, a *regulative harness*, on vital and possessive values. They define 'duties', and 'duty', we all know, is easiest to recognize when it runs counter to inclination. Interpreted in this way, the account could hardly be presented as complete in itself. Rather, rational values would be added to possessive and experiential values as their ethically necessary corrective.

On the other hand, the precepts of rationality can be interpreted in an *expansive* way. Thus the traditional oath requires telling the whole truth as well as telling nothing but the truth. Where, more generally, regulative rationality requires only that *inasmuch as* we happen to judge, believe, feel, act and pursue, we should do so rightly, appropriately and effectively, expansive rationality involves such open-ended injunctions as: seize the day; see further and more, as far and as much as you can; develop your understanding towards its limits; exploit your knowledge to the full in your experience; cultivate depth and refinement of feeling; aim at achieving much, not just a well-done modicum; love the world.

There are three things to note already about these injunctions. First, though open-ended in character, they are not unlimited in their scope. For they refer us to our abilities and opportunities. They demand that we perceive, feel, understand and achieve not an impossible everything, but what we can. Indeed, since they will often conflict with each other in practice they must be taken rather in the spirit than the letter: collectively they require of us our general best (a familiar demand among those teachers make of students). Second, they have ethical, as well as vital, force – an integrated vital and ethical appeal. Third, they would begin to bring to the fore the value of the objects with which we rationally engage – as will become clearer presently.

Peters never decided finally between these interpretations of an educated rationality, it seems to me.[21] We must, however, prefer the second. The argument I shall advance for this is indirect. Its nub is that a regulative ethic actually presupposes an expansive ethic. Only in the context of an acceptance of open-ended formulations can the *ethical* force of the negative or regulative formulations be secured. I shall attempt to demonstrate this for that rational value that is most obviously ethical – and most widely associated with the work of Richard Peters – respect for persons.[22]

We can take it that *respecting a person* – her decisions, beliefs, feelings, in general her assertive point of view, involves, first, acknowledging her, and their, independent *existence* and, second, *taking account of* her and them in the sense of allowing her and them to have a certain kind of influence, namely a limiting influence, on what one does oneself. From this comes the connection in philosophical tradition between respect and rationality (which implies, at the least, an ability to acknowledge what is real), and its particular connection with practical reason. But respect involves more. Politicians, demagogues and secret police interrogators may be highly skilled at taking people's points of view into account in their work. We must add that to respect persons is to set a value on them in themselves, to treat them never only as means but always (also) as 'ends in themselves', as Kant put it.[23]

It is because of this condition that the concept of respect easily passes over into that reverence defined by Kant as 'the awareness of a value that demolishes self-love'. Nevertheless, there is a difference between respect and reverence. While they both involve setting a value on the object in itself, 'reverence' picks out a kind of contemplative regard for the valued object, whereas 'respect' picks out a reluctance to interrupt or interfere with it. Respect is, in that way, a negative attitude. But it remains that it is the negative side of a primarily positive coin, a positive valuing of persons – without which it is not respect in an ethical sense.

This fact tends to be concealed if we take as our paradigm of respect for persons that respect we owe those we don't know, hardly know, or dislike, for in these cases the practical consequences of our valuing them as ends in themselves consist entirely or mainly of restraints that we impose on our conduct for their sakes. Now even in these cases the restraints are based on a positive recognition of them as ends in themselves. But have we not here chosen the extreme cases as paradigms, ones that involve relatively thin and abstract modes of respect? We could not have first learnt that meaning and value of 'person' that is involved in respect for persons in relation to the stranger or the enemy – just as, in a Wittgensteinian example, we could not have first learnt to calculate in our heads, and then gone on to do it aloud or with an abacus. I am suggesting that respect, like charity, begins at home. If we more reasonably choose as our paradigm that respect which is an integral part of good family life, authentic collegueship, friendship and love relationships, then the conceptual connections become clearer between respect, on the one hand, and the more positive aspects of valuing somebody, like reverence and concern, on the other. Then, too, we might be bold enough to assert that respecting the stranger or mere acquaintance as a person, though it certainly does not imply that we love her in any ordinary sense of the word, does involve the acknowledgement that someone could find a world in her. We might also be rather less inclined to consign love to the realms of the non-rational, contrasting it in this with respect. (No doubt there is some stipulation in this use of the term 'love', some tightening up in relation to the variety of common uses, but so is there in the term 'respect' as used ethically in 'respect for persons'.)

What this shows is that there is something inherently unstable about a position that makes respect for persons the central virtue in our dealings with others. The ground on which it tries to stand has a way of vanishing. If it is too embarrassed to acknowledge its subsidiarity to love, it risks collapsing back into a prudentially motivated regard for others, a subscription to a social contract that promises respect in return for respect given. It will lose that independence of fear and inclination that Kant emphasized. But if it insists on its properly ethical quality, then it will have to underline its basis in a positive acknowledgement of the independent value of other persons, the paradigm of which is a loving relationship.

An analogous thesis relating to *truth* as an ethical value can be more briefly indicated. On the one hand there is a pragmatic concern for truth, perhaps a wariness of it lest it take one unawares and frustrate one's designs, or, perhaps, an acknowledgement that it provides a necessary point to the exercise of intellectual muscles, as goal scoring gives point to football. On the other hand there is a love of truth for its own sake, of which Simone Weil rightly observes that it is really an inaccurate expression for a love of reality, or an aspect or a part of reality, for its own sake.[24] Between these two sorts of regard for truth there is no middle ground, unless it be a love that is still too weak honestly to call itself anything but a sense of duty. Though this may in fact be the ground most of us stand on, it is an inherently provisional one.

Our line of argument again brings us up sharp against the idea of persons, objects and aspects of the world having value in themselves as a condition of their being values for us, and of love of the world as a rational condition of our other prizings. In this vein, the religious believer can acknowledge that the praise of God, just because He is God, is his primary religious response – more fundamental than his search for salvation through relationship with God (ultimately making sense of that search and constituting his side of that relationship). The scientist can feel that the order of the universe is worth investigating because it is marvellous – this being what makes the enquiry exciting rather than, vice versa, the excitement making the world marvellous. The artist may maintain that beauty is for contemplating and highlighting just because it is 'there' and there to be revealed. The historian may justify his work, not primarily in didactic terms, but because people are everywhere in history and people are, in themselves, worthy of our interest. And education can be conceived as, in large part, the loving initiation into these, and other such, mysteries.

INTELLECTUAL VITALITY, CONSCIENCE AND OBJECTS

Ray Elliott has sought to secure due recognition in philosophy of education for each of these three forces in intellectual endeavour. Our interest is in the way they converge and 'grow into' each other.

Elliott describes intellectual *vitality* as a composite of eros and energy that has its own characteristic virtues of involvement, ambition, adventurousness, tenacity, endurance, hope and faith.[25] It includes a reference to hedonistic notions like enjoyment and pleasure, but as part of a larger whole. Success for it is more fundamentally 'victory' than 'pleasure'. Intellectual *conscience* or probity, he suggests, is expressed in such virtues as authenticity, integrity and truthfulness. Whereas vitality functions in an expansive way, conscience in isolation is typically regulative. Third, there is a sense of the importance of certain kinds of *object* of enquiry, and a corresponding respect for them and love of them.

> It is a matter of some significance that the disciplines are concerned with the various worlds or regions of worlds which are essential to man's being, or on which his being depends, or which may shed light on the nature of his being, or which express his being with such force

and comprehensiveness that they are essential for his self-understanding; and which reveal, also, that which is other than man but with which man is necessarily concerned, or upon which his well-being depends, or which is relevant to his well-being as a valued or threatening part of his environment, or which is worthy of his care and attention for its own sake, or which claims his attention as having a being superior to his own.[26]

These three factors can be characterized independently, and they can function independently, or even against each other – *up to a point*. We have just given them some independent characterization, and it will not be difficult to imagine cases where they function independently, or in opposition. (1) Intellectual games are paradigms of the relatively pure exercise of intellectual vitality. Neither conscience nor the world penetrate very far into chess (though – and it is worth noting – a simulacrum of each does: the rules and conventions of chess in one case, and in the other case the way players imaginatively project the legal possibilities on to the physical board and pieces, almost to the point of seeing around each piece a series of pathways determining its possible moves). Where conscience focuses on chess from the outside it might even be with disapproval: one might consider it disgraceful that one devotes so much time to it. (2) There can be a lack of proportion in the importance attached to the objects of some enquiry that turns love of them into idolatry – and one can suppose that the enquirer has an uneasy conscience about this. (3) An enquiry can be pursued as a matter of intellectual conscience, without interest, and without attributing intrinsic importance to the object of enquiry. This may be justified as part of a larger enquiry – so, much history writing consists of routine enquiries entered into for the sake of completeness. But in the absence of a larger context we might speak of a scrupulosity or excess of conscience that drains vital energy and narrows vision to a pinpoint.

Thus independent to a degree, each of these three is 'most itself' when working with the others; they are 'meant' or 'made' for each other, and they cannot be *profoundly* characterized, nor *ultimately* justified, in isolation.

(1) Consider, first, the relationship between *intellectual vitality* and *the importance of objects*. Whatever the range of factors, from food and rest to peace of mind, that enable this vitality, its fundamental summons comes from objects. We might say here that objects activate, stimulate or trigger the natural potentialities of mind. But that is insufficient, for it is not the case that once started up mind could then function without objects. We might then add that objects are the material and the energy source of enquiry. But that still omits something. In an objectless world, mental life would lack not only energy, but *point*. Perhaps all one can say in the end is that objects are objects; the mind–object relationship is *sui generis*. Again, taking faith and hope, say, as virtues of intellectual life, ask what they are placed in: the enquirer's own abilities? While the scholar is still standing off from his enquiry that answer may seem appropriate. The clever school-leaver who is making up his mind what to take up at university might have faith in his ability to master any of several disciplines. But if we go on to imagine him – his choice made – actually engaged on some enquiry, a deeper intentionality emerges: the intelligibility of things. What sustains him primarily now is his trust that objects which pose questions will also yield answers, and that the answers will be worth having.

(2) Consider, next, the relationship between *vitality* and *conscience*. Understood regulatively, the 'demands of reason' discipline vitality *ab extra*, but they do not command it. They get no purchase on the person who cannot bring himself to go on living,

and not much on the one who lacks the appetite for a full life. But understood expansively, as we have argued they must be to have any ethical force, they set a value on life itself, and they also make fullness of life a matter of some obligation. Now conscience seeks to stimulate, to conserve and to select the objects for intellectual vitality, and to develop the specific virtues of intellectual power.[27]

(3) Consider, finally, the relationship between *conscience* and *objects*. We touch here on a fundamental issue in moral philosophy, for the coupling of these would imply the rejection, ultimately, of a Kantian-style formalistic ethic, in particular of 'universalizability' as the fundamental criterion of morality.[28] Instead of saying that killing, for instance, is wrong because it is non-universalizable, we should say it is (pretty) universally wrong because of the ontological importance of what is destroyed by killing. Similarly, the virtues and principles of intellectual conscience are to be justified fundamentally by reference to the importance of the objects with which intellectual life deals, and they have force in proportion to that importance. There is something fundamentally wrong with conceiving it otherwise, with taking precision, clarity, relevance and care for truth as having a value that is quite independent of what is being investigated. The idea, for instance, that science is educationally valuable because it develops such virtues in the pupil is, to some extent, an insult to science. The truth of the matter is more nearly the reverse, that those virtues are necessary because they are required for science (among other disciplines) – but then it should be added that science is not itself an autonomous value, but a response to the value of the physical universe.

CONCLUSION

We shall shortly track these value considerations into different approaches to cultural analysis, and in later case studies into some specific curriculum areas. But the line of the general argument is clear: 'security of possession' is a rational value only when subordinated to that of 'richness of experience' which, in its turn, becomes a pursuit of one's tail unless, first, it allows itself to be constrained and limited by the demands of truth, respect and justice, and, second, it transcends both itself and a negative conception of its ethical limits, in an acknowledgement of the world that is properly called love. The converse implication is that only from the perspective of love of the world can the values of the ethical life, of the rich or the full life, and of possessions be balanced and integrated. In an adaptation of a biblical text that is lighter than it may appear, we might say that if we seek first the world and its justice, all these things will be added unto us.

NOTES

1. From a 1918 address cited in Pirsig (1974, pp. 105–6). Compare: 'The order of the world is the same as the beauty of the world. All that differs is the type of concentration demanded, according to whether one tries to conceive the necessary relations which go to make it up or to contemplate its splendour. It is one and the same thing, which with respect to God is eternal Wisdom; with respect to the universe, perfect obedience; with respect to our love, beauty; with respect to our intelligence, balance of necessary relations; with respect to our flesh, brute force' (Weil, 1949, p. 281).
2. See Chapter 10.

3. 'Ideology' is particularly complicated. Though it probably oversimplifies, we might usefully distinguish three current senses: a pejorative non-technical sense, where it refers to 'the uncritical' or 'the dogmatic' in belief; a pejorative technical sense, where it means a 'false consciousness' that is the product in some way of class, or other sectional, interest; and a non-pejorative sense, where it means 'a philosophy'. For a more complex and historically sensitive account, see the entry in R. Williams (1976).

4. See, for example, Skilbeck (1976) and Lawton (1983, Chapter 1).

5. Thus, for example, Pring (1976), as he surveys some of the main contemporaneous movements of ideas – Hirst's theory of the forms of knowledge, the child-centred movement and the sociology of knowledge – draws from each elements that might serve some (in his view) more satisfactory synthesis. And Dewey in his classic 1938 essay, which is both restatement of progressivism and critique of the excesses of some of his followers, attempts to present progressivism, in and by its focus on *experience*, as the transcending (Dewey was a youthful Hegelian) of either/or dichotomies: authority or freedom; past or present and future; individual or society.

6. See, for example, Aristotle's *(Nicomachean) Ethics*, Book 1.

7. Dewey (1916, Chapter 23), White (1982, especially Chapters 4 and 5) and most recently Pring (1987) all evince appropriately complex approaches.

8. Dewey (1916, p. 311).

9. See White (1982).

10. Dewey (1916, p. 307).

11. These are mentioned in Pring (1976).

12. See the papers of R.K. Elliott alluded to later in this chapter (e.g. 1977, pp. 9–13).

13. Dewey (1916, p. 54). Dewey also expresses this thesis in terms of 'meaning': 'the chief business of life at every point [is] to make living . . . contribute to an enrichment of its own perceptible meaning. We thus reach a technical definition of education: It is that reconstruction or reorganization of experience which adds to the meaning of experience, and which increases ability to direct the course of subsequent experience' (p. 76).

14. Dewey (1938, p. 35).

15. Kierkegaard articulates this stance in the first volume of *Either/Or*, and in the second volume criticizes it, directly and indirectly, from the point of view of the more humdrum 'ethical man'.

16. *Critique of Pure Reason*, I, 2nd part, 1st division. See the interpretation of Strawson (1966, pp. 47–152).

17. See especially Dewey (1916, Chapters 4–6, 1938, *passim*).

18. See Dewey (1946, Introduction and Part III, Chapter 5). The Introduction in particular, specially written for a republication of some of his papers, shows him at his eloquent and profound best, but is still wrong, I believe, inasmuch as it sets its face against any 'givenness' of value, any priority of value to experience.

19. There may also have been a simple confusion in his thought on this matter. In the Introduction of his 1946 work, Dewey argues that the doctrine of intrinsic value is incompatible with the empirical presuppositions of modern scientific method. This is simply a mistake that rests on a confusion of the necessary or essential with the certain and/or the *a priori*. An essential truth can be both a discovered truth and one for which our grounds do not justify certainty (see Kripke, 1972). The confusion is easily understandable inasmuch as, historically, the former regularly consorted with one or both of the latter – and Dewey's historical sensibility was profound.

20. See especially Peters (1966, 1973, 1977a, 1981). These represent, it should be noted, a continuous revision and development of the account.

21. Broadly, his *descriptions* of education and the educated person tended, often beautifully, towards the open-ended and expansive ideal; while his main *argument* tended only to the regulative ideal (and, indeed, does not succeed, I believe, in giving the desired *ethical* force to that ideal). See Peters (1966, Chapter V) and the reconsidered and more mature case in 'The justification of education' in Peters (1973).

22. See Peters (1966, Chapter VIII).

23. *Groundwork to the Metaphysic of Morals*.

24. Weil (1949).
25. R.K. Elliott (1975).
26. R.K. Elliott (1977, p. 13).
27. On the other hand, this is, so far, to say nothing very precise about the dialectic of vitality and conscience. It may even be true, as Simone Weil often argued, that pure attentiveness to the truth (as to affliction) is a 'supernatural' thing, involving a kind of death to the natural man. But two things would then need to be added. One is that this idea is far removed from the picture of conscience as a kind of check or harness on vital values; it is altogether more radical, and would probably involve the 'death' of conventional conscience as well as of vitality. The second is that the death in question, without subtracting from its painfulness, would not be just any kind of mental destruction, but one that had some kind of 'life after death' in view.
28. The essence of the Kantian view can be put in the following way, perhaps. Posing the question to ourselves, when confronted with a moral choice, of how it would be if others followed the tempting course of action – did it to us perhaps – is more than an *imaginative aid* to gaining a moral perspective. It actually *constitutes* the moral perspective and it intimates escape from self-contradiction as the essential *reason* for moral action. So, not only 'do unto others as you would be done by', but do this *because* only thus can you be consistent with yourself. This is the view I am challenging here. Kant himself, however, fudged the issue by adding to the above some glorious rhetoric about treating people always as ends in themselves!

Chapter 9

Elementary Maps for Ordering Cultural Capital

SETTLING THE CURRICULUM

A curriculum is always a selection. The question for this chapter can be seen as the last in a series of five that immediately attends this observation. The first two of these are political. First, who is to select, or – assuming some articulated system of education – *who is to participate in the process of selection, in what ways, at what stages, and to what degrees of influence?* Second, who is the selection for, or – granted universal education – *what is to be the balance, and the mutual articulation, of common and differentiated education?* From these questions I shall regretfully abstain as beyond my scope. The third question we have already addressed in effect: *what are to be the criteria of selection?* For us these would be, obviously, the values we have just discussed, ordered and coordinated as we have argued they should be. The fourth question is: *from what 'pool' is the selection to be made?* Two answers to this are suggested in the literature. One is 'the disciplines of learning', whether as potential 'items' with those selected then mapped straight on to the curriculum, or as principal or exclusive 'resources'.[1] The broader, more outward-looking answer is 'culture', using the word rather in its general sense than as 'high culture'.[2] It commends itself to us as making fewer initial assumptions, safeguarding the links between curriculum and education in the widest sense, and suggesting the reasonable hypothesis that the cultivation of possessive, experiential, ethical and ecstatic values is not restricted to the learned disciplines. Of course it is compatible with regarding, and invariably does regard, academic disciplines as *among* the important resources and items. But it would be more generally comfortable with the notion of 'practices'. 'Practice' not only embraces building and housekeeping as well as science and psychology, and, more generally, suggests a broad view of the possible uses of the cumulative, 'drip-feed' approach of curriculum; it is also firmer about the organic links between theory and practice, between studying music or poetry, say, and making music or poetry. Our preference for the broader answer will be clear in what follows and we shall come upon some of the distorting effects of the narrower answer.

But our principal focus will be on the fifth question: *how are we to 'map' culture (including the disciplines) for purposes of curriculum selection?* The general assumptions of this question are that there are categories of things to be learnt which are severally important (e.g. sciences, arts, humanities and technical subjects make up a familiar, if rough and ready, set), and that from each of these categories basic and/or representative excerpts can be so taught that the student learns a feel for the category as a whole, is enabled to communicate with people who have studied different excerpts, is inclined to pursue further excerpts on her own initiative, etc. We shall also address the important sub-question of whether one map only is needed or many. Sub-questions that are beyond our scope include what the balance should be among the identified categories in terms of time and other resources, and whether, and how, we may attribute here *precise* degrees of importance, e.g. distinguish the essential, the important and the merely worthwhile. (We shall not, however, be forsaking the general category of the valuable; indeed some of the main distinctions of Chapter 8 will re-emerge and be further clarified in this chapter.)

No mapping exercise is even hinted at in the UK's Education Reform Act of 1988, which proceeds *directly* from the general goals of mental, physical, moral and spiritual development to a rather disconnected and arbitrary-seeming list of subjects and themes constituting the new National Curriculum. This omission has since come to be felt at the National Curriculum Council. Subject working parties report and subject programmes are settled (and reopened and resettled), but issues of omission, overlap (when does 'valuable reinforcement' become 'wasteful duplication'?) and general adequacy to the statutory goals are proving a struggle, one hears,[3] in the absence of any considered and endorsed picture of cultural resources and possibilities. This is not at all surprising. In whole curriculum planning the analysis of knowledge intervenes crucially between deliberating over goals and designing the curriculum itself, overlapping with each of these and translating them one to the other. In its absence grand statements of goal come all too quickly to be regarded as ignorable rhetoric.

KINDS OF MAP

There are different analyses in circulation and, more than that, different kinds of analysis with different kinds of aspiration. Three kinds may be distinguished.

First is the kind of map that is essentially *deliberative and pragmatic* in character: perhaps a matrix of areas of experience, elements of learning and structural principles, designed by an inspectorate newly conscious of its whole-curriculum responsibility, and keen at the same time to loosen the stranglehold of 'subjects';[4] or an outline 'core curriculum', a matrix now of life areas, learning processes and learning environments, offered by a federal development centre to autonomous states as a flexible 'working model' for the 1980s.[5] Such maps emerge from particular situations, involve some degree of consultation with practitioners, and take deliberate account of local challenges and constraints. They are essentially exercises in practical and political responsibility; if sometimes conceptually complex and theoretically well-informed, they still aim more at the next major step forward than at logical rigour and utopian ideal. Of them we shall only say that they are to be judged, like deliberative discourse generally, from two directions at once, from the point of view of their feasibility and practical appeal on the one hand, and from the point of view of educational ideals and more theoretical maps on the other.

Another kind of map is, by contrast with the first, *grandly theoretical*: Bloom's taxonomy, Phenix's realms, Hirst's forms, and Lawton's cultural systems.[6] We shall consider two of these, one at considerable length, later in the chapter. They are ambitious, not only in the measure of validity across contexts and times that they claim, but also in seeking to project – misguidedly, I shall argue – all the really significant distinctions on to a single master-map or taxonomy.

Modesty on that latter score is a feature of a third kind of map, the *elementary map* based on some set of simple distinctions. As we shall see directly, maps of this kind come at culture and knowledge from obviously different angles and never look like pieces from some one-dimensional jigsaw set. Resisting theoretical synthesis with each other, what they yield in combination is matrices, i.e. practical devices for the simultaneous deployment of diverse theories. Another of their features is familiarity. They are deep in our language and our thought about ourselves, and more or less venerable in our philosophical traditions. This is *not* to say, however, that we effortlessly appreciate their curricular significance; there are inhibitions to overcome in our present value systems and epistemologies. The main positive intention of this chapter is to display in the case of each of some key 'elementary' maps its analytic reach and its critical and reconstructive power in relation to standard curricula and standard cultural assumptions, and so to make a case for it being a useful guide and a criterion of adequacy in relation to some particular dimension of the curriculum. This revives the pluralist approach to mapping of Joseph Schwab. In his day he also reminded people of the first two elementary maps we consider, which we shall, however, develop in rather different ways from him.[7]

The crucial starting point is that just as things have many aspects, so collections of things to be classified have as many potential bases of classification. A crowd of people, for example, may be grouped and regrouped endlessly according to sex, age, hair colour, nationality, interests, income levels and so on. This elementary point of logic also applies to cultural achievements and disciplines of knowledge: they too may be validly mapped in an indefinite number of ways. Our concern, however, is limited to classifications that have *educationally significant* bases and so identify categories that are important enough severally to have a serious claim on the curriculum maker. The number of these maps should not be endless. But could it be just one? On the face of it that is unlikely. And it takes no more than a rummage in the history of philosophy to come up with a number of maps that differentiate in ways that, intuitively, seem valid, important, and quite different from each other.

Three such shall occupy us fruitfully. Let us preview them together before getting down to each in turn. First is the Aristotelian division of thought *by aim*, into science, art and politics – that is to say (since each of those terms was meant very broadly), the differences between thinking aimed at:

- good (or better) understanding of how things are;
- making good artefacts;
- good decisions and good living.[8]

This division can be a stick for the traditional liberal curriculum with its overwhelming emphasis on the propositional, its downgrading of art and still more of technical education, and its neglect of the ethical, political, legal, economic, ecological and family studies that bear most directly on deliberation and policy.[9] And we shall find subtler uses of it besides. But cutting right across that division are the historical variants (Greek, neo-Platonist, medieval, Comptean) of another elementary division of knowledge, this time by reference to the *layer of reality* engaged with, e.g. thought, studies and practices specifically relating, in turn, to:

- the physical world;
- the biosphere;
- the animal kingdom;
- the human;
- the transcendent.[10]

Our ordinary curricular distinction between sciences and humanities, and the sub-distinctions that go with it, can be most naturally located here. But it may be queried whether these standard school subjects sometimes act to *screen* their objects from the gaze of students, and so to frustrate the underlying point of this division. Finally, and from yet another direction, a modern philosophical and educational tradition employs age-old psychological distinctions to urge the necessity of educating *the whole person, in her varied dimensions and powers*:

- physical as well as mental;
- moral as well as cognitive;
- imagination and emotions as well as memory and intellect.

But, some may ask, is this tradition now in some disarray and retreat, in part because of an inherent vagueness in its 'zoning' of the person and in the 'folk psychology' on which it relies, and in part because of a tendency in it to narcissistic excess? We shall consider how it may be defended and reaffirmed.

In sum, taking knowledge and culture as sets of relationships between us and the world, we anticipate elementary but interesting divisions based in turn on the precise nature of the relationships, the part of the world that is most involved, and the part of us that is most involved. (Putting it that way suggests that, after all, the maps may fit together, though *three*-dimensionally, and amount to a broadly complete analysis, but we shall not pursue any claim of that sort.)

MAPPING COGNITIVE AIMS

The immediately obvious practical interest of our first map is, to repeat, as a reproach to our traditional curricular neglect of both making and deliberating. Of course, theoretical school subjects give some opportunities for technical construction, as in experimental work, and for deliberation, as over the reliability of an historical explanation. But these are subordinate to the theoretical purposes of those subjects. The significant thing is the lower status, if not the absence, of subjects that are *primarily* to do with making or deliberating. In Chapter 11 we shall consider at length the importance of 'making subjects' of one broad kind. Here we might advance some simple propositions regarding an important part of an education in deliberation, *an education in social issues and causes*, as it might be called.

There exists a whole range of causes, all profoundly matters at once of prudence and of justice, which are of more or less critical importance for the future that our pupils (and their children) will live in. They are captured in labels like 'world hunger and North–South relationships', 'disarmament and nuclear deterrence', 'ecology, energy and the green movement', 'racism and a multicultural society and world', 'patriarchy, feminism and women's rights', 'relationships, the sexual revolution and AIDS', 'localism, nationalism and internationalism'. All of them are complex, requiring patient and sustained reflection towards a multidisciplinary understanding (part scientific, part historical, part economic, etc.). Aside from a proper care about them, if the various kinds of relevant concept and information are not being imparted in school, it is unlikely that many will go to the large trouble of seeking them out in later life; surely, a substantial start must be made at least in secondary school. Second, these causes are so many foci of propaganda and counter-propaganda in the battle for public opinion. It would be an educational challenge to avoid indoctrinating students, indeed to arm students against indoctrination, as one set about provoking their sustained concern. Third, and further, they are all matters involving powerful and deeply entrenched interests, political and other. So we may expect to have to fight a rearguard action here for the legitimate freedom of schools – as in connection with that more general 'frightening' thing, a practically minded political education. Fourth, there are specific curriculum projects that relate to these issues: peace studies, black studies, women's studies, energy studies, etc. Where these are taken up they struggle for time with traditional subjects, and it is a nice question how much effort should be put into them and how much into opening out existing subjects towards these issues, into the pursuit of a just astuteness as a cross-curricular theme. Fifth, we must not overestimate the contribution of 'lessons' here – that indeed is very much the point. An education in deliberation, to be authentic, must involve *actual* deliberations, just as we make students read literature itself and not just commentaries on it, or do science experiments and not just read them up in the textbook. Thus some of the study, criticism and discussion of our issues should be in the context of real student participation in, for example, the running of a school and its sub-systems.[11]

These propositions are among the many that would find root-room and comfort in Aristotle's triad of cognitive aims. But so much for broad brush-stroke. If we pursue this map now to two of its sub-divisions (well known already to Aristotle himself), we highlight some further fundamental issues.

The first sub-division is of 'science' (thinking about the world as it is, rather than as what it might become through the thinker's art or action) into *investigative* and *appreciative/contemplative* modes of thought. On the one hand, there is acquisitive enquiry that seeks to extend the human stock, or one's own stock, or one's students' stock, of knowledge. On the other hand, there is a knowing which has the character of a resting in the object – and this is something else of which the very mention raises the suspicion of neglect. In a profound paper Ray Elliott expresses both the distinction and the suspicion:

> But a student might say, with some justification, that he has been taught to love Criticism *rather than* literature or history *rather than* the past, if literary works and the past become for him nothing but objects to enquire into in accordance with the methods he has learned. If a student of philosophy thinks of philosophy as enquiry for its own sake, enquires into whatever the other philosophers enquire into, and is unclear about the point of the whole activity, he is at best a lover of enquiry, hardly a lover of wisdom, which is something

beyond enquiry. . . . [In philosophical aesthetics] it is frequently taken for granted that when a work [of art] ceases to offer any further scope for enquiry one ceases to have any further interest in it, and turns to something else. No account is taken of the lover of art who after having come to know a work returns to it again and again, not with the hope of discovering anything new in it but to live in it and take it to his heart. This tendency to regard acquisitive enquiry as their sole or chief aim makes the practitioners of the humanities seem more like hunters than shepherds.[12]

The second sub-division is of 'art' into the *aesthetic* and the *functional*: two kinds of product (or aspect of product), two kinds of making and two kinds of the thinking that inhabits making. We shall touch briefly on this, a prime site for cultural and educational reflection, in a later chapter. But note that, whatever its nature and importance, it remains a *sub*-distinction here. Considered as a whole, this map more associates the arts with than dissociates them from other kinds of manufacture, and would certainly not preclude some association of the arts and the technology sections in schools.

Our first map allows us, next, to identify some discourses and practices as involving unique and valuable *integrations* of elements from more than one of its categories and as having a consequent *prima facie* claim, among other claims they may have, on the general curriculum. Thus, as we saw in earlier chapters, 'utopian' discourse combines a commitment to good action with a theoretic-type interest in the ideal, and the human sciences embody a (controversial) balancing act between detached understanding on the one hand and relevance to human values on the other. To mention another example, technology, though it obviously centres on making, also draws integrally both on many parts of science and on many kinds – commercial, environmental, legal, ethical – of deliberation. (The original three categories remain basic, even archetypal, however. These integrations imply only that they are not quarantined from each other.)

Finally, it is also to this map's credit that we can find educationally significant *cross-distinctions* that derive simultaneously from it and the next map. Thus the distinction between the human and the natural sciences remains in some part the result of applying the human/physical distinction from the list of layers of reality (the next map) to the category of 'science' here. Again, we might draw a distinction, intuitively significant, between *software* and *hardware*, using these terms in a generalized way to refer to artefacts that are primarily linguistic or symbolic (books, newspapers, television pro-grammes, computer programs) on the one hand, and those that are not primarily symbolic (houses, vehicles, food, weapons) on the other. Such a distinction emerges as the result of applying the human/physical distinction, this time to the category of making. For the essence of 'software' is meaning (not paper, ink, discs, etc.) and so it is an extension of mind, while 'hardware', though it has human (including inhuman) purposes, is in itself purely material. This distinction, incidentally, would cut across our earlier distinction between aesthetic and functional and be *positively* hospitable to such associations as of building with architecture in its hardware division, and of journalism with literature – or of most of the things brought together in the school subject 'English' – in its software division.

To end on a more formally philosophical note, this first map is replete with practical implications precisely because its distinctions are – as it seems to me – profoundly archetypal. They are even in some way anterior to the categorization of values. Each category of values has a purchase on (can be pursued in) each of theorizing, deliberating and making (we shall demonstrate this for making in Chapter 11), and from that would seem to follow at once the fundamental importance of each of the three and the artificiality of any attempts (ancient and medieval philosophy offered several) to place them in an order of importance.

MAPPING THE INTELLIGIBLE WORLD

Our second map will prove suggestive as a pointer, less to particular imbalances and gaps in standard curricular provision, and more to a possible general malaise in that provision. The main question, we shall see, is whether we rather neglect the 'extrovert' spirit of this map even if we generally observe its letter.

The map, it will be recalled, distinguishes layers of reality such as the material, biological, animal, human and divine. There are purely conceptual relationships among these. Each category after the first one, excepting the last, is, extensionally, a sub-class of the preceding, while, intensionally, it includes the preceding within itself. The class of animal, for example, contains the class of human while the meaning of 'human' contains 'animal'. More interesting, and very much more problematic, are the metaphysical relationships between the layers. Of each of the distinctions between non-living and living, non-conscious and conscious, non-rational and rational, one may ask whether it is of kind or of degree, ultimate or not. Is humanity sufficiently described as a more developed animal species? Is the mind a brain? Is an animal a complex machine? And what is to count for and against answers – what, for instance, is really entailed by the evolution of each layer from the preceding, or, were they to occur, what would laboratory syntheses of living substances and silicon intelligences imply? Three broad approaches to these questions may be distinguished, one of them pluralist, the other two monist. We may attend to the differences between the levels and insist upon them as final. We may instead attend to, and insist upon, the continuities. This latter we may do either in a levelling down spirit – mind is 'nothing but' brain, the human being 'no more than' a sophisticated animal, and so forth – or in a levelling up spirit – matter can think, evolution reveals the extraordinary potentialities of matter, biology and psychology tell us more about matter than physics, and so forth. Levelling down is usually called 'reductionism', and we might call levelling up 'elevationism'. Moving now to the divine, in our culture there is of course a question of its real existence. Beyond that there is the perennial question of its proper characterization. It is only very crudely thought of as one more ('the highest') level of reality – since it would be the *source* of all levels, and as such would enter our experience. The main issue is sometimes thought to be between transcendent and immanent conceptions of God. In fact each of these may entail the other: *because* God is whole in all space and time, He has to be 'outside' space and time, or *because* He is, as the medievals were fond of saying, more in us than we are in ourselves, He has to be totally Other.

Using this map as a check on curriculum breadth does not actually commit us to the pluralist approach and it excludes only an arrogantly confident version of reductionism. For the distinctions in question are not clearly unreal, and that, combined with their cultural significance, is enough warrant for representing all the layers on the curriculum. On the other hand, the metaphysical questions are not then educationally irrelevant. One would expect some actual engagement with them somewhere in a decent curriculum – and not only as contextualized in (say) literature, history and science, but directly and for their own sake.

The curriculum's 'metaphysical involvement' is not, however, primarily a matter of adding bits of philosophy to the student's other subjects so as to sensitize her to certain historic controversies. What is primary, and determines curriculum 'relevance' in its deepest sense, is the bearing of her school subjects generally on the student's *lived relationships* with Nature, Man, and God, which may include a lived sense of the *unity* of these as constituting her world and entering into her identity. Do her studies in history, literature and religious studies, for example, really allow the student to observe all this in others – at arm's length so to speak – and then attend to it in herself as a matter of critical self-development? If it is required of her curriculum, first, actually to 'make a connection' with these lived relationships and, second, to walk the fine line between quizzing them and blasting them, would we be more anxious about the second if we were better at meeting the first requirement?

Not long ago two leading philosophers of education were converging on these matters from different directions. Richard Peters, in some of his later writings, sought to capture a kind of enquiry and knowledge whose main – and great – significance was neither theoretical nor practical but lay in its bearing on the framework of our beliefs and attitudes regarding the general conditions of human life.

> Suppose a man is exercised about why his friend is rude to him, worried about his own prejudices and uncharitable feelings, or concerned about whether he should be patriotic or feel awe for the sea or at the sight of death. Suppose that he is led by such uneasiness into studies in psychology, ethics, politics, and religion. . . . Notions like 'knowledge for its own sake' and curiosity suggest a stance that is too detached and disinterested to do justice to his concern about such questions. On the other hand, answering them is not obviously connected with any particular course of action or further end to be achieved. . . . What is he to make of objects in the natural world and of phenomena such as the dark, thunder, the tides, time and the changes of the seasons? What is he to make of other people and of their reactions to him and to each other? What is he to think about himself and about questions of ownership? What attitude is he to take towards the cycle of birth, marriage and death? In what way is he to react to authority, suffering, and violence? These are questions arising from the general conditions of human life.

By neglecting such questions and such uses of the disciplines of learning, traditional education had switched off a great many students, Peters suggested.[13]

More than frameworks or 'general conditions' are involved here, however. It is as much a matter of mental vitality – the mind's teeming engagements with the natural, the human and the divine – as of wisdom. In a well-known paper[14] Ray Elliott wrote of the Understanding's need to live, with fertile intellectual *eros*, in close contact with its chosen objects, and suggested that progressive educators might be interpreted as proclaiming just this. A distinction, non-rigid but real, may be drawn between natural understanding and the understanding provided by the learned disciplines. Natural understanding can be of a very high order – Elliott reminds us of Shakespeare. It is also far from impossible that a discipline may lose its way for a time, its relationship with its objects become distant or distorted – too exclusively that of the hunter as opposed to the shepherd, for instance, or too concentrated on a single feature, or too manipulative. At one time or another, the quality of theology's relationship with religious life, of science's with our experience of nature, of literary criticism's with our response to literature, of psychology's with our ordinary intersubjectivity and of academic history's with our love of the past have all been reasonably challenged. These facts entail not that we drop the disciplines from the curriculum, but that we 'problematize' their role. We must consider how they might best be used (here a discipline's own history may sometimes suggest escape routes from its contemporary orthodoxies and odiums), and how they might need to be supplemented, if the Understanding's life with its objects is to be developed rather than cramped. Elliott also postulated an experience of 'a primitive synoptic unity' of Nature, Man and God. By their abstracting nature the disciplines will diminish this, breadth of disciplines by itself being a breadth without unity, unless education also teaches a method of 'recall' to its naivety. Without these attentions to natural understanding, Elliott suggests, 'the educated person' comes to fulfil his own tragi-comic caricature: one whose mind moves in tracks that he neither contributes to nor fully understands, which he cannot relate to the common experience that he somehow despises or is no longer interested in, and which have already been superseded in the disciplines themselves.

Let us draw some conclusions from these reflections.

(1) Like others, this map may be used as a simple check on curriculum breadth, to *spot the omissions*. Thus it highlights the absence, or the minimal presence, in standard curricula of ethology, the young science of animal behaviour (and this despite people's involvement with pets, concern about various forms of cruelty to animals and interest in wildlife) – zoology, which is generally on offer, being about as adequate a representation of the animal kingdom as physiology is of the human world. It marks, similarly, the usual omission of any productive involvement with the biosphere, e.g. gardening or farming, from technology education.

(2) Its more profound use is as a reminder of the values that undergird it, the cherishings of material, living, conscious, human and divine worlds for their own distinctive sakes. The particular map of the 'ecstatic' category of values, it is essentially extrovert. But disciplines, like churches, may be introverted, turned in on themselves to the point of forgetfulness of the being of their proper objects. There is a corresponding responsibility on the educator *to look out for this introversion in the disciplines*, teach them in a way that offsets it and supplement them with more informal approaches as necessary – not only in primary schools or with 'non-academic' students, but in all schools with all students. (It is probably the case that the concern for relevance in the curriculum development movement has increased awareness of all this among teachers, subject associations and examination boards. But the battle has to be constantly renewed if the costs of institutionalizing disciplines are not to outweigh the benefits.)

(3) One kind of introversion to guard against is a discipline's concern with the recruitment, selection, training and assigning – and all-pervadingly with the status – of its professionals. This concern is quite proper and responsible provided the result is not to distract itself too much from research and enquiry, but it is a notorious threat to general education and to future amateurs and 'consumer–users' in its area. For the institutional *self-interests of disciplines and the interests of education in disciplines do not coincide*, though they overlap. Providing opportunities for youngsters to try themselves out at various things and passing on some critical appreciation and respect for disciplines are, doubtless, shared interests. But, to speak ideally and from the point of view of this map, education's great interest in a discipline is its potential to develop the appreciative consciousness – eye, heart and hand – of students in relation to its segment of reality, and it is not clear how large the discipline's own stake is in this. The community of scientists,

say, may take a cheerful view of a science curriculum that is ordered and sequenced so as to steal a march for its future specialists and burn the rest off. But education cannot share this arrogance. It has 'apostolic' duties to the world's grandeur which, as much as straightforward egalitarian considerations, give it a deep interest in limiting failure and the significance of failure and keeping everyone in the game. If the selection of professionals is 'norm-referenced' in the end – though it is true this end can be delayed – then education is 'criterion-referenced', welcoming late as well as early development, average as well as high achievement, and breadth as well as depth.[15]

(4) Points (2) and (3) need careful handling lest they become a cover for Luddites. Thus forgetfulness of its object is not the same thing as *a discipline's essential abstractness and impersonality*. These qualities may actually ennoble our everyday relationship with the object. The following is perhaps an example of that. Once, we placed ourselves at the centre of the universe. That cosy anthropocentrism may already have contained the seeds of its own supersession, inasmuch as what it arranged around us was not less than everything. In any case, science came along to admonish us of the extreme immensity of the universe and the randomness of our location in it. But we may eat this humble pie and still manage a mischievous humanism. Our location in the universe seems irrelevant to our entertaining, and being entertained by, its infinitude. Indeed, we sometimes feel, infinitude makes it only just big enough for us, and the wastes of space join the breezes and the sunshine of planet Earth in making the universe 'our home'.

(5) Finally, there is the issue if education's relationship with the unity of the world and of our experience. We have Elliott's suggestion that unity is available only in natural understanding, and not also across the disciplines. In Chapter 7, I suggested that fragmentation was indeed a feature of our intellectual culture, but implied that this was not in the nature of things. A unity of archetypal ideas and images across disciplines, such as the Greeks may have enjoyed in their use of concepts like 'form' and 'proportion', remains an intellectual ideal. And where such mutual echoes and resonances linger on, or new ones start up, it would be important to attend to them in education.[16]

MAPPING SELF-EXPRESSION

If the previous map related particularly to realizing values in the 'ecstatic' category, mapping the zones of human being can be seen as instrumental, especially, to what we called experiential and vital, and might also have called self-expressive, values. We shall in turn, remark upon

- the logical informality of our discourse in this area;
- the perspective on personhood that is fundamentally involved;
- the possible relationships between specific 'zones' of the person and specific curricular disciplines and practices.

First, then, we have here not one division, but an *overlapping, intersecting cluster of divisions*: mental/physical, moral/cognitive, intellect/memory/imagination/feeling, and perhaps a few more. It would seem that education borrows these schemata, with occasional adaptations, from ordinary language, where the 'psychology' they represent is pervasive and subtle but quite unsystematic. If, by some shoving and hauling, they were overlaid on a single map, it would be at a cost to nuance and overtone. Again, complex interrelationships among the items distinguished, a feature already of our first two maps (e.g. between material and human, or between science and intelligent making), combine here with some instability in the meanings of terms. Thus, from Aristotle to Kant to Sartre, there have been philosophers to argue that imagination is routinely involved in *all* understanding. But this would not preclude some acts of understanding being conspicuously imaginative (in a perhaps slightly different sense of the word), our ordinary sense that 'imaginative' is just the right word for some acts, rather than, say, 'precise' or 'lucid'. Nor would it preclude the educationist from criticizing a curriculum or a pedagogy for neglecting this kind of understanding. Again, philosophers point out that feelings like fear, envy, anger and so forth embody *cognitive* appraisals of situations, e.g. as dangerous, or as of someone having what one does not have oneself. But this omnipresence of the cognitive would not justify a treatment of students as 'brains on stilts', as though the education of the feelings would then look after itself.[17] Yet again, in education 'the physical' refers to bodily skill, fluidity and force primarily as *expressions* of the mental, but it remains important to distinguish these from other expressions of the mental and to cater specifically for them.

In passing, we may distinguish proper and improper uses of this unsystematic 'psychology' in education. Properly, it provides key words and key contrasts to the plain-language plans, descriptions and evaluations that are our ordinary means of lighting our way. Improperly, its schemata might be decontextualized and burdened with systematic theorizing, as perhaps by Benjamin Bloom in his famous project to create a complete taxonomy of educational objectives under separate cognitive, affective and psycho-motor heads[18] – as though, to mention the main difficulty, these three zones were not conceptually interpenetrative. (This informality suggests to some, however, that we should work towards replacing this 'folk' psychology with something more scientific, something that would take a full theoretical strain. They envisage not just a scientific psychology that continued to develop its specialist applications and to tinge our general awareness with some of its more speculative ideas, but one that *overran* our awareness of ourselves and others, and so overran our history, literature and, of course, educational discourse.[19] I am sceptical about this idea. If some future flowering of our minds could make Shakespeare seem primitive, I doubt that it would resemble contemporary psychology in form as much as it would Shakespeare. But I am conscious that the argument for thus backing the informal over the 'scientific' for the long run would not be easy to assemble – in addition to taking us far from our present tasks.)

There is a further and more basic ambiguity to note, *a narrow and a broad rendering of the idea of a harmonious development of the whole person.* Narrowly, the idea is rendered through the psychological schemata alone: it proposes, simply, the due and proportionate development of each of the zones that these schemata pick out. Broadly, it would be articulated additionally through our first two maps. That is, 'all-round fulfilment' would also include a balancing of our relationships with the material, animal, human and divine, and of the three main modes of relationship, i.e. understanding, disposing and fashioning. After all we may be 'starved' of human companionship or contact with Nature, and 'ache' for an opportunity to make something or, again, to influence the course of events. Indeed classical fulfilment theories, like Aristotle's, tended to *restrict* themselves to an articulation in terms of objects and modes of relationship. But the psychological schemata surely do amount to an independent criterion of breadth and balance, though it may have taken the Romantic movement and Idealist philosophy to draw them out from the shadows of the first two maps.[20] After we have said that a balanced education will include making and deliberation as well as the propositional, and will deal with each of material, living, animal, human and divine, do we not *still* need to say that in all this we must provide space for the body as well as the mind, the feelings and imagination as well as the intellect, and the character as well as the brain? On the other hand, considerations of this third kind should not be allowed to swamp those relating to the objects and the modes of relationship, what may be dubbed 'the Californian fallacy'.

This merits further reflection. There is a particular side of personhood, of what it is to be a person, that is represented and safeguarded by this third map: *its self-expressiveness*. The person is, among other things, the centre of an assertive point of view, in Richard Peters's phrase, who seeks to put her stamp on things. And one aspect of disciplines and cultural practices is that they are so many expressions of the assertive human spirit and vehicles, endlessly, for the self-expression and self-discovery of their practitioners. So the point of the psychological schemata is to map a self-expression that would be full and balanced. Again, with Marx, we may view human life as, through all its historical forms and phases, essentially *productive* activity. Not only technology, commerce and the economy, but politics, religions, arts and philosophies are products of our work. And in Marx's concept of 'alienation' and his project to overcome the alienation of the worker from his products, and, relatedly, to heal the split between manual and mental labour, the ex-Hegelian shows his continuing commitment to the idea of a rounded and coherent self-production.

The contrast, of course, is with the limpidly receptive side of personhood, by which it mirrors, reveals, facilitates the world – what we might call *the person as 'friend'*. Notice that this contrast cuts across the triad of understanding, making and doing, though not perhaps at a full right-angle. Understanding lends itself very readily to a description in terms of receptivity. What we come to know, we take in, entertain, assimilate, digest, even (as the Greeks had it) become, and truth is the shaping of the mind to the world. But making and doing also have, or ought to have, their own receptive sides, as our new 'green' consciousness brings home to us. Technology and art may be seen as *revelatory*, releasing the latent powers and revealing the latent meanings and beauty of things. And proper action is a kind of *obedience*, it might be said, even when it is transformative. In the natural law tradition, it is obedient to a law inscribed at the heart of things by God. On the other hand, it is not only making and doing that have their active side; as the Greeks were already well aware, so does understanding, and we call it 'enquiry'. And from that point of view, which is our present one, the enquiring mind is – like the creative urge, the determined will, or the active and agile body – a fit *expression* of human personhood.

These two interpretive keys, expressiveness and friendliness, are not mutually exclusive perspectives on personhood, but complementary. The aspects they pick out degenerate, surely, if cut off from each other, the one into a kind of narcissistic desperation, the other into an abnegatory quietism. It is along these lines, I think, that one would develop a fuller case for complementing our first two maps with this more narrowly psychological approach to curriculum balance.

What kinds of *curricular action and adjustment* does this criterion of balance involve? There might be disagreement over this. First, we have the old, but persistent, idea that subjects may be classified according to the aspects or powers of the person that they especially draw upon and develop – at its crudest and clearest, the arts for imagination, drama for empathy, the humanities for affectivity, physical education for the body, and the sciences and mathematics for sheer bloody intellect. But this at once attracts rejoinders of the kind that dwell on the amount of sustained, critical analysis in history and literature, the ways in which mathematics and science reward passion and imagination, and even the perspiration of piano playing. These may come from either of two general positions, themselves opposed. One claims that any one of many curriculum areas and, for that matter, of many non-curricular pursuits, could be sufficient in itself for the development of *all* the mental powers, if properly handled and sustained (part of a case, perhaps, for specialization). The other, instead, insists on the *different ways* in which the mental powers are exercised in various subjects and pursuits: thus, imaginative thinking is 'one thing' in the arts, 'quite another' in personal relationships and 'different again' in mathematics, so that the proper development of imagination will require its exercise in each of these, and other, pursuits.[21]

The tolerant view, which I think is right, is that each corner of this triangular debate contains a kernel of truth. Stripped down and persuasively qualified, they yield propositions (a) to (c).

(a)   Of its logical nature, discipline D (say, literature) makes a specially large demand (relative to other disciplines) on psychic area A (say imagination), and more modest demands on many other psychic areas.

(b)   *Within limits*, the sizes of the demands D makes on A and other psychic areas vary with pedagogy and related factors.

Clearly (a) and (b) are now compatible (and the question is left open of the relative importance of the variables of logical structure and pedagogy).

(c)   Qualitatively, D makes *fairly distinctive* demands on A and other psychic areas.

Here, the word 'fairly' makes (c)'s qualitative point compatible with both (a) and (b). It suggests a degree of distinctiveness that limits the significance of informally 'quantitative' comparisons (say, with imagination in mathematics), but does not make them nonsensical. (And if these were nonsensical, could we still be sure we were talking about the same psychic area?) In practical policy, too, these lines are naturally harmonized. Suppose an agreement in a school to correct a curricular imbalance by a more vigorous targeting of the imagination. It would cause little surprise to gloss this as involving, at one and the same time, more work in the arts because of their overall significance for imagination, a reconsideration of pedagogy across the curriculum, and attention to some designated modes of imagination (empathic understanding, fertility in problem-solving, open-ended creativity, etc.) and to the disciplines, or parts of disciplines, in which they may be particularly exercised.[22]

A MASTER MAP? HIRST'S THEORY OF FORMS

Our reflections, summary and exploratory though they were, have tended to vindicate each of the three maps and, with them, the multidimensional approach to curriculum design. But might there be, after all, some way of bringing everything into a unified theoretical vision, some basis for a curriculum 'masterplan'? Paul Hirst's well-known theory of the forms of knowledge aspires, it seems, to just such a bold economy. First, it presents other kinds of knowledge as either reducible to, or thoroughly dependent upon, *propositional* knowledge. Then a division of this knowledge is proposed according to certain *'purely logical'* criteria which are to absorb whatever is not simply to be discarded of traditional criteria relating to levels of reality and aspects or powers of human being. This division yields *seven Forms of knowledge*, at once distinct and interconnected, which together constitute the fundamental prescription for a rational core curriculum. In addition to its economy, the theory is attractive by virtue of the quasi-intuitive plausibility of many of its aspects (insufficiently acknowledged by its critics). Some would add as a merit the fact that it endorses the broad intellectualism and the main distinctions, though not the actual subjects, of the traditional liberal curriculum. For others, this arouses their deepest suspicions.

I will formulate and review the main steps in Hirst's argument.[23] Indeed I will, to an extent, *re*formulate some parts of the argument the better to expose some of its considerable strengths and with a view to some refinement of my own position. In the end, however, I will be confirmed in my preference for the 'divergent' approach to mapping. (Very recently Hirst has changed his position – in one respect drastically – and we shall refer briefly to this in a postscript.)

The primacy of the propositional?

The prolegomenon to the theory proper, in which propositional learning is made pivotal to learning in general, is already of far-reaching curricular consequence. One of Hirst's starting points for this is a standard classification of kinds of knowledge under three heads (which is similar to the first of our maps, though lacking Aristotle's discrimination between making and deliberation):

- propositional knowledge or *knowledge that*, where what is known is a truth or a set of truths, e.g. 'London is the capital of the UK' or the seven times table;
- procedural or practical knowledge, often called *know-how*, where what is known is how to carry out a performance or activity of some kind, e.g. to ride a bicycle or to remove a brain tumour;
- knowledge with a direct object or *knowledge by acquaintance*, where what is known is an object, like a person, a place or a work of art.[24]

Plausibly enough, Hirst claims that knowledge by acquaintance (our contemplative/appreciative knowledge?) is analysable into some combination of 'knowledge that' and 'know-how' plus an implication that these are founded in part on direct experience of the object in question. Less plausibly, Hirst also claims that because some 'knowledge that' is always presupposed in 'know-how' – thus knowing how to ride a bicycle involves being able to identify some things as bicycles, understand some statements about the purposes of bicycles and of some bicycle parts, etc. – it is the more fundamental of the two, and therefore the most fundamental kind of knowledge. And a similar conclusion is reached starting out from kinds of development and, again, from the concept of meaning.[25]

Hirst infers from this that education should consist centrally, though not wholly, of propositional-type learning[26] – a matter, of course, not just of piling up facts, but of the mastery of those processes by which propositions may be generated, related to each other and tested.

> No matter what the ability of the child may be, the heart of all his development as a rational being is, I am saying, intellectual, and we must never lose sight of these ends on which so much else, nearly everything else, depends.[27]

He would add that the importance of the intellectual is not only strategic. Propositional learning also constitutes 'a liberal education' – as illuminating and making sense of our experience it is worth pursuing 'for its own sake'. It is not clear, furthermore, that he accords that self-justifying status to making or to deliberation. The educational primacy of 'knowledge that' may thus be doubly insured, once by reference to its strategic role in practical living, and again by reference to its intrinsic value.

Some of our earlier discussions have prepared us to see why this line of argument is shaky. It would seem to assume that dependence has to be a one-way street. Thus it overlooks the likelihood that the affective, the moral, and the practical are properly *inter*dependent with the intellectual – in a great variety of ways, depending on the context. The result is a view of the autonomy of the propositional with which few, or none, of the following sit at all easily:

- the evidence from psychology that 'enactive' understanding is a frequent condition of propositional understanding;
- as a particular case of that perhaps, that priority in some respects of educational practice over educational theory on which, as we saw previously, Hirst himself now sets much store;
- the fact that advances in engineering can stimulate, as well as result from, scientific advances;
- the role of values, and the dialectic between interest and detachment, in the very structuring of a proper human science;
- the engagement of the heart to the propositional in contemplative–appreciative knowledge in the humanities, if not also in other areas of knowledge;
- the extreme subtlety of the relationship between evidence and faith in some religious believing;
- the common belief that moral insight is as much a fruit as it is a condition of good will and right action;
- the contribution of the experience of practising and performing in the arts to the understanding of works of art.

This first step in Hirst's argument seems the least considered. It is, however, the most fateful. It would legitimate not only the traditional low status of 'practical' subjects, but also that distortion of many subjects that has resulted from isolating their propositional from their deliberative, technical and contemplative elements. It also has a diminishing effect on the next step in Hirst's theory, his identification of the criteria of a Form. For it conceals from him the likelihood that the relationship of propositions to value and action within forms of knowledge is just as integral to their logic or 'grammar', and just as distinctive in each form and as significant a variable across forms, as those features of propositions on which he fixes. None the less, this next part of his argument is of

great interest. I shall endeavour to do it justice, while giving myself a fairly free hand
in the way I assemble it.

The criteria of a Form of knowledge

If propositional learning is the crux of the curriculum, as Hirst believes, then the
classification of kinds of proposition will be the crucial guide to curriculum planning.
But propositions, like everything else, can be classified in a great many ways: as positive
and negative, categorical and hypothetical, according to tense, etc. What we are after
is a classification according to the *most fundamental logical properties* of propositions
as such. These would seem to be truth value (the proposition's being always either true
or false) and meaning (which is carried by the concepts of the proposition). Thus, the
two most fundamental questions about any proposition, it might be said, are: 'What
does it mean?' and 'Is it true?' Can we then find among propositions different kinds of
meaning and of truth?

Let us try at once to point and to answer this question. We know that there is a
variety of strategies for *testing* truth and that this corresponds with a variety of kinds
of proposition. Thus, Pythagoras's theorem, '$E = mc^2$', 'Napoleon lost the battle of
Waterloo', 'you don't understand me', 'lying is generally wrong', *'Crime and Punishment*
is a great novel' and 'God exists' are each to be argued for in significantly different ways.
Again, as Wittgenstein remarks in criticizing behaviourism, we really do *see* consciousness in another's face, including particular shades of it like indifference or excitement, the glance he casts at someone else, the look in his eye, etc. – but *not in just the
way* that we see the colour of his eyes.[28] More generally, the seeing that is believing
comes in many modes. We may say, then, that there is variety in the *truth criteria* of
different kinds of proposition (and duck the question of whether that entails different
kinds of truth). If we ask, next, what determines this variety, the answer can only be
the different *kinds of meaning and concept* involved. And if we press that idea, will we
not come to different forms and degrees of *networking* of concepts, definitions and
propositions?[29] Perhaps we should go on to say that there are four, not three, ideas
here which belong together in a particularly fundamental way, namely kinds of truth
criteria, kinds of meaning and concept, kinds of inter-propositional and inter-
conceptual relationship, *and* kinds of (propositional) knowledge. In any case, definitions of the last that use the first three as interdependent criteria will indeed be pretty
fundamental. (Whether they touch actual rock-bottom, however, is something we will
query shortly.) We may consider some examples of the interdependence of these ideas.

(a) By nature, the concepts of mathematics form a relatively tight structure. Thus we
can define the range of natural numbers in terms of just the three concepts 'one', 'plus'
and 'equality' ($2 = 1 + 1$; $3 = 1 + 2$; $4 = 1 + 3$; etc.), a large number of operations by
reference just to addition, and all the concepts of a geometric system in terms of a few
primitive ones. But one cannot thus interdefine, and organize into a set, aesthetic
epithets like beautiful, fine, graceful, elegant, majestic, monumental, pretty, neat and
picturesque, though they do belong together in some kind of family. Now in the
mathematical case the interdefinability of concepts is clearly a condition of such a
typically mathematical mode of *validation* of propositions as reduction to axioms. And
the quite unsystematic relationships among aesthetic epithets are similarly reflected in

the informality and the variety of the ways in which the choice of one epithet rather than another, 'monumental' rather than 'picturesque' say, would be defended.

(b) Compare the mathematical statement $32 = 2 \times 4^2$ with the scientific one $E = mc^2$. Despite the identical mathematical operations, quite different kinds of relationships between the constituent concepts are being affirmed. We are safe in saying that in the first case the relationship is *perceived as necessary* in a way that in the second it is not. And this difference is intimately related to the presence in the scientific case, and the (at least relative) absence in the mathematical case, of an appeal to empirical evidence, that is, to a difference in the truth criteria of the two statements.

More generally, then, what we are faced with in the domain of knowledge is not just a matter of different families of propositions and concepts, with parallel relations between the concepts in each area, and parallel truth criteria, but rather with families that are in these internal respects quite dissimilar – so dissimilar indeed, we might add, as to make us appreciate the elasticity of words like 'family' or 'form' in embracing them all.

Hirst has sweeping ambitions for these criteria. One aspect of this is that they would provide us with not only a fundamental classification of kinds of *proposition*, but thereby (since propositions are taken to be the original home of all concepts) of kinds of *concept* as well, and therefore a fundamental analysis of *experience* too, since it is only as 'concept-soaked' that our experiences come to us and can mean anything.[30] We are offered, then, what purports to be the fundamental analysis both of knowledge in its developed, disciplined forms and of the elements of relatively undifferentiated commonsense knowledge.[31]

The seven Forms

Applying the criteria to knowledge in our present evolutionary phase is said to yield us some seven basic Forms of knowledge and experience. In its mature form, the theory identifies these as: *logico-mathematical, empirical, interpersonal, moral, aesthetic, religious* and *philosophical*.[32] Each of these has a decent, though not in all cases an unassailable, claim to constitute an area of possible objective enquiry and knowledge. Each has its own distinctive kinds of concept, of networking of concepts and of touchstone of truth, and so each may claim to be a separate logical form. This does not mean, however, that they are logically isolated from each other. Hirst (increasingly) acknowledged, as he had to, that the autonomy of each was limited by myriad relationships and dependencies among them.[33] Thus we may remind ourselves of the relationship between the empirical and the mathematical in the physical sciences; of the various ways in which the interpersonal depends on the empirical and of the fact (a necessary fact?), at bottom, that the human person is, among other things, a material object; of the interrelationship of the interpersonal and the moral, which is controversial but in any case very close, to the point where from different perspectives each can seem even to enclose the other; of the similarly controversial, but on several accounts close, relationships of the moral to the religious, and to the aesthetic; of the relationships of the philosophical to all the others, the perception of which varies with differences of view on what 'philosophy' encompasses; and so forth. Many of these relationships, it will be noticed, are precisely loci of traditional philosophical controversy. The theory of Forms should not be read as foreclosing on these controversies. It presumes only that none of the specified Forms may be simply identified with another.

It should be acknowledged that Hirst's derivation of criteria and of Forms is persuasive as well as subtle. Once grasped, its more argued aspects have a high intuitive appeal. Indeed they represent, I suggest, not so much a set of new 'discoveries', as, like a lot of good philosophy, a making explicit of what we already knew, and indeed had to know in order to see the force of the argument. But the theory is open to important criticisms in relation to the more vaunting aspects of its claims: that not only may Forms be distinguished, but *there is some definite, unambiguous number of them* (probably seven, at our present stage of development); that there are these criteria *and no other*; that the truth of propositions counts *and no other kind of truth*; that this classification *pre-empts metaphysical and psychological classifications*. In addition, the theory has lacked an adequately developed theory of value. Let us take these points in turn.

(1) A good case can be made on the criteria for each of the seven Forms. Furthermore, they would seem to encompass everything collectively; one would be hard put to it to find an eighth Form that is not already in some way included. All the same, there is some arbitrariness in allowing no more and no less than these seven, indeed in insisting on *any* definite number.

This is a matter, first, of *an uncertainty in the abstract as to how far to carry the division of knowledge in each sphere*. Thus Hirst divides the general area of the humanities into interpersonal, moral and religious Forms of knowledge. Doubtless the criteria permit this, but it is not clear that they require it, considering the closeness of the relationships between the three, especially on some accounts of them. On the other hand, Hirst's list does not distinguish among the sciences, nor among the arts. But we can envisage a case, on the criteria, for counting some of our usual distinctions in these areas as distinctions of Form. Thus the biological might constitute a Form in its own right, and the ethological may constitute another. Their heavy involvement in physical science would not be enough to preclude this, for, as we have seen, the autonomy of a Form does not preclude close relationships with other Forms. More positively, these areas are demarcated by such apparently fundamental concepts as 'life' and 'consciousness'; again, one could say that such special features of the observation of animals as that they can observe themselves being observed and that they can, indeed, come to 'relate' to their observer, constitute it a logically different form of observation to that of, say, the astronomer. Some scientists may entertain the ideal of one day representing the whole of biology and ethology as logically quite continuous with physics and chemistry, but certainly they have not got there yet, nor is it clear as to what form this continuity would take and precisely what reinterpretations it would force upon us. In similar vein, we might find good reasons for pronouncing music and art as different Forms, though with significant common features. Our uncertainties all along here are a function of some indeterminacy in the criteria of a Form. This is not necessarily to be judged a weakness in them – to be overcome by seeking a greater degree of precision. It might be thought a positive advantage that it allows us to have broader distinctions and fewer Forms in contexts where the interconnectedness of knowledge is the point, and finer distinctions resulting in more Forms in contexts where the relative autonomy of kinds of knowledge is the important thing.[34]

Second, Hirst does not consider the possibility of *logically 'compound' Forms*, as opposed to fields of study that are logical 'mixtures' of different Forms. The analogy here is with the difference in chemistry between a mixture, like a solution in liquid, in which each substance retains its own properties, and a compound, like water, in which the elements combine to form a quite new substance with its own distinctive properties. Geography, for example, is more 'a mixture' of its physical and human elements, inasmuch as these remain easily distinguishable within it. But other complex subjects seem rather to be 'compounds', with a claim to be forms of knowledge in their own right. Thus the human sciences apply scientific method to an area delimited by interpersonal concepts, but if we have learnt anything from their development it is that both method and concepts are transformed in the process.[35] Consider, too, the case of narrative literature. A great novel, like *Crime and Punishment*, combines affective, aesthetic, moral and religious elements and its greatness resides, among other things, in the *unity* it achieves among these elements. Is that a reason for regarding narrative literature as an additional Form, or a reason for reducing down the interpersonal, the aesthetic, the moral and the religious to a single Form of the humanities? Either way, the insistence on an exact number of Forms becomes, again, problematic.

It is to be acknowledged that these queries do not challenge the broad lines of Hirst's distinctions. But they add up to a case for a much more flexible application of the concept of 'a Form', and one that is probably less prescriptive in curriculum terms. The next point strengthens that case.

(2) Should we not add to the three acknowledged criterial variables of meaning, truth and logical structure a fourth: *the point (significance, interest) of a form*? It would seem to be as fundamental as any of them and as implicated in them as we have seen them to be in each other. Adding it would have three effects. First, it would fruitfully complicate the profiles of, and the comparisons between, the originally acknowledged Forms. It would bring to the fore the relationships between knowledge of persons and personal relationships, religious beliefs, worship and good works, critical appreciation, artistic practice and performance, and right thinking and right living, and it would bring out the contrast between the points of these Forms and the more 'intrinsic', or exclusively propositional, points of mathematics and science. Second, it would let in deliberative and technological discourses. Their propositional elements are so clearly not their most prominent features that even Hirst was not tempted to distort them into purely propositional Forms, yet his inclusion of moral, aesthetic and religious Forms might well be thought to have prepared the way for them. Third, it would force broader interpretations of the three original criteria. 'Meaning' would no longer be restricted (somewhat artificially?) to the meaning of propositions. 'Truth' would include, alongside the truth of propositions, such practical analogues of truth as the virtues of accuracy in application and execution, authenticity, integrity, fidelity and truthfulness. Finally, 'logical structure' would embrace the role of action and/or making in relation to propositions.

A good case for adding this criterion and accepting these consequences has been made, in effect, already. Earlier in this chapter we listed many realities that sit uneasily with Hirst's prioritizing of the propositional. In previous chapters we have argued the following claims more fully: that the human sciences are importantly distinguished from the natural by the greater intimacy, in principle, of their involvement with values, arising from the proper resonance between the values that give point to their enquiries and those that their enquiries confront; that within the general sphere of practical reason utopian, deliberative, evaluative and scientific discourses may be distinguished, as well as related, on the basis of their different relationships to value and action; and that there is a 'trialectic' in ethics, implicitly recognized in much ordinary moral consciousness, that involves action as well as vision and argument in a constant interplay with each other.

(3) We may challenge, next, Hirst's claim to have surpassed 'metaphysical' and 'psychological' divisions of knowledge in absorbing them into a single 'logical' division.

In respect of the psychological, this amounted to the idea concerning powers of mind, like imagination and feeling, that they varied quite irreducibly in their action across the Forms. Earlier we represented this type of claim as one tendency in a three-cornered debate, opposed both by the tendency simply to correlate individual powers with individual Forms and by the tendency to make the powers of mind altogether independent of the variation in forms. We proposed a softening of each of these three positions, thus allowing them to combine harmoniously into a synthesis more plausible than any of them. Here, the implication of that would be that our psychological distinctions and maps remained significantly independent of the distinguishing of Forms.

In respect of the metaphysical, one understands, of course, the scruples of the post-Kantian philosopher in basing any division of knowledge on supposed levels of reality. For the Greeks this basis had been essential for their conceptualization and justification of their version of a liberal curriculum. But it presupposed a realist position in epistemology, the view that we may know things about the world as it is in itself, and that, properly speaking, 'knowledge' entails precisely the conforming of our judgements to aspects of objective reality. We, however, might be considered the heirs of Kant, and, in particular, of Kant's 'Copernican revolution' according to which knowledge is the conformity of the world to the laws of the mind. Impressed by this part of Kant's philosophy, perhaps, Hirst argues that the old realism in epistemology is too speculative a basis for curriculum construction. We can no longer be confident that knowledge is the understanding of reality. We can be sure only that it is the understanding of *our experience*; that is, the coherent organization of our experience.[36] And as experience is the stand-in for reality in this view, so there is a surrogate for the old objectivity in the new idea of the essentially shared or 'public' nature of our concepts and our criteria of truth. Thus the theory of Forms, in its putative strictly 'logical' character, is presented precisely as a substitute for a division of knowledge according to levels of being, and a substitute that offers a more secure basis on which to build the liberal curriculum.[37]

We should not be taken in by these substitutions. At bottom, the project of the 'Copernican revolution' is scarcely even a coherent one. For it promotes experience at the cost of falsifying experience. The following is the argument for that claim, in summary form. In our *judgements* we implicitly affirm precisely the reality of this or that state of affairs as independent of our judgement of it. But judgement may be deemed a crucial element in our experience (in a properly full account of 'experience'), a fact not generally disputed; indeed, we can say that our experience is simply shot through with understanding and judgement. It follows that we may be said to *experience the independence of states of affairs of our experience of them*. That is just the kind of experience we have (as indeed Kant himself brilliantly and inconsistently insisted in another passage of his philosophy). Of course many of our judgements turn out to be wrong and the experiences of which they are part illusory. But that fallibility institutes no 'divorce' between experience and reality. On the contrary, the business of refutation and correction revivifies the relationship. Note that it is not just a matter of a sense of reality forming some sort of 'background' to our experience, or of our experience conveying 'intimations' of a reality beyond experience. For of what do we experience, or seem to experience, the independent reality? Of those particular states of affairs, those distinctions and relationships between particular things and kinds of thing, even those particular values of particular things and kinds of thing (sometimes intrinsic ones) and those particular orderings of these values, on which we confidently pronounce.

This argument suggests that there is no 'third way' threading between, or somehow 'transcending', realism and scepticism. The 'Copernican' way is no more in the end than a camouflaged form of scepticism. Unabashed scepticism makes a better alternative to realism, inasmuch as it is at least open and clear that there is an ordinary assumption in ordinary experience that what is being experienced is independently real. To refuse scepticism is, then, to reinstate realism. In the present context, it is to reinstate the possibility of some basis for the Forms in independent reality, the idea that some significant proportion of the differences in logic between the Forms is necessitated by, and derivative from, differences in the way things are, the kinds or levels of reality. It is to reinstate, in principle, the second of our three earlier mapping exercises.

Hirst's exposition of the logic of the Forms is genuinely valuable (though incomplete). But we have, in effect, undermined his attempt to project all the significant differences on to a single logical map. First, the resultant ignoring or marginalizing of considerations relating to powers of mind and aspects of personality seems illegitimate. Second, the attempt involves some conflation of considerations that are better seen as separate and cross-cutting. There are considerations, on the one hand, that are ultimately based on differences between kinds of being which are probably the most significant in distinguishing empirical, interpersonal and religious Forms of knowledge. Thus an elaboration of the criterion of 'meaning' would surely involve some reference to what a proposition refers to, or is about, and this in turn, as we have argued, should be given a realist interpretation. On the other hand, there are considerations relating to the differences of point between 'science', 'art' and 'politics', which are probably the most important when it comes to distinguishing the aesthetic and the moral from each other and from the other Forms. (This argument implies that the criteria, though implicated in each other, do not function in a wholly interdependent way. Thus within the enlarged set of Forms that I have proposed we would get different divisions into sub-sets depending on which criterion we emphasized.)

(4) Our final criticism of Hirst's position is for its lack of any developed theory of value. We have outlined one such theory in the previous chapter, and we have kept it warm in this chapter in noting the special relationships of the 'reality' map to 'ecstatic' values, and of the 'personality' map to experiential values. Furthermore, by stressing here that values and distinctiveness of value should be seen as *internal* to the logics of the Forms, we have indicated the 'handles' by which the general theory might get to grips with the Forms. Some such strategy is essential to an evaluation of the worth of individual Forms, and, therefore, to the least curricular prescription relating to them. We cannot require people to climb the mountain of mathematics, for example, simply because it is 'there' and because it is not quite like any other (though if it is magnificently there and shiningly unique, there begins to be a case). But in Hirst's writing there is very little either about general kinds of value or about the values that are internal to the Forms to back up his broad curricular prescriptions.[38]

Postscript

Hirst has recently abandoned one part, in curricular terms perhaps the single most significant part, of his theory of Forms, namely the doctrine of the primacy of the pro-positional. Indeed he now affirms in its place the primacy of the practical. In place of the claim that 'know-how' always presupposes 'knowledge that' there now seems to be the claim that 'knowledge that' is ultimately based on 'know-how'. The Forms of propositional knowledge and their criteria may be identified much as before, but they should now be thought of as themselves 'practices' of a particular kind – theoretical practices – alongside the social practices of daily life, personal relations, vocational practices, etc. Furthermore, it is practices in general that are now the starting point for mapping curriculum objectives and 'theoretical practices' are no longer accorded an ultra-privileged position. In advance of Hirst's published text[39] I can offer only some brief and provisional comments on this about-turn. In view of our general argument I would obviously find agreeable both the broader starting point (in our earlier terms, 'culture' rather than 'the disciplines') and the ending of the downgrading of the practical. I am pleased, too, that Hirst has *retained* his criterial approach to the identification of Forms – by which we were impressed at the same time as we proposed developing it fur-ther. My reservations also follow from the general line of this chapter. As regards the relative status of the practical and the theoretical I have argued that it is not a matter of the priority of *either*, but of a mutual interdependence that takes different forms and strikes different balances in different contexts – and this connects with my proposal to add the variable of point (significance, interest) to the list of the criterial variables of a form. Second, we should not forget intelligent making ('art'), the third member of Aristotle's triad, and its relationships to the other two as, for example, in technology. Finally, Hirst continues to take a line in epistemology that disallows any consideration of different levels of objective reality and on this score our positions still differ rather profoundly.

A MAP OF CULTURAL SUB-SYSTEMS

Denis Lawton proposes an adaptation for curriculum purposes of a technique of cultural analysis originally developed in anthropology. All societies may be said to have certain cultural sub-systems: socio-political, economic, communication, rationality, technology, morality, belief, aesthetic and maturation sub-systems. This thought allows us not only to develop a properly multi-faceted understanding of a society, but also to begin to plot a curriculum provision that might be adequate to its culture. Lawton goes on to make shrewd and telling use of this instrument, first to provide an educationally relevant analysis of contemporary British culture, then to criticize conventional British curriculum practice in relation to his analysis, for instance, for its neglect of economic and political education, and, finally, to suggest ways in which the deficiencies might be made good in practice.[40]

In contrast both to our three elementary maps and to Hirst's theory of Forms, this instrument of analysis is to some extent empirically based. If that fact places the full evaluation of the approach outside our scope, it can also provide a focus for some brief observations about its general character.

(1) The adaptation of anthropological tools for curriculum purposes is in principle appropriate inasmuch as culture in general is the business of curriculum. One is impressed by the *breadth* of curriculum consideration that results in this case. The map allows Lawton to carry through his commitment to a general, as opposed to a merely academic, conception of education.

(2) In its original 'scientific' context this map is an analytic instrument and prescribes nothing. Necessarily, therefore, it needs supplementing with a theory of value if it is to be used for curriculum prescription, and all the more if it is to be an instrument of cultural critique and reconstruction as Lawton also intends. Lawton (like Hirst) does not provide such a theory in any very systematic form.

(3) Considered as an instrument of *social* science, it has some inbuilt bias towards the social, as opposed to the individual, aims of education. 'Sub-systems' are seen in the first place as things shared, bonds that hold some people together and distinguish them from other people, and only in the second place as organizing individual experience and developing individual minds. In this perspective individualism is itself seen as a social construct and a phenomenon of particular cultures. But some emphasis on the development of the free mind, individualism in its broadest sense, connects up with the values of truth and amplitude of truth and, like them, may be seen as transculturally normative whether widely acknowledged or not.

(4) Although it is a theoretical construct in anthropology, the map may be presumed to have emerged in some contact with field experience and its usefulness in the field may lie partly in such considerations as its dividing up the project of understanding into tasks of a roughly equal size, the sort of practical cognitive advantage that might then be carried over into the different businesses of cultural critique and curricular prescription. This should be put into the balance against some impression of a conceptual untidiness (e.g. the extensive overlaps between belief, rationality and moral sub-systems) that might worry the fastidious philosopher. Empirically derived maps may be muddier than the intuitive products of the philosophical armchair but have some advantages of their own.

SUMMARY

Mapping or analysing culture is one of the tasks implied by the fact that a curriculum is always a selection. Acknowledging the utility of context-specific pragmatic maps, and the ambition (at any rate) of grandly theoretical maps, a good case may be made for the basic significance of each of three relatively elementary bases for mapping knowledge and, in the process, for taking a multidimensional view of curriculum balance. The Aristotelian triad of 'science', 'art' and 'politics' (each very widely understood), together with some of its sub-divisions, remains potent in curriculum terms. In particular it draws attention to the relative neglect of both making and deliberation. The equally venerable division of knowledge according to levels of being also spots some gaps in the usual curriculum, but has a more telling use as a basis for evaluating the relationship of the developed and institutionalized disciplines to their natural objects. Those maps, informal in character, that are associated with the modern emphasis on developing the expressive personality make their own further contribution to our concept of a balanced curriculum. Paul Hirst's theory of Forms may be seen as an ambitious attempt to subsume this range of considerations under the single heading of logic. But the (extremely significant) variables of truth criteria, meaning and conceptual relationship that he isolates are compatible with other identifications of the Forms than his list of seven. More important, Hirst's failure to realize the equal significance of the variable relationships of propositions to value and action led him to distort some, and to ignore other, Forms. Again, the theory conflates considerations that are better kept apart – especially if one takes, as one should, a 'realist' view of knowledge. Thus his endeavour serves in the end to confirm the initial plausibility of the multidimensional approach to mapping.

NOTES

1. Hirst (1966, 1974), Phenix (1964) and Schwab (1964) – and the new National Curriculum in the UK – all lean in this direction.
2. Smith *et al.* (1957), Lawton and Skilbeck in their writings generally, Hargreaves (1982), Her Majesty's Inspectorate with their 'areas of experience' (e.g. 1985), and the Australian Curriculum Development Centre (CDC) with its proposed core curriculum (described in detail in Skilbeck, 1984) all deliberately choose this second starting point.
3. Paul Black, then Deputy Chairman of the National Curriculum Council, in a public lecture at the London University Institute of Education, Autumn 1990.
4. See especially *Curriculum Matters 2: The Curriculum from 5 to 16* (HMI, 1985).
5. Malcolm Skilbeck, who was Director of the Australian Curriculum Development Centre at the time, describes the model at length in Skilbeck (1984, Chapter 7).
6. Bloom *et al.* (1956), Phenix (1964), Lawton (1983, 1989).
7. Schwab (1964).
8. Aristotle's *(Nicomachean) Ethics*, Book 6.
9. The humanities, as taught in schools, tend not to fit this bill. First, they are not deliberative in any immediate sense; their crucial significance for deliberation is long-range and contextual in character. Second, I suspect this significance is too rarely drawn out in classrooms, mainly because of the 'theorization' (sometimes inappropriate in form?) of the humanities. Third, they are somewhat hidebound in their range, often omitting altogether law and economics, for example.
10. The matrix produced by taking this map and the first map together would look something like this:

	PHYSICAL	BIOLOGICAL	ANIMAL	HUMAN	DIVINE
THEORY ('science')	*physics*	*botany*	*ethology, zoology*	*human sciences, history*	*theology*
TECHNE ('art')	*engineering*	*biotechnology*	*animal training*	*literature, 'software'*	*Gregorian chant?*
PRACTICE (*'politics'*)	*environmental planning*	*ecology*	*pet-care*	*relationships, civic life*	*prayer*

These cells would vary in their degree of educational importance, of course.
11. Progressive education takes this as read, especially in America – where schools in general may be ahead of UK schools in student involvement. Kohlberg's experiments with 'cluster' schools are particularly interesting. They are described in Wasserman and Garrod (1983).
12. R. K. Elliott (1974). He restricts the point – needlessly, I think, and unlike Plato – to the humanities.
13. Peters (1977b, pp. 53–4). He remarks here that when Whitehead famously appealed for

'useful', as opposed to 'inert', ideas in education, he meant by 'useful' the broad 'illuminating of ordinary life and its objects' rather than the narrower 'instrumental to ordinary purposes'. This is certainly right, and Whitehead is another contributor to our line of thought here. See Whitehead (1932).

14. R.K. Elliott (1975).

15. In practice, schools are places where the educational and the selection/training motives combine and compete, often subtly. A series of examples can be taken from the new National Curriculum in England and Wales. Its 'grammar school' general format was seen as soft-pedalling 'the vocational' by comparison with immediately prior policy (TVEI, etc.). But this observation overlooked the training and vocational dimensions of traditional subject teaching. Later the working parties appointed to draft curricula in mathematics and science proposed broad profile components such as 'communication', and 'science in action', alongside the more academic 'contents' and 'processes', just such additions as would bring the disciplines into everyday life and reveal their human as opposed to their specialist significance. The Minister, however, used his new powers firmly to reduce this threat to the traditional hegemony of 'content'. 'Communication' and the other novelties were 'absorbed back into' content and process. This is rightly seen as something of a defeat for the educational motive. On the other hand, the Minister's reaffirmation of 'content' as against 'process' is more ambiguous. There may be some degree of emphasis in promoting 'thinking scientifically', say, at the expense of 'knowing science', beyond which the future professional is still well served, but the future amateur is not.

16. The 'cult' writings of Fritz Kapra are suggestive in this connection. See also Maxwell (1984).

17. See Dunlop (1984).

18. Bloom *et al.* (1956).

19. Evers and Walker (1984) in particular promote such a line.

20. John White has expertly traced the Idealist influence on both British and American versions of the progressive or child-centred education (White, 1978).

21. See the exchange of papers between Elliott and Hirst that follows on, in the same book, from R.K. Elliott (1975).

22. Note that the plausibility of the claim that different disciplines exercise the imagination (etc.) differently turns on the intuition that they exercise such *particular functions* of imagination to some special degree – as drama does empathy, without being the only disciplines to exercise those functions – history also develops empathy. Thus interpreted the claim just forces refinement on us: we have to distinguish different forms of the important exercise of imagination (etc.), and ensure that each is catered for. And note that this would supplement, rather than replace, such grosser associations as that of the arts in general with imagination in general.

    This differs from the interpretation that powers and sub-powers, like imagination and empathy, may be securely identified only within, and not across, disciplines. That would be tantamount to a dismissal of the 'psychology' of ordinary language which, cheerfully and pretty unequivocally, applies terms like 'imaginative' across disciplines and intentional objects, and it is implausible in the exact measure that this ordinary vocabulary is illuminating.

    Of course, the general notion of 'a mental power' needs the general notion of 'an intentional object' as a correlative, and that different disciplines exercise mental powers differentially relates, no doubt, to differences in their intentional objects. If you will, classifying intentional objects by the powers on which they principally draw, one way of classifying them, can be related to other ways of classifying them, for instance by level of being (thus empathy's special association with drama and history will connect with their association with the human). But this, clearly, is quite different from a claim that this classification would *coincide* with any other, and so could be ignored.

23. The theory was first published in a 1965 paper, republished with most of the other key papers in Hirst (1974). See also Hirst (1973, 1979), and Hirst and Peters (1970, Chapter 4). Its long innings was never uncontested. See, for example, R.K. Elliott (1975, 1982), Pring (1976), Wilson (1979), O'Hear (1981) and Evers and Walker (1983).

24. Hirst (1979). See also 'Realms of meaning and forms of knowledge' (Hirst, 1974).

25. (1) *Kinds of development*. The proper analysis of, say, emotional or moral development can only make us aware of its dependence on intellectual development: emotional responses involve cognitive appraisals of situations; and moral commitment presupposes moral knowledge.

    (2) *Kind of meaning*. Although many things besides true propositions have meaning, e.g. false propositions, questions, commands, actions and events, the meaningfulness of everything else ultimately depends on that of true propositions. This is because, in turn, meaning requires concepts, concepts require agreed criteria of their application, and such criteria require agreed judgements. See Hirst (1974, pp. 63–4).

26. Ray Elliott (1982, p. 51) challenges even this inference: Hirst might legitimately have inferred the *fundamentality* of propositional knowledge to the curriculum, but not its *centrality* in the sense of its commanding the most prominent place. It is true, I think, that Hirst needs an additional premise about the *extent* of the propositional knowledge needed by other kinds of knowledge to make his case. Such a premise, however, would not be too difficult to supply.

27. 'The nature and structure of curriculum objectives' (Hirst, 1974, p. 28). Here, and elsewhere, Hirst criticizes the 'anti-intellectualism' of many curriculum proposals, especially those for the average and less-able pupil. But it is unlikely that these would have advocated the impossible course of eliminating propositional learning and it may well be, indeed, that they could be seen as 'anti-intellectual' only from the point of view of that high intellectualism that makes everything non-propositional secondary.

28. *Zettel*, paras 220–3.

29. Hirst's accounts of this third criterion are in general less developed than his accounts of the first two, but in at least one passage he conveys the general idea clearly. '[T]here is a network of relations between concepts in each case which will in certain respects be distinctive. Moral concepts involve complex relations with each other and with other kinds of concepts that produce a unique structure. If there are different kinds of criteria for truth in the areas concerned, then, for instance, moral arguments, being concerned with the application of moral concepts, and not the application of physical world concepts, must have a different logical structure from that of arguments in science. The idea that the relations between concepts and propositions in all forms of knowledge must conform to those of mathematical or scientific knowledge is a matter of pure dogmatism. We must examine these relations for their own structure in each case. Looser forms of relations are not necessarily suspect as these may be of the nature of the concepts. Nevertheless, certain elements within a moral argument may be identical in form with those in a scientific argument' (Hirst, 1974, p. 90). See also Hirst and Peters (1970, p. 65).

30. 'The forms of knowledge revisited' (Hirst, 1974, pp. 91–2).

31. *Ibid.* p. 90.

32. See, for instance, Hirst and Peters (1970, Chapter 4).

33. See 'The forms of knowledge revisited' Section III, and 'Curriculum integration' (Hirst, 1974).

34. I owe this last observation to a discussion with R.K. Elliott.

35. Hirst comes close to acknowledging that the human sciences have this strictly 'compound' character, but then drifts away from the point (Hirst, 1974, p. 86).

36. 'To acquire knowledge is to become aware of experience as structured, organised and made meaningful in some quite specific way . . .'. It is a mark of some ambivalence, perhaps, that Hirst follows this sentence up directly with one that is much more 'realist' in tone: 'To acquire knowledge is to learn to see, to experience the world in a way otherwise unknown . . .' (Hirst, 1974, p. 40).

37. This is clearest, perhaps, in the original proposal of the theory of forms in Hirst (1974), e.g. 'justification for the concept [of a liberal education] must now however stem from what has already been said of the nature of knowledge as no metaphysical doctrine of the connection between knowledge and reality is any longer being invoked' (p. 41).

38. The argument as to value that he did try out originally was of the kind loosely called 'transcendental deduction': any serious challenge to the value of knowledge and enquiry will, as an intellectual exercise itself, bear implicit witness to the very thing it challenges. But this

argument falls well short of a justification for pursuing, or imposing, the forms – as I believe Hirst has long acknowledged. First it is much too general. It would establish only that value cannot be denied to enquiry in general, not that it cannot be denied to this or that form of enquiry, say, mathematics. Second, it would fail to establish that *intrinsic* value of enquiry that 'liberal education' asserts. Our challenger, after all, may be seeking a justification for enquiry from us in an entirely pragmatic spirit. He may wish to be sure that the life of the mind has some practical use before going to the trouble of embarking upon it. What we catch him out in, in that case, is the implicit assumption only of the practical utility of at least this enquiry.

39.   My sketch of Hirst's new position is based on a paper he read at the London University Institute of Education in the spring term 1991 and on subsequent private correspondence.

40.   Lawton (1983, 1989).

Part 4

Curriculum Case Studies

Chapter 10

Literacy and Intellectual Power

[Reading] is a quest for meaning and one which requires the reader to be an active partici-
pant. It is a prerequisite of successful teaching of reading especially in the early stages, that
whenever techniques are taught, or books are chosen for children's use, meaning should
always be in the foreground. . . .
    Teachers should recognise that reading is a complex but unitary process and not a set of
discrete skills which can be taught separately in turn and, ultimately, bolted together.
                    (The Cox Report: *English for Ages 5 to 11*, from paras 9.4 and 9.7)

In Chapter 2 we noted the centrality of literacy and basic 'letters' to (formal) education
as conventionally understood. At the end of Chapter 7 we remarked how the idea of
'the academic', i.e. the literate and concentrated, is made to carry excessive responsibility for the unity of our curricula and our intellectual lives. We have since then rallied
the main defaulters from this responsibility: overarching educational values (ordered in
relation to each other) and maps which can relate these values to our cultural capital
and provide directions for exploring the distinctiveness and complementarity of different parts of that capital. Obviously, however, it remains that literacy has cross-
curricular, and therefore some unifying, significance. How that is best understood will
be our principal interest in this chapter. A second concern will be to study an instance
of the (often camouflaged) penetration of general value questions into 'technical' questions in education, and that will provide our starting point.

CHOOSING A READING SCHEME

Viewed from a distance, learning to read and learning to write seem straightforward as
conceptions, at any rate if tied down to some definite context. Up close, they fairly
bristle with question marks. We have noticed something of this as regards writing in
Chapter 7. We shall look at reading here.
    Imagine a staff meeting in a primary school to decide on an approach to the teaching
of reading. Many schemes are available ready-made, or something home-made may be
mounted by drawing eclectically on the ready-mades and leaving some room for a less

structured 'real books' approach. The participants would quickly agree that a good scheme is one that produces good readers in a relatively speedy and economic way. But someone – probably the 'post-holder' for English – asks, 'But what is a good reader? Is it enough to read correctly and fluently and score well on standardized reading tests? Mustn't comprehension come into it as well?' She gets the reply *'Well of course it must!'*, and the dialogue is off and running:

'Can we really take it for granted like that? Banal materials and a phonic pedagogy may freeze the pupil's consciousness to the written words – "things-out-there-in-themselves" – and dislocate his reading from his centres of pondering, feeling and understanding. Maybe he will finish a reasonably accurate and quick reader – but also an inattentive one who doesn't read and think at the same time. People can be subliminally responsive to road signs and advertisements but need the double-take of "listening to themselves reading" if they are actually to *think* about what they read.'

'All that means is that we monitor for comprehension as well as accuracy and fluency and most of these schemes have built-in comprehension tests. They are way ahead of you.'

'Those tests might not catch my inattentive reader; we should have to consider redesigning them. And, anyway, what is comprehension?'

'We recognize it when it's there and spot its absence when it isn't. Let's not make a philosophical meal out of it.'

'No mystification intended. The point is only that the "quiz-and-precis" type of test (even in its more developed forms[1]) embodies a pretty limited concept of comprehension when set against the range of reading materials: stories, poems, prayers, newspapers, shopping lists, instruction manuals, etc. It's the same question as arises with speed-reading techniques: they are advertised as increasing speed without reducing comprehension, but if one were to 'whip through' the Combined Works of Shakespeare or the Bible isn't it exactly the kind of *meaning* that makes these volumes special that one would miss?'

'In the teaching reading context, that limited sort of thing is just what "comprehension" does mean. It goes without saying that in other teaching contexts we do take on appreciation, imaginative response, criticism, understanding the topic itself, and so forth.'

'Reiterating the standard usage begs the question, surely. You're ducking the issue of whether conceiving separately of "language" and "literary" skills – "training in literacy" versus "educating in the uses of literacy" – might not be dangerous for many of the most important uses of reading. We can't just presume it could not be.'

'You might have said that that's what's been bothering you. Now, what's the research picture on that question?'

'Risking your further irritation – what is to *count* as research in this area? We should certainly have to consult more than the "hard" end of the scale. We could start by evaluating the *forms* of research that lie behind these schemes in front of us.'

'You are being irritating – and not very realistic! Whatever happened to the division of labour? We can't consider everything simultaneously here, and we can't teach everything simultaneously in the classroom. Besides, doesn't your train of thought come, in the end, to the claim that one has "read properly" only when one has thoroughly grasped everything, indeed that failures to appreciate or criticize what one

reads should be counted as "reading" failures? That's a massive load to put on one little word – especially when we have all those other words – interpreting, understanding, appreciating, criticizing, etc. – perfectly willing to pull their own weight.'

'I have claimed only this: that some kinds of reading habit are inappropriate for some kinds of text; that that forces us to reflect from the beginning on which uses of reading we think important; and that these obvious truths can be concealed behind uses of "comprehension" and "reading well" that are educationally too undemanding, whatever their technical precision. As to the division of labour: it is not in question, though the particular division we have may be. Getting it right requires some kind of overview or philosophy of literacy. As to language use: in our ordinary and professional lives we need *many* uses of "reading", "comprehension" and similar terms, for our many purposes – sometimes more open and sometimes more loaded uses for different contexts, even psychometrically loaded uses for the odd suitable occasion.[2] What we must not assume is that uses which can be rendered quantitatively are *ipso facto* the most significant. And why should any of all of this be difficult to swallow? Only because of the notion that imparting reading skills has become a kind of autonomous science and technology, so that all the teacher has to do is "operate" a scheme and consult the teacher's "manual" when problems arise.'[3]

'We'll never get to the "operating" if we carry on like this. We really must move to choose our scheme.'

'As Wittgenstein said in a similar context, the fly is still going to buzz in the fly bottle.'

This dialogue follows a pattern also found in discussions of, say, class control or mixed-ability teaching, and in teachers' deliberations on their tools and tackle generally. A discussion is launched as relating to methods and means, but it reaches an impasse and cross-purposes are suspected. The presumption of a shared understanding of the ends and values in question begins to yield, as ambiguities emerge in the meaning of such expressions as 'an orderly class', 'a proper learning environment', 'a good reader'. The uncertainty may spread to the meaning of 'education' itself – and therefore probably further since education is a matter (more like love than the jam jar) on which views tend to vary with variations of view on many other matters. On the other hand, this broadening of the debate is resisted by some participants, not only for reasons of time[4] but also, more fundamentally, because they doubt the real relevance of the broader questions. This is particularly likely when, as with reading, the issue has been the subject of a great volume of empirical research, much of it of the 'hard' variety. Then an insistence on bringing philosophy to bear can seem positively 'medieval'.

In fact, however, as our staffroom philosopher was implying, in education *questions of value, of a medium to broad range, are properly prior to, and also closely involved in, technical research and development.* So, in the first place, they determine what the technical questions are and what priority they deserve – or, as we could put it, what they must be if they are to be important. It is no real objection to this that, in practice, professional and technical enquiries often proceed happily without the intrusion of matters like the true meaning of education. In a particular group there may be agreement over the relevant deeper issues – a full, or a sufficient,[5] or a 'working',[6] agreement. But deeper issues may not arise only because none of the participants perceives their relevance, with the consequence that any of them may unknowingly work against her own values. As Simone Weil observes, we and our world are so constructed that we can seldom pursue our goals without becoming more or less distracted from them by the demands that the choice and the execution of means make on our powers of concentration. As simple a task as the search for a spanner that fits can interrupt our attention to what we need it for. And as tools require their own attention, so they acquire their own disciplines and institutions, with their own prestige and their own momentum – the 'technological imperatives'. A general impression is created of a degree of autonomy that, rationally speaking, the technical quite lacks.

Second, it is actually owed less autonomy in education than in most other areas of life. Technology, as a human practice, as 'ours', should always operate within a parameter of goals and constraints derived from human values. But this may still allow it an internal life of its own in, say, farming or engineering, with some issues and tasks being 'purely' technical in the sense that philosophy and values, having contributed to the setting of purposes and restraints, should then keep a respectful distance. But the specifically *mental* nature of educational 'techniques' changes this picture. Here the deep values need to interact *continuously* with the technical enquiries and the technical deployments. That is one of the things we shall be arguing for in the particular case of literacy!

TWO CONCEPTS OF LITERACY: BEREITER VERSUS FREIRE

Carl Bereiter, in his work with disadvantaged children, contributed to the development of a 'mastery method' of teaching reading for which he made the following claims. First, it was remarkably effective: it enabled *virtually all* children, whatever their backgrounds, to read well by between six and nine years of age. Second, though high-pressuredly behaviouristic, it was humane – indeed, children found it fun. Third, and crucially for Bereiter (whose suspicion of 'education' we met earlier, in Chapter 7), precisely because of its behaviouristic orientation it 'left kids alone' save in the one respect of providing them with this skill. It did not, of itself, alter their beliefs, attitudes, character, did not 'make them over' into something other than what they started as. For instance, it did not make them more (or less?) amenable to classroom discipline, nor give them a taste for any particular kind of reading material. 'Lower-class black kids remain lower-class black kids, only they become literate. We don't try to condition them in the process to some ideal of middle-class childhood or to some romanticized form of black culture.'[7]

This is to conceive reading as pure instrument or skill, taking its value from its empowerment of the individual in relation to the options which it opens up, but does not condition towards. That is not without intuitive appeal. Let us suppose, as regards Bereiter's mastery method, that all his claims for it stood up and came to be generally accepted. Suppose, too, that training in what different educationists might variously take to be the proper uses of reading did not have to be deferred until the 'basics' had been acquired, but could proceed *pari passu*, where it is thought desirable to lose no time with them. Would we not now have a tool that was uncontroversially useful, one that held its value through the spectrum of general views on education and the uses of literacy? And such matters as improving it and evaluating the relative merits of its variants would then seem authentically technical.[8]

None of this could happen, however, if Paulo Freire is to be believed. For him, training in literacy had been fundamentally mishandled if it had not produced an explosion of a highly active kind of awareness of oneself and of one's general environment, what he called 'conscientization'. So what Bereiter insisted on separating, Freire insisted on binding together. 'One must not think, however, that learning to read and write precedes "conscientization" or vice-versa. Conscientization occurs simultaneously with the literacy and post-literacy process. It must be so!'[9]

Freire is, of course, aware that something *ordinarily* called the ability to read and write may exist without any such dramatic expansion. So we understand this as a particular normative conception of literacy (and post-literacy), a claim that what *deserves to be worked for under this title* will include conscientization as an intrinsic part, as indeed the heart of the matter. It stands diametrically opposed to Bereiter's instrumentalist conception.[10] Reading and writing do not derive their main value from extrinsically conceived ends – which might, or might not, include conscientization. Rather they are to be conscientizing, or enhancing, in themselves. They are not just skills that become unconscious with proficiency. For Freire they are special modes of the *experience* of oneself in the world (thus far, indeed, a claim that might also be made for such an apparently instrumental skill as riding a bicycle), more specifically *special modes of making sense of the world and oneself in it*. Put another way, reading and writing should bring a greatly heightened awareness of the intentional possibilities of language. Thus these abilities are precisely not to be pursued as merely technical achievements – by contrast, perhaps, with learning to read in a second script or learning to type when one can already write long-hand.[11] On this analysis, then, to build 'consciousness raising' into literacy training is no mere piece of educational opportunism.

Nor, further, is it the political opportunism it might seem to build into the training a critique of the prevailing social and political orders – or not, at any rate, with regard to some societies and teaching contexts. For oppressive political structures are seen as fostering in the people what Freire calls 'a culture of silence'. And this is incompatible with the full flowering of these new modes of consciousness and self-consciousness, manifesting itself as a mental blockage with regard to them. Furthermore, this, of its 'intentional' nature, can be overcome only if the student is himself brought reflexively to focus his attention on it and its political causes. Hence, for the oppressed at least, political consciousness raising is to be seen as an integral aspect of the more general conscientization that belongs with literacy.

Bereiter's political views actually concur with Freire's in some relevant respects. Both criticize conventional education, including much literacy training, for being 'domesticating', and both are emphatic that literacy skills can be valuable augmentations of the individual's power to run her own life and find her own way in society. That they still come up with flatly opposed approaches would seem to be mainly because of the presence in Freire's reflections on literacy and freedom, and the absence in Bereiter's, of a phenomenological dimension. Put crudely, the one is sensitive, while the other is not, to what goes on 'in the head', to the *mental* concomitants of literacy.[12] We need now to give these our full attention. I think our intuition (unless perhaps we are language specialists) is not quite comfortable with the heavy loading in Freire's conception. We are tempted, like the staffroom interlocutor earlier, to recast it as a thesis about the *uses* of literacy, since large claims under that rubric no longer surprise us. But this would miss Freire's point. He means to challenge not, of course, a simple distinction between the possession and the exercise of a set of skills, but our habit of conceiving training in literacy and education in the uses of literacy as separate tasks, and the attendant assumption that there are processes called 'reading' and 'writing' which remain univocally the same through all their various exercises, regardless, for instance, of the specific qualities of the texts with which they engage. Now really to threaten that habit and that assumption will call for some determined argument.

LITERACY AND MENTAL DEVELOPMENT

Freire writes:

> Learning to read and write ought to be an opportunity for men and women to know what *speaking the word* really means: a human act implying reflection and action. . . . Speaking the word is not a true act if it is not at the same time associated with the right of self-expression and world-expression, of creating and recreating, of deciding and choosing and ultimately participating in society's historical process.[13]

We are accustomed to attaching this climacteric significance to the child's acquisition of *speech*, to viewing *that* as an appropriation by the child of herself and the world. Thus we quickly dismiss the suggestion that oracy is a matter only of techniques for more efficiently trading in ideas that are in principle independent of language. But now we are asked to approach literacy as a new and more reflexive phase in the development of oracy *and all that 'takes off' with oracy*. Why should we regard it as a watershed of this kind and importance? Our argument will fall into two main stages.[14]

(1) The written word, by comparison with the spoken word, involves us in a new relationship with language, specifically *in a more concentrated attention on language itself*.

In the first place, the text generally *requires* a more exclusive attention to language. The utterance is typically an embodied, and otherwise embedded, thing, in the sense that part of its meaning either is logically to be determined, or is at any rate determinable, from non-verbal cues in the immediate context. This may be true even if it refers to the past or the future. Hence it typically assumes, invites or allows an attention that is in part directed away from itself as a form of words. 'Do as you're told, please!' 'Which of you broke this window?' 'The dog seems pleased to see us.'[15] The text, by contrast, is typically disembedded in that its whole meaning is to be discovered in itself; that is, in language. A particular sentence or paragraph is, of course, likely to take its sense in part from preceding and succeeding ones, but that context is itself linguistic. Again, the meaning of the text will certainly presume, more or less remotely, on lived experience, but on the reader's *previous* experience, the links with which still have to be forged exclusively in the text itself; that is, in words. It does not typically depend on the reader's *immediate* non-verbal experience, which has the character, indeed, of a potential distraction. Illustrated stories and instruction manuals are among the exceptions, to varying degrees, to this rule of the disembodied, disembedded text. The book provides the rule.

Second, the text *facilitates* a more controlled and concentrated attention to language. Some of its advantage here is shared with the audio-record up to a point. Both text and record exist quasi-permanently and independently of their producers, which put them at the disposal of their users in ways that the primary utterance cannot match (though, needless to say, it has advantages of its own). But even this probably shades towards a crucial advantage of text over both live and recorded utterance. A particular paragraph is generally easier to recall to perception than a particular snatch of recorded utterance, and this edge may be founded on the more general and intrinsic advantage of the visual over the aural so that it would not yield to improvements in 'playback' technology. In any case, there is such an intrinsic general advantage of the visual: the aurally intelligible is necessarily transient and (pretty well) one-paced, the visually intelligible is generally multi-paced when it is transient, and it is not necessarily transient. Utterances, recorded or not, do not admit of being perceptually 'held'. But texts permit an attention that is continuous, or nearly so. Sentences and groups of sentences can be isolated, scrutinized and rescrutinized. They approximate the picture in their contemplative accessibility. On the other hand, texts can also be raced through at a speed at which utterances would be gibberish. The pacing possibilities in reading are wide and in the reader's control. (Thus, much the most convincing candidate for the 'successor to the book' is the interactive video, and this because it continues to incorporate all the advantages of the text.[16])

In sum, then, the typical text as against the typical non-recorded utterance requires, and as against utterances in general facilitates, an attitude to language use that is more controlled and more concentrated. It is these features of texts that are developmentally crucial. The text-as-process is the thing, it is tempting to say, rather than the access it provides to vocabulary and ideas outside the reader's oral environment. But this special process, we shall see, makes possible special language and ideas, from which the developmental significance of the process is not to be divorced in the end.

(2) Why, now, should a concentration on language be developmentally more important than a concentration on any number of other things? This question is revealingly misleading in form. It would have us think of language as just another feature of our environment, something else to be learnt about in a world that has much else to compete for our attention. There is evidence of a tendency, especially among pre-literate people, to think of it in just this naturalistic way, in particular to see the names of objects as among their objective properties. The Russian psychologist Vygotsky tells of a peasant who was less surprised that it had been possible to discover the size of certain stars than that it had been possible to discover their names![17] In some cultures this linguistic naturalism combines with an animistic view of the world[18] to yield another well-attested phenomenon, believing that words have magical properties, that objects will 'respond' to their name-callers provided the names used are the 'true' ones. A proper literacy may involve some weaning from these tendencies. Quite apart from the text's more reflexive relationship to words, the very realization that the same words can be rendered visually as well as orally, that is in altogether different perceptual forms, would suggest a view of them as conventional signs rather than natural properties.[19] Furthermore, this 'unsticking' of words from the realities they represent, as the anthropologist Robin Horton refers to it – correlatively an awakening to the activism of the human mind – may prepare the way for the idea of new or alternative theories and belief systems, and so contribute to the 'unsticking', also, of *ideas* from reality.[20]

We can be more direct in our argument. We can say flatly that language is not just another feature of the world 'out there'. Rather it is a possession of minds, an intentional reality, and indeed an embodiment and a tool of thought about all features of the world.

Simply, *a use of language that is more reflexive, controlled and concentrated means thought that is more reflexive, controlled and concentrated.* The growth will be in two interdependent directions: noetic, i.e. in relation to the thinking subject, and noematic, i.e. in relation to the content of thought.

Noetically, writing is particularly significant – and reading as it provokes to rewriting one's own text or to written comment on another's. The objectification (more or less) of one's thought process, in a form that is at once stable and modifiable, has a quality of open-ended self-revelation.[21] It heightens awareness of one's thinking and oneself and, interrelatedly, allows a more deliberate control of one's thinking and oneself.

Noematically, the text embodies a greatly heightened ability to transcend the immediate, the concrete and the commonsensical. This can be observed, first, in the dependence on texts of the more sophisticated forms of enquiry. How far into mathematics could the school-learner get without written calculations, or into science without these and record-keeping? Could history have become a critical discipline, such that even at school level the learner can be asked to consider different interpretations and theories, without it having ceased to be a purely oral tradition? And so on. Even literature, which has had its rich oral masterpieces,[22] is at the very least freed from mnemonic encumbrances by writing. The precise ways in which the text enters into the development of a discipline, and into the pupil's development in a discipline, vary from case to case and could, no doubt, be analysed for the length of a book in each case. But the general dependence is obvious. It is obvious, too, that texts are more than external conveniences, more than 'banks' of knowledge opened by the 'key' of literacy. Rather they condition and enter the thought processes that characterize these disciplines. Thus, famously, a diagram in the sand and Socratic questioning 'draws out' a geometric theorem from a non-literate slave boy, but, as Plato observes, his understanding remains 'dream-like' and 'untethered' unless it advances from the stage of following Socrates through each individual step, to the autonomy-conferring realization of the overall strategy.[23] What Plato does not remark is that this probably needs a form of demonstration that can be perused at leisure and as a whole, and the (definitely non-innate) capacity to peruse it. That is to say, it needs a text and literacy.

A critical understanding of social and political systems also requires the kind of controlled and concentrated thinking that may originally have to be acquired from working with texts – perhaps actually political texts. For these systems are not immediate to experience (rather, their effects, or the effects of their effects, are), and their understanding requires piece-by-piece assembly. Again, their critique is bound up with the envisaging of alternative systems or parts of systems, a degree still further removed from immediate experience. Yet again, they are not only abstract and complex, like geometric systems. They are also ideological, more or less. Understanding them involves 'catching oneself on', 'waking up', 'seeing through them' – in general a 'denaturalizing' of them and the beginnings of a shift from a passive to an active stance towards them. And it may be that the new relationship to language that literacy brings is, as Freire believes, also crucial to this, its essential prototype so to speak.[24]

The effect of a rightly designed literacy on our powers of thinking is more pervasive still. Just because the text is not merely an external auxiliary to memory, that which was originally accessible only on paper thereafter becomes the personal possession of mind and may be entertained in the absence of texts. It can inform the educated eye, hand and heart in relation to the ordinary and immediate environment. It can also be discussed and developed in new forms of oral transaction. Hence there is a dialectical relationship between chalk and classroom talk and between books and the disembedded oracy of the seminar, and from here also, perhaps, come the 'elaborated codes' of quite unacademic conversations in some circles.[25]

There are two caveats to append to this general picture of a literacy-based mental expansion. First, I have represented literacy as pervasively significant, but it would be something quite different (and no part of my argument) to claim that it was constitutive of 'rationality' itself and of everything properly to be called 'civilization'. This needs saying because of a tendency to hyperbole in some of the literature.[26] Second, we must go on remembering that the kind of mental expansion we have been describing here is no inevitable accompaniment of literacy – everything depends on the way literacy is conceived for teaching purposes, is taught, and is then used. (Thus Scribner and Cole researched the cognitive effects on members of the Vai people of north-western Liberia of each of three forms of literacy found in their society, and found different specific effects for the three forms.[27])

TEACHING LITERACY

In an influential paper of the 1970s, Michael Young once characterized usual education as biased towards the literate, the individualistic, the abstract and the remote from ordinary experience.[28] Our argument tends to confirm his intuitive association of the final three of these traits with the first. But Young seemed to doubt at that time that there was a reason intrinsic to knowledge and education, as opposed to one based on the interests of certain social classes, for thus heavily involving the curriculum with literacy and its attendants. Our argument would seem to meet this challenge: the development of thoughtful, critical and self-critical modes of thought in various spheres of learning, including the political, is at the least greatly facilitated by the proper uses of reading and writing. On the other hand, we have held no brief for average current conceptions of the balance between literacy and oracy, or of the relationship between literacy and oracy, or of the relationship between both these things and action. What we have done is to defend a conception of literacy on which the importance of all these practical issues is advanced. (Thus it is important that there may be potential losses to guard against, as well as gains to be anticipated, in an education for literacy, e.g. some loss of spontaneity and sensitivity in our face-to-face dealings, and a weakening of the 'primitive synoptic unity' referred to in Chapter 9. The views taken of our literate modernity by remaining non-literate societies can be suggestive in this regard![29])

On this conception, too, learning to read and write are not over and done with in the early years of schooling. The significance of early achievements is not denied – the moment when the apprentice reader first reads a line without her prompters, her joyful discovery that she can read books other than her school readers, and so on. But we are invited to see many developments in later schooling, or indeed in adult life, as continuous with early literacy training and its achievements, as we are invited to define the tasks of early literacy training with these later developments in mind – and they might not then be as much later!

As to usage, we certainly need those general or open uses of 'read' and 'text' that allow us to observe that readers may be thoughtless and uncritical, and texts as vacant as the

Sun newspaper. But when it comes to *setting objectives*, it is the thoughtful and critical reader or writer who is the 'true' reader or writer that we ought all along to have in mind.

What, finally, do we make of a behaviouristic method like Bereiter's? Could we not still use his techniques as part of a larger package? This needs a nuanced answer. It is not necessary (though the idea dies hard) that techniques for imparting 'the basics' that are highly effective on one conception of literacy must remain useful on another, but, at most, that techniques *in some respects similar* to them must be useful. Doubtless, there are considerations, whether specific to one language or referring to languages in general, that must be taken into account in any programme; for instance, that materials should be sequenced with an eye to their degrees of phonetic difficulty. Freire does not pretend magically to avoid such considerations. In particular, he exploits deliberately and largely the syllabic code structure of the Portuguese language. As much as Bereiter's, and surely in partly similar ways, his methods would require considerable adjustment before being usable in relation to a language that was very different in structure, Chinese for example.[30] But such commonly binding considerations do not imply the common usefulness, without modification, of any single *technique*. For techniques are not usually, and certainly need not be, responses to only one kind of consideration at a time. They can be, for instance, responses simultaneously to graphaphonic, syntactical, semantic and aesthetic considerations. And, even where we have what looks like the adoption of a whole technique by one programme from another, it is likely to be a nice question whether or not, set in its new context, amid different companion techniques and different overall purposes, it will remain what we should really count as 'the same' technique as before. But, all that said, it is not that a Freire could learn nothing from a Bereiter. It is rather that what he may coherently adopt or adapt from him would be a matter for an investigation of the techniques in question that, as befits his own paradigm, is more phenomenological than psychometric in character. On the one hand, it is right that the rationale should rule the pedagogy; on the other hand, it should exercise its rule 'non-ideologically'.

CONCLUDING SUMMARY

We caught an issue on the rise in an imaginary staff meeting: the vulnerability of an apparently top-heavy educational conception of literacy to a more common-sensical, and at the same time technically sophisticated, instrumental conception. (In political terms, this corresponds roughly to the vulnerability of the specialist English establishment to the critical interest in this subject of the general public, generalist primary teachers and educational psychologists.) Having extended the discussion into a contrast between Bereiter's emphasis on humane efficiency and Freire's on conscientization, we then sketched a defence of the educational conception in two stages. First, literacy requires, and to a unique degree facilitates, a direct attention to language. Second, in principle such an attention enables more reflexive, controlled and concentrated kinds of thinking, and the subjective and objective consequences of such thinking. This has consequences for the importance, the duration and the terminology of literacy education, and for the evaluation and adaptation of technical aids relating to it.

NOTES

1. More developed forms include any or all of multiple-choice questions, the reading 'work-shop' or 'laboratory', and the hierarchical taxonomy of comprehension skills. See the excellent critique in Moy and Raleigh (1988).

2. Note that ordinary language sanctions uses of 'read properly' which do imply good under-standing, or appreciation, or criticism – as well as less loaded ones. There are many uses for many contexts, contexts which in turn help to determine how the uses are to be interpreted! The trick is not to mismatch use and context. Thus 'reading without understanding' is a useful phrase for diagnosis but not for naming an educational objective. Its legitimacy in one context does not entail that reading a text and understanding it are quite separate processes that may be separately taught for. It helps us resist this particular temptation to note that 'reading without understanding' itself can describe a range of situations, from somebody reading a text in a foreign language he does not understand (though a listener might be following it), through a large number of intermediate cases, to an unbeliever reading the Koran. Neither what is affirmed ('reading') nor what is denied ('understanding') is precisely the same for each situation.

3. See de Castell (1981) for, among other things, a comparison of this technocratic model of literacy – now dominant, she argues – with the previously dominant progressive and classical models.

4. It will be appreciated that philosophical construction and conversion are not usually the work of an afternoon. Or it may be believed (and nowadays this belief can have the taken-for-granted quality of common sense) that value disputes are interminable because in principle undecidable. In the meantime some decision is, or seems, necessary. Even the clarification of differences that a true compromise would need is likely to be fought shy of. For experience suggests that, in matters like this, clarification itself can take quite some time, and is not guaranteed even with time. (Besides, clarified dissent may not altogether appeal as a working atmosphere.)

5. Sufficient, that is, for a joint conception and conduct of the enquiry – for agreement on its formulation and on what is to count as evidence in it. This may coexist with different kinds and degrees of interest in it.

6. For example, the 'official' philosophy of a school or of a discipline. Such working agreements are commonly needed in cooperative ventures precisely in order to restrict debate to manageable proportions.

7. Bereiter (1973). See especially pp. 64-7.

8. Bereiter flirts with the idea that much of what we currently regard as social, emotional and aesthetic education could also be replaced by a training in skills (sensitivity skills, body-awareness skills, honesty skills, skills of discrimination, etc.), that would avoid 'making pupils over' in the process (Bereiter, 1973, pp. 36-7).

9. Freire (1972, p. 42). The Brazilian educator is directly concerned with adult students. But his view of how children should be brought to literacy would undoubtedly be closely analogous (if throttled back).

10. Also, of course, normative, for what is seen as only instrumentally valuable – or, perhaps, as most valuable when conceived only as an instrument – is still seen as valuable.

11. The trouble with Bereiter's position from Freire's point of view, it might be said, is just that he does conceive primary literacy skills on the models of such secondary and parasitic ones.

12. The phenomenology in Freire's main works remains embryonic rather than developed and systematic. It is, none the less, an essential element in his general approach. It comes out, for instance, in his use of such student comments on the significance for themselves of learn-ing to read and write as 'Before, letters seemed like puppets. Today they say something to me, and I can make them talk!' (Freire, 1972, p. 44).

13. Freire (1972, p. 30). Hence the prominence in Freire's teaching methods of consultations with, and among, students.

14. Freire is himself strangely inexplicit at this point, but we can attempt the sketch of an answer that would follow the implicit grain of his position. In places it leans heavily on Donaldson (1978). (I formulated the argument that follows before reading more widely in the literature.

Later I found I had been anticipated by Olson (1977), who draws on still earlier work by Havelock (1973) and Goody and Watt (1968). Perhaps independence of discovery says something about the worth of an argument! Olson's presentation is, however, more historically based and less purely philosophical than mine. I am indebted to my colleague Margaret Meek for guiding my late reading in this area.)

15. The tendency of young children in interpreting utterances, including those of the logically self-sufficient kind favoured by some psychological workers, to help themselves liberally to non-verbal clues in the environment, and to make mistakes in the absence of such clues, is well-documented in Donaldson (1978).

16. See Clarke (1984).

17. Cited in Donaldson (1978).

18. There may be already a weak animism in the naturalism, whose implicit theory would be that an object's name is originally the sound it utters, its self-revelatory noise. Think of our spontaneous uses of expressions like 'bow-wow' and 'moo cow' in very early language training.

19. In this respect, presumably, learning a second language would be similarly subversive, at any rate where the learning was 'indirect', i.e. involved the experience of translation.

20. R. Horton, 'African traditional thought and Western science', in Wilson (1970).

21. '[T]hey can write down ideas in order to reflect on them and reformulate them; they can elaborate complex arguments which require written support' (The Cox Report, 3.14, from its list of the developmental benefits of writing).

22. However, most of the originally oral masterpieces we possess are not simply transcriptions of oral traditions, but literary redactions of them – in some cases (e.g. in many 'Biblical books) redactions of redactions.

23. Plato, *Meno*, 85c and 97d–98a.

24. So that a proper literacy would condition political awakening, as well as (at least for the oppressed) being conditioned by it. This idea has achieved a high degree of respectable currency. Thus the Kingman Report – in a passage quoted in the Cox Report – is not far from the argument of this paragraph: 'People need expertise in language to be able to participate effectively in a democracy . . . A democratic society needs people who have the linguistic abilities which will enable them to discuss, evaluate and make sense of what they are told, as well as to take effective action on the basis of their understanding . . . Otherwise there can be no genuine participation, but only the imposition of the ideas of those who are linguistically capable' (Kingman Report, Chapter 2, para. 2).

25. B. Bernstein, 'Social class, language and socialization', reprinted in Bernstein (1971). Scollon and Scollon (1981) remark that to the Alaskan Athabaskans the English speaker '*talks* like a book'.

26. For example, Greenfield (1972) and, to an extent, Olson (1977). See the critique by Street in Mercer (1988, volume 1).

27. 'Unpackaging literacy', in Mercer (1988, volume 1).

28. M. F. D. Young, 'An approach to the study of curricula as socially organized knowledge', in Young (1971).

29. See especially Scollon and Scollon (1981).

30. On the other hand, 'structure' here should not be interpreted behaviouristically. Differences in language structure are, in the end, differences in thinking.

Chapter 11

Upgrading Technology: A Value Clarification

To put a youth with a vocation for manual work on an assembly line is a crime as great as putting out the eyes of the young Watteau.

(Simone Weil)

TERMINOLOGY

Our subject is a diffuse one. It is that part of the curriculum which relates to working in woods, metals, plastics, textiles, foodstuffs and other materials, to making from materials what the National Curriculum classifies as artefacts, systems and environments, and to practices that are built around this making, such as carpentry, mechanics, cookery, fashion, building, decorating, electronics, design, by extension gardening, farming and biotechnology, and by an extension of another kind programming – whose business is software. Among established school subjects home economics, CDT (craft, design and technology) and IT (information technology) are central to this area. Art, science and business studies, and, perhaps to a lesser extent, mathematics, language and environmental studies, overlap with it.

This diffuseness has made for some difficulty in finding the right label for this curriculum area. 'Practical', though often used, would be better restricted (in the Aristotelian terms discussed earlier) to those subjects that focus on deliberating and deciding, like moral and political education and business studies. The focus here is, rather, *making* – 'to operate effectively and creatively in the made world' is the overall objective for this subject[1] – and, we should surely add, *growing*. It is true, of course, that these interact with deliberation and decision-making in real-life practices like housekeeping and engineering; the obligation imposed upon such practices to be 'functional', to relate to human needs, ensures this. Reflecting this fact, the new National Curriculum in Technology for England and Wales has one clearly deliberative target out of the four attainment targets it adopts as together defining a design and technology capability:

Identifying Needs and Opportunities: Pupils should be able to identify and state clearly needs and opportunities for design and technological activities through investigation of the contexts of home, school, recreation, community, business and industry.

This target then dictates roughly one-quarter of the new statutory programmes of study.[2] Interaction is not identity, however, and the distinction between making and deliberation remains a profound one in educational, as in other, contexts. To say that the subject technology, for example, is *primarily* to do with making, while business studies is *primarily* to do with deliberating, is to indicate no mean difference between these subjects. The matter ought to be seen as parallel to what obtains between making and science. The interaction between those two, quite fundamental though it is, does not inhibit us in the least from insisting on the underlying distinction between them. We could say that the status of science sees to that. If we are more inclined to fudge the making/deliberation distinction in our curriculum analysis, this probably reflects the traditional begrudging of status and time to both of them, as much as any fine sense of the interplay between them.

'Productive activities'[3] and 'materials' are each too general as titles since they are not apt for distinguishing this area from the arts. 'Technical subjects' and 'technical education' have historical support, but also, perhaps, an historical association with special schools and institutions that makes them problematic. 'Craft, design and technology' has been used in the UK to refer to a particular set of these activities and usually excludes, for instance, cookery and textiles. 'Technology' is now the officially adopted general title in the UK. In many of its uses it is too redolent of applied science – even of applied physical, as opposed to biological, science – happily to suggest *all* of this area. But there is a broader anthropological sense of 'technology' as, simply, *the use of tools for meeting human needs and achieving human purposes*, and in this sense (which is gaining in currency, I suspect) it makes an appropriate general title. I shall use it principally in what follows.

THE UPGRADING OF TECHNOLOGY

The traditional contrast was with 'academic subjects', a ragbag that included mathematics, the sciences, the humanities, languages and – though somewhat uneasily – the fine arts. These corresponded with what were once called 'liberal pursuits', and they made up the core, if not indeed the whole, of 'the liberal curriculum'. Compared to them, the traditional status of technology was low. But now it is being upgraded, and there is wide agreement that this is not before time. In the UK, formerly a particularly low esteemer, it has recently achieved the rank of one of the eight National Curriculum Foundation Subjects, with an extensive and demanding set of programmes and objectives that are mandatory for all maintained school pupils up to the age of 16.

This is the culmination of a process going back a quarter of a century in which, with hindsight, several stages may be distinguished. First, the introduction of comprehensive schools was generally accompanied by a common curriculum for the 11–14 age group in which *everybody* studied some technical subject or subjects. Then, the new awareness of gender issues in the 1970s and 1980s challenged the division of the area into 'boy' and 'girl' subjects. At least in coeducational schools, it became the norm for boys to take home economics and for girls to take craft, design and technology – though with a strong tendency to regress to stereotype in choosing options at 14. Next, there was the government's massive Technical and Vocational Education Initiative (TVEI) of the 1980s. Initially viewed by teachers with suspicion – it seemed an enormous bribe by a government that was otherwise starving education of funds – TVEI came to be an accepted part of school life. Schools came to see it as reasonably open to an 'educational' interpretation while still prodding them into new lines of reflection and practice. These lines included, in particular, the development of a wide 'problem-solving' definition of 'technology', and – associated with that – a deal of interaction between secondary school departments that had previously stood aloof from each other.[4] Both of these trends are fully endorsed in the National Curriculum Technology. The official literature for this stresses that the mandatory programmes will of their nature require the cooperative involvement of a wide range of departments and subject areas. And the emphasis falls not on the kinds of material on which pupils are to work, but on the stages of the technological process – which are defined as identifying needs and opportunities, generating a design proposal, planning and making, and appraising the result. These are made the basis of the quartet of overarching attainment targets alluded to already, which come with an added caution that they are to be interpreted in an interactive and holistic, rather than a linear, fashion. This broader and more abstract view of it may be seen as part and parcel of a reappraisal of the value of technology education, and also as a device for accommodating a large increase in its share of total curriculum time by giving almost everybody some stake in this increase. The increase itself is the most dramatic expression of upgrading, in particular the two facts that a quite serious involvement with technology is henceforth required all through primary school, and that 'academic' and clever children will henceforth be prevented from dropping this area at 14. Another significant sign of the times is that independent schools in Britain, though legally exempt from the National Curriculum, have been rushing to add technology to their curricula.

It is, however, as vital now as ever to reflect on the unreason of the previous low status of technology, and, positively, on the real educational values of this area. This is partly to inhibit backsliding, considering the venerability and pervasiveness of the prejudices involved and all we know about the difficulty of consolidating curriculum change.[5] It is even more to clarify the *directions* in which technology may best develop – in case our reaction to the former unreason should become another piece of unreason.

EQUALITY INSUFFICIENT

What then was the case for upgrading?[6] As a preliminary, we should note that considerations of equality provided no short-cut. From the principle that all citizens are owed an equal respect, the conclusion does not immediately follow that an equal respect is owed also to their jobs and to the kinds of activity which constitute those jobs. For equality is formal, in the sense that it relates to the distribution among citizens of goods or activities that are *independently* evaluated, and does not itself judge the relative values of those goods or activities. In the name of equality the Renaissance writer Campanella once proposed, in his *City of the Sun*, that lowly manual work should be distributed equally among all, so that every citizen should have time for the liberal and spiritual pursuits that 'really mattered'![7] That was to reject the elitist element in the classical conception, the idea that the work of the many should support the elevated contemplation of a privileged few, but to retain the classical belief that non-manual contemplation was supreme among human activities.[8] More philistine spirits, on the other hand, might take the view that only wage equality counted for much, and the nature of the paid activities for little or nothing: if the drudges of industry were paid at the same rate as the captains, would it matter any longer that they were nothing but drudges? In this form too, though it is radical like the first, egalitarianism prescribes no regard for technology as such.

We should note, too, that familiar rhetoric about the 'equal dignity' of manual work may be used to quite opposite effects. For example, it can be used to whitewash the assembly line, or to condemn it. The harsh mindlessness of at least some of its forms may be glossed over and condoned, or it may be highlighted and opposed in the name of technology itself – as in Simone Weil's fierce remark quoted at the head of this chapter.[9] But for a conception of technology to function as a critical tool we must build norms or standards into it, as we have more firmly done with our concepts of art, science and literature. And we certainly will not find such dignifying norms for technology, any more than we found them for those 'liberal' pursuits, in a bare principle of equality.

What we can say for equality, however, is that an egalitarian climate may allow the suppressed values of things to emerge. In the early comprehensive schools, we have seen, everyone had to take some technological subject from 11 to 14. This might have been left as a matter of teaching all students to pull their weight technologically, while continuing to see these subjects as the humble ones. In fact it turned out to be the first step in an upgrading of the subjects. This was at least partly because their educational potential became more obvious in the experience of teaching them across the ability range. But though equality may facilitate upgrading in this way, it does not dictate it, logically speaking.

THE LIBERALITY OF MAKING

What can dictate upgrading? A much more promising idea is that we may find in technology those very values which the liberal tradition had associated exclusively with its 'academic' and 'humane' pursuits – and, finding them in that unexpected place, gain a broader view of those values at the same time.

The values in question were generally held to be encapsulated in the notion of the pursuit of knowledge 'for its own sake'. Only that kind of pursuit was thought to have much educational value. Technical knowledge and enquiry could not qualify, it was further assumed, because they were by definition a matter of utility. A line of rebuttal suggests itself here. Might we not show, first, that technology is in fact pursued for its own sake as well as for further ends and, second, that in any case educational status cannot properly be restricted to activities pursued for their own sake? Now we shall start out on this line more or less. As we progress, however, we shall find the underlying distinction – between the pursuit of knowledge for its own sake and its pursuit for some further end – itself beginning to unravel. Each leg of it conflates important subdistinctions and, more than that, an effect of drawing these out is to blur the main distinction considerably. At best it is crude and its service to liberal values doubtful.[10] But all this is to anticipate.

Let us start by asking what motivations were *permitted* in the liberal position. What could count as pursuit 'for its own sake'? Our categorization of values in Chapter 8 suggests four possibilities, of which at least the last three would have gained approval in the liberal tradition:

- the pursuit of knowledge out of greed or addiction, where the point of pursuing it is to have it as a possession, without much thought to using it or living through it;
- the pursuit of knowledge in the spirit of play, where the paramount considerations are the joy of exercise and mastery, and the experience of full and powerful living in the cognitive dimension of one's being;
- the pursuit of knowledge in the dogged and scrupulous spirit of an ethically conceived devotion to truth;
- the pursuit of knowledge out of love of the object of which knowledge is sought, where the value of the object itself is primary and where it is seen under concepts like the wonderful, the dreadful, the glorious, the beautiful, the good and the important.

It is already clear, then, that 'knowledge for its own sake' is an ambiguous slogan. As a form of words in isolation it is perhaps most suggestive of the somewhat dubious first motivation, while as actually used in the tradition it covered the other three, or perhaps all four, motivations – this without clarifying what they had to do with each other or how they should be ordered. Now we have developed a position on the general ordering of these values, it will be recalled, but for our immediate purposes it will be quite sufficient to show that whichever emphasis is preferred, no downgrading of technical subjects will be entailed. Setting aside the first motivation, each of the other three can be found as well in technical as in traditional liberal subjects, as the following considerations will show.

(1) The actual process of making can be a thoroughly experiential and *vital* business with its own tribulations and joys in the meeting of challenges and its frequent experience of absorption and, again, of power. In the longer term it can truly enter into the drama of personal history, as one's technical skills develop with practice, perhaps to mastery – or stagnate and diminish. Add to these features the possibility of a continuing lived involvement with the product: it may be a lasting occasion of pride, or disappointment. Now all this can have a thoroughly intellectual character. One may think of the far-reaching theoretical enquiries that may be set in motion by a practical problem, the range of a Freud's speculations about the minds of the patients he was concerned to heal,[11] or the excursions into physics, philosophy and religion that might take off from motor-bike maintenance.[12] This is one side of that dialectic between theory and technology that is so fruitful for each. But at a more commonplace level, and with much less turning aside from the practical task in hand, activities such as curing a patient, repairing a machine, building a house, cooking a meal or tending a garden may require from us, and reward us with, a great deal in the way of intellectual effort, audacity and fulfilment. There is the articulation of a conception, the translation of this into a design, the constant mutual adjustments of conception to design and of design to execution, and the growing intimacy of one's knowledge of the product. Of course, technological activities are liable to have a physical dimension in addition to the intellectual. But if

building a house, for example, calls forth physical – as well as mental – power, courage, dexterity and communion, that should only be a reason for valuing it the more in terms of vitality and engagement.

(2) Technical activities have *conscientious requirements*, often severe ones. As we engage in them we can properly regard ourselves as bound by standards that are analogous to the demands of truth and related values in theoretical enquiries. To truth, consistency and clarity as intellectual virtues, do effectiveness, economy and good workmanship not correspond as virtues of making? These, too, are virtues of reason, i.e. virtues with a peculiarly rational content and appeal. And the further fact that much technology imposes a physical discipline as well, that it promotes a controlled fluidity of body as well as a controlled attentiveness of mind, only adds to its ethical significance. Furthermore, we must not omit (and we shall return to it later) the possible ethical significance, in personal, social and environmental terms, of the product – the food, the shelter, the new or repaired machine, the new drug or the healed body – a significance which may well be present to the worker's intention and attention.

(3) Through technical activities we may express and develop an appreciative sympathy and *love*, not only of the finished products, but of the 'materials' which we work upon and work up. We may think here of a carpenter's love of his timber, his respect for its grain, and of how this has been fostered by his actually working with it and could not have been developed to the same peculiar degree by his just looking at it attentively. We could go on to consider the feeling for her land (much more than simply 'naked proprietorship') that a farmer develops, or of the artist's relationship to her materials. We might dwell on the strange mood of sympathetic solicitude for a machine that a good mechanic gets into and that is a condition, often, of correct diagnosis and proper repair. This is distinguished from what the machine's user, e.g. the 'easy rider' of a motor-bike, might feel by its connection with understanding: it seeks an understanding of the fault against the marshalled background of a general understanding of the machine's working. But, just the same, it too is a kind of physical communion with one very individual machine.

The general truth in such cases can be expressed in Simone Weil's terms: we can only command nature by obeying it, having first understood it; and we, free beings, can bear to obey constantly only what we can trust, respect and feel some affinity with. Weil would add that it is in work with a hard manual dimension that we are most vividly, perhaps painfully, made aware of this. In line with the monastic tradition of Western Christianity, she argued that manual work should be an intrinsic complement of contemplation, this combined physical and mental involvement, with its attendant pain and toil, a means by which the hard 'necessity' and, therefore, the ordered beauty of the world might bite into one's soul.[13] The deep Benedictine adage *laborare est orare* ('to work is to pray') can be understood in this way – and thereby made available to the non-theist while still being open to the traditional theist interpretation as well. Whitehead refers to this adage and 'strips it down' to 'the essential idea . . . that work should be transfused with intellectual and moral vision and thereby turned into a joy, triumphing over its weariness and its pain'.[14] I would want to add to that an explicit reference to the role in this vision of the worker's engagement with the world.

Once, then, the different values of 'liberal' pursuits emerge from behind the veil of the 'for its own sake' formula and parade themselves, we discover more or less the same values in technology, plus additional physical values, or, as it might be better to say, we find the same values in a broader register. These values represent ways in which technical engagement too can be prized 'for its own sake'. What we have yet to find is even the hint of a good general reason for the omission of technical subjects from the liberal curriculum.

ARBITRARY EXCLUSIONS

The ulterior motive

We may now consider the other leg of the liberal distinction, the pursuit of knowledge *for some further end*. What exactly did this include, and by the same token seem to exclude, from educational status? Most obviously disdained – ever since Plato railed against the Sophists for training young men 'to get on in this life', and much of the Christian West followed Plato in this (ostensibly at least) – was *worldliness*; that is, such long-term considerations as wealth, power and status, and such short-term ones as passing an examination, gaining a teacher's approval and outscoring a rival. These are often called 'extrinsic' motives, to contrast them with the immanent aims that enter into the definition of an activity.

The first thing to say here is that excluding such extrinsic motives does not entail the exclusion of technology. On the one hand, those motives are as ulterior to technology's intrinsic or immanent aims – the meal, the machine, the garment, etc. – as they are to the immanent aims of acknowledged 'liberal' subjects – the theory, the proof, the poem, etc. On the other hand, they can just as well be the real motives, or among the real motives, of the scientist, artist or scholar, as of the craftsman and technologist. This latter fact may be easier for us, among whom science, art and scholarship are recognized livelihoods, to perceive than for those, like the Greeks, among whom 'liberal' pursuits were generally the privilege of persons whose livelihood and social position were independently secured. But even if, as some argue, the existence of a leisured approach and a leisured class was a precondition of the establishment of liberal pursuits – necessary to boost them into orbit, so to speak[15] – it remains that *present* engagement with them is consistent with quite high levels of extrinsic motivation. Furthermore, some technologies might similarly require, and promote, a disinterested attitude if they are to get going. Indeed 'alternative', 'intermediate' and 'green' technologies tend precisely to define themselves as against the forces of a rampant materialism. Whatever we might think of their feasibility, they make our point nicely that an opposition to those forces need not translate into an opposition to technology as such.

Second, we should want to know why extrinsic motives are to be *presumed* extra-, and even anti-, educational. It is not just that we should ask whether a teacher may not justifiably use them as a tactic for drawing students into a pursuit, believing that the internal *telos* of the pursuit will then gradually take the students over. Considered even as *permanent* elements in a pupil's motivation, are there not cases and cases? Compare wealth, power and prestige, on the one hand, with earning a living and doing a responsible job on the other. The former connect with the potentially evil human tendency to distort what are naturally means or enabling conditions into engrossing ends-in-themselves, at the cost of other people, and peoples, who are real ends-in-themselves. We can see why education should be put on its guard against them (and we shall not fool ourselves that this will be at all easy). But earning a living, doing a responsible job, and, for that matter, *creating* wealth, would seem to be honourable and important aspirations if considered as conditions of the good life and of doing good. They should not be deemed anti-educational as motives just because they can be regarded as extrinsic (perhaps only partly extrinsic) to the educational task in hand. Nor should they be denied all influence in shaping the curriculum. It is not, then, the extrinsic/instrumental as such that is the enemy, but certain kinds of extrinsic motive and thinking.

Dualism and the socially useful object

The liberal tradition was also disdainful of technology's rather more integral stake in physical objects that served human needs and wants. This attitude derived from a combination of that dismissal of the instrumental that we have already noticed and a further suspicion of matter and the material, and it had several strands to it. First, both the physicality (the 'blood, sweat and tears') of the processes and the materiality of the products – artefacts, systems and created environments as opposed to theories, poems and proofs – were alike held in some contempt. Thus far, indeed, even art was tainted insofar as it too was materially embodied. Second, unlike art, technology did not redeem itself by investing its materiality with intrinsic meaning: it was not meaningful in itself but only in relation to some human need beyond itself. Third, the human needs and wants that technology serves were seen as paradigmatically bodily in character and, as such, not of comparable dignity to the spiritual needs served by other activities.

What are we to make of these ideas? As a preliminary, we might split some not altogether trivial hairs. Even if a concern for the social utility of products were foreign to education, it would not follow that the making of them was foreign to it. The making need not be, and often is not, motivated by the product's social usefulness. For that matter, the maker might know a product was useless or harmful and not care! Making may be engaged in for fun, as a challenging exercise of wits and skills. The end-product still shapes the activity here, but it is the activity itself that is valued – just as goal scoring is the aim in football but does not constitute its whole enjoyment. Again, the product may be valued more for its aesthetic than for its useful quality. Presumably this was the view taken of architecture, and if architecture can be liberal 'despite' its usefulness, then so can cookery, needlework, carpentry and boat-building for the aesthetic qualities of their products.[16] Yet again, it may be the engagement with the materials that really appeals, the feel of the wool and the knitting needles more than the resultant socks.

Points like these have some force *ad hominem*. It must be admitted, though, that they are otherwise limited. For they suggest a non-engaged kind of relationship with technology in which it is not *qua* technology that it is valued. Like all flirtation, this would miss much of its object's character and point. We must, then, challenge the liberal prejudices more directly.

To go for the jugular, the idea that attention to basic human and social needs is foreign to education was surely a mistake. Studies and activities that are instrumental to feeding, clothing, sheltering, transporting and healing ourselves and others – not to mention those whose products carry our 'software' and serve our information and communication needs – are, as such, valuable, and that is already a strong *prima facie* reason for regarding initiation into them as properly educational. We may be grateful to the liberal tradition for its insistence that there is more to life and education than such concerns, its underlining of the truth that man does not live by bread alone. But its *exclusion* of them from education was really an abdication, exempting vast areas of life from serious critique and reconstruction – inhibiting to this day, for instance, the development of a proper consumer education.

The challenge laid down here is *both* to the blanket dismissal of the instrumental and to the suspicion of the material. As to the first, it is to say, again, that the discrimination of instrumentalities by reference to their *destinations*, what they are instrumental to, is essential. (Of course, the *form* of instrumentality involved, in particular its place on the mindful–mindless continuum, is also crucial in the educational context, and we will return to it.) As to the second, it is to begin a reinstatement of the material and physical which we shall now take further.

What is required fundamentally of us here is the displacement of implicit and explicit forms of dualism by something more holistic. For disdain of the material is rooted in the doctrines of dualism. The great classical exposition of these doctrines is in the dialogues of Plato. There, an all but complete divorce between matter and spirit is engineered in a series of dimensions. Metaphysically, the intelligibility of matter is separated from matter itself: what science understands is pure ideas or forms, thought of as inhabiting a heavenly domain while their shadows alone inhabited the Earth. At the psychological level, body and soul were divorced. Only the most tenuous of connections between them was acknowledged – and it was lamented! This dualist refrain was sustained through Plato's ethics and politics. From all this it was no step at all to the view that technical capability belongs to a low order of achievement inasmuch as its processes are physical, its expressions hardware and its functions intimately related to bodily need.

As it happens, there was an immediate response to Plato. Aristotle de-radicalized the matter–spirit distinction and worked up an unsurpassed counter-series of holistic, though internally complex, perspectives to combat Plato's. He failed to carry this through, however, to any ringing endorsement of technology. No doubt his social position in an Athens in which manual work was left to slaves inhibited him from seeing that far. But in any case Aristotle was to be less influential than Plato in the formation of Western consciousness. The bulk of his work was lost for a crucial half millennium during which Christianity found a Platonic form of self-expression – sadly, a form less authentic to its own biblical roots in the respects we are considering than an Aristotelian one would have been.[17]

Modern culture is not consistently either dualist or holist (and is perhaps more casually reductionist than anything else). In a self-critical mood we are likely to be troubled less by the bodiliness, and more by the triviality or artificiality or plain harmfulness of many of the needs and wants that technology serves. And the physicality of technological processes bothers us less than the enforced mindlessness of much of it. Our operative criterion in these critical judgements is not the either/or of dualism, but a catch-all ideal of widely distributed, environment-friendly, all-round human fulfilment. But dualism lingers on *in what we are reacting against here.* As well as the traditional educational bias against technology, we struggle with the division of mental from manual labour in industry, with a concept of leisure as heavy consumption and with the still faltering state of our green consciousness. And should anyone think that Plato's view of science depended on the then rudimentary state of science, let her examine the constructivist theories in contemporary philosophy of science, which also minimize science's connection with the real world and also leave matter itself largely a blank. We might say that the potential of technology education, in the picture of it that we have been drawing, requires the context of a realist view of knowledge, a holistic psychology, a green ethic and a reorganized working life if it is to be fully realized. And each of these has to be fought for.

COMBINING THE USEFUL AND THE AGREEABLE

The role of the aesthetic in our lives is a further relevant issue. Our basic functions and needs are associated with various symbols, rituals, skills and art forms, and we may notice two different conceptions of this association.

One, the dualist conception, is of the aesthetic as *extra-functional ornamentation*: the primitive functions and needs are seen partly as 'occasions' for the ornamental exercise of liberal skills and arts, and partly as crude realities to be softened, socialized, civilized or even concealed by them. It seems that the traditional liberal is logically committed to a view like this. He can claim some support from ordinary language, for in calling something 'functional' – a table, a garment, a meal, etc. – we do often seem to be distinguishing sharply between this quality and aesthetic qualities.

On the other hand, we have in current architecture, say, an activity where good functioning is itself seen as an aesthetic ideal and, even, where the functionally superfluous may be viewed with artistic suspicion. This suggests another general conception, namely, one in which the symbols, rituals, skills and art forms are seen as *internal dimensions* of the need or the function. Instead of being extrinsic adornment, they are in some cases a natural part or extension of the expression of a basic need, and in other cases part of the satisfaction of the need. This implies broader accounts of the needs and functions themselves, from the vantage point of which the narrower accounts would then seem artificially abstract. 'Eating' would be a form of communing with the world and, often, with other people – rather than just an act of physical assimilation – and thankfulness might be an intrinsic element of the pleasure it gave. The desire to cherish and be cherished would be a part of sexual desire rather than something supervenient upon it. And so on. This conception, too, can claim support from ordinary language, for locutions like 'making love', 'making a home' or 'going out to dinner' suggest a view of activities as combining in *natural units* what the earlier conception divided. Doubtless, we need both kinds of conception at different times and for different contexts. But it remains that by ignoring the useful, the liberal tradition not only denied its own values what we earlier saw to be a perfectly appropriate field of operation, but – perhaps even more seriously – rendered itself unable to exploit the *healing and integrative* potential of its own values.[18]

CONCLUSION

We have been turning up a variety of values in making activities. Apart from 'ulterior' advantages, not all of which are to be disdained, these are:

- vital values connected with personal fulfilment and development and a sense of power over the environment;
- quasi-ethical values like workmanship and effectiveness;
- serious contemplative potential;
- intrumentality to basic individual and social needs;
- aesthetic and integrative power.

Perhaps we should also be clear as to what we have *not* been doing. We have not made thinking in general subordinate to making. So, we have not disputed the liberal view that the pursuit of knowledge without regard to technical pay-off can be worthwhile, and this not only because an untrammelled basic research can make a more powerful contribution to technology in the end. Again, we have not simply identified thinking and making. The immanent *teloi* of theory and production remain distinct. Knowledge and understanding, because of their essential receptive intentionality, cannot be *adequately* regarded as just particular kinds of 'product',[19] while from another point of view products are certainly more than just thoughts.[20] We have argued, indeed, that certain kinds of value are shared by thinking and making, but we have also referred to differences of register here and to some values, relating to basic human needs, as specific to technology. Since our concern was with technological subjects we have not considered the specific values of other curriculum areas. Were we to do so, we would again find the formula 'knowledge for its own sake' an obstruction – this time by its insensitivity to the differences among traditionally acknowledged liberal pursuits, the sciences and the humanities for instance.[21] We might sum up our position in two conclusions:

- a description of educational values that is *broad* enough to apply to the whole range of traditionally acknowledged subjects will be *found* to apply also to the technical subjects;
- a description of educational values that is *specific* enough in relation to the values of particular categories of subjects (the sciences, the arts, etc.) to guide our interpretation of a proper breadth, must be *made* to include the specific values of the technical subjects.

APPENDIX: BALANCING TECHNIQUE AND UNDERSTANDING

Educationally, it matters hugely that something is the fruit of the initiative, thought and labour of an individual or a small group, as opposed to just rolling off an assembly line. Understanding, in particular, is almost non-negotiable for education. But efficacy is also a value. So blending these is a major challenge for technical education. Its success in this, if experienced by a sufficiently large number of students, would, in turn, be the strongest possible incentive for pursuing the same ideal in the technical aspects of everyday life and in a reorganized industrial life.[22] Let us consider this challenge for technical education, while noting, at the same time, its wider curriculum application.

In an interesting passage[23] Simone Weil argued that there is one insuperable obstacle to a completely consummated marriage of theory and practice, thought and action. It is that the sequence of steps by which theoretical reflection must proceed does not coincide, unless accidentally, with the sequence of movements by which a practical task is methodically executed. The mind works on a problem by proceeding from the simpler to the more complex, from the clear to the obscure, but the order of a worker's movements are determined by what must be done first, whether simple or complex, as a causal condition of doing the next thing. Hence it is, she says, that we all experience that if in the middle of a practical task we are faced with something we do not understand, we have to stop working to think. More generally, unless the conception behind a task is very simple or the task itself requires only minimal attention, we cannot hold the conception in mind at the same time as we work. Rather than working directly from the conception, we work, as it were, from an abstract diagram that indicates a sequence of movements to be carried out – much as if we were following a magic rite. It is this ultimate distinctness of theory and making that makes possible the situation where one person thinks and another executes according to a conception that she need not herself grasp. Beyond that, it makes possible the assembly line and the computer, where mindlessness and efficiency are fantastically combined.

There is something right and something wrong about this account. What is wrong, I suggest, is its rather stereotyped view of the thinking process. Even in its purely theoretical engagements thinking is not as linear and predictable as this. But, more to the point, the account seems to miss out altogether on specifically technical intelligence and thinking. This is the intelligence and thinking that actually figures out what should be the next movement, or series of movements, in a technical task – and that may go on then to construct assembly lines to help routinize those movements, or automata and computers to mimic them. This figuring is likely to apply theoretical knowledge, often in its own thoughtfully eclectic way, and it may even switch in and out of actual theoretical thinking – bent, still, on a technical solution more than on any theoretical advance. At such times it may indeed down tools, fold arms and stand back from the task for a while – but even so it will remain spiritually connected with the task. At other times – as is equally obvious and equally essential to recall – this figuring proceeds with tools very much in hand, using them as exploratory probes, trying out alternative sequences, manipulating materials this way and that, searching for what works or works best – and at more sophisticated levels constructing full-blown prototypes. By omitting the essential problem-solving aspect of technology, Simone Weil contrives (though this was not her intention) to overstate the problem of the mental–manual divorce, even to make it seem insoluble.

What is right about Weil's account, however, is that successful technical thinking does indeed usher in the possibility of a more or less mindless execution of technical tasks and of separating execution and executioners from conception and conceivers with the social inequalities normally attendant upon that separation. But should we not immediately add that it also ushers in a different possibility, namely of using the solution achieved as a stepping stone to the solution of further, and often more complex, technical problems? Thus tools are embodied solutions to technical problems that we then use to solve other technical problems – first, problems of the everyday kind and, second, problems in the construction of more sophisticated tools in the upward spiral of technical advance.

Brute efficacity, otherwise known as 'productivity', is a central value in industrial life. In the *educational* context it is not altogether objectionable inasmuch as the purely routine performance of technical tasks can still have a perceived ethical significance in relation to the meeting of human needs and retain a communion of sorts with the natural world. What education could not tolerate, however, is a *systematic* divorce of efficacy from understanding. And there are perhaps three broad ways in which it can head this off. One, just alluded to, is by the use of achieved understanding to tackle further and more complex problems - as with progression in any other curriculum area. A second is to engage students in the intelligent maintenance and, very particularly, the repair of artefacts and tools. The third is by the deconstruction in class of artefacts, including the tools used by students, with a view to understanding how they work - this to be carried far enough, and to be repeated for a wide enough range of artefacts and tools, to leave students with a consolidated sense of themselves as masters rather than slaves of the technological world they are inheriting.

It is illuminating to notice that the challenge to balance efficient technique and understanding is not confined to technological education. Thus in aesthetic endeavour there is a broad distinction to be drawn, and an educational balance to be struck, between solving technical problems and achieving a manual technical proficiency, on the one hand, and using achieved skills to seek and to express an artistic feeling or vision, on the other hand. Nor is the issue confined to manual subjects. In the passage already alluded to, Simone Weil goes on acutely to observe that something very similar arises in mathematics, where there is a simple distinction between applying a method - of long division, say, or finding the square root - and understanding why the method works. In working out a difficult division sum it would scarcely be possible, and it is certainly not normal, to have the theory of division simultaneously present to mind. Rather, we might ponder over this theory after the event and think about each step in the sum until we saw why it was required, though in many more advanced mathematical operations the effort this involved could be enormous. This presence of technique in mathematics, as in technology, makes possible the benefits and the costs of the division of labour: the benefits to efficiency, the costs to holistic understanding and thought. And, of course, this has implications for science, considering the degree of its dependence on mathematics - to which we should then add considerations, first, of the contemporary extent of science's own division of labour and, second, of the excruciatingly sophisticated nature of the instruments and hardware on which science now relies.[24] Thus mathematics or science teachers might sometimes have to resist the seduction of magical techniques that pupils might readily learn to apply, but which they (and perhaps the teachers) could not understand - just as craft teachers may decide against the use of a sophisticated tool on the grounds that, in this context, it would be a kind of cheating.

In this appendix to our main argument we have identified the educational aim of keeping a constantly renewed balance and a fruitful complicity between efficient technique and understanding, and we have seen this as a challenge, first, for the technology teacher but, second, for teachers in some other curriculum areas as well.

NOTES

1. Report of National Curriculum Working Party on Design and Technology for Ages 5 to 16.
2. The other three general targets cover: generating a design proposal; planning and making; and evaluating. The last of these is also deliberative in part, for it involves the constant review of progress in relation to the other three targets. Again, there is much stress on the interplay between these targets and programmes (National Curriculum Council Consultation Report, Technology, November 1989; this report followed up and revised the Working Party Report referred to in note 1).

3.   Schwab (1964).
4.   Cotter (1992, Chapter 6).
5.   As I write, there is in fact quite a lot of official retreat from some provisions of the National Curriculum. But so far technology has escaped – and has indeed found itself promoted to the status of an 'extended core' subject.
6.   What follows is to a considerable extent a 'rethink' of a previously published paper (Walsh, 1978). Past philosophers of technical education, in their day voices in the wilderness but who can now be seriously consulted, include Marx, Dewey, Whitehead and Weil. Their views on the technical are situated in, and vary with, broad epistemological, metaphysical and ethical contexts: Marx's dialectical materialism, Dewey's version of American pragmatic empiricism, Weil's corrected Platonism, Whitehead's metaphysic that includes, *inter alia*, Platonic and pragmatic elements. What is striking, however, is the degree of shared feeling and intuition among them as to the significance of technology.
7.   Cited in Vasquez (1977, p. 20).
8.   See, for instance, Aquinas, *Summa contra Gentes*, Book III, Chapters 25 and 37.
9.   See 'Human personality', in Weil (1962).
10.   See Peters's essay, 'Ambiguities in liberal education and the problem of its content', in Peters (1977). My general approach in this chapter owes much to this important paper.
11.   As Peters does (Peters, 1977).
12.   As in the interesting, and philosophically sophisticated, cult book, *Zen and the Art of Motorcycle Maintenance* (Pirsig, 1974).
13.   Weil (1949).
14.   'Technical education and its relation to science and literature', first published 1917, reissued in Whitehead (1932).
15.   See, e.g., Whitehead (1932, pp. 70ff.).
16.   And why weren't these recognized as art forms by educationists? Why, indeed, were even 'non-useful' practices, like flower gardening, not given this status? Could it have been because of something as laughable as a prejudice against sweat and dirt?
17.   Dewey offers further historical reflections on the prejudice against technology. He relates it, first, to a separation by the Greeks of 'theory' from an actively conceived 'experience', and, second, to a different separation of a passively reconceived 'experience' from 'action' by classical empiricists in the seventeenth and eighteenth centuries (Dewey, 1916, Chapter 20).
18.   Dewey emphasizes the intellectual side of this integrative potential. ' "Intellectual" studies instead of being opposed to active pursuits represent an intellectualizing of practical pursuits' (Dewey, 1916, Chapter 20).
19.   Which would be the direct contrary of the classical thesis (see note 8 above) that production is justified ultimately by its contribution to the contemplation of truth.
20.   Thus our position is distinct from: (1) Dewey's, which, in the tradition of American pragmatism, did come close to denying the distinction between thought and action, science and technology; (2) that 'sociological scientism' which regards the sociological perspective on knowledge as a social construct as the *only* illuminating one; and (3) Habermasian critical theory, which, with its roots in both pragmatism and sociology, tends to discount the autonomy and disinterestedness of the sciences in particular – which he sees as orientated technically as opposed to contemplatively. (To the extent that modern science in fact lent itself to that reading, would it not be in danger of losing its soul? See note 24 below.)
21.   See Peters (1977, pp. 53–4).
22.   '[T]he occupations of the household, agriculture, and manufacturing as well as transportation and intercourse are instinct with applied science. . . . It is true that many of those who now engage in them are not aware of the intellectual content upon which their personal actions depend. But this fact only gives an added reason why schooling should use these pursuits so as to enable the coming generation to acquire a comprehension now too generally lacking, and thus enable persons to carry on their pursuits intelligently instead of blindly' (Dewey, 1916, p. 275).
     Whitehead, also writing 70 years ago, argued for the economic necessity of this: 'alike for masters and for men a technical or technological education, which is to have any chance of

satisfying the practical needs of the nation, must be conceived in a liberal spirit as a real intellectual enlightenment in regard to principles applied and services rendered. In such an education geometry and poetry are as essential as turning laths' (Whitehead, 1932, p. 70).

23. Weil (1958b, 1972 edition, pp. 91ff.).

24. To the extent that a mathematician's thought does not, perhaps cannot, catch up on the refinements of his technique, mathematics for him ceases to be a form of knowledge and becomes either a game or a tool, as would the science that depends on this mathematics. Efficacy (theoretical rather than technological) would take over from understanding as the main operative ideal. Simone Weil develops such thoughts into a critique of contemporary science. See the two audacious and erudite essays, 'Classical science and after' and 'Reflections on quantum theory', in Weil (1968).

Chapter 12

History and Piety

It is common to distinguish two principal motives for the study of history. The love of the past, or 'history for its own sake', is one. The other is the desire to understand the human present in the light of its past or, more fully, the desire to understand, assess and direct the human present – and thus shape the human future. Let us focus on the relationship between these two motives, an organic relationship as it will transpire. I propose that in this relationship the first kind of motive should be interpreted in its strongest sense and then be given priority over the second. Put provocatively, history should be approached primarily as an extension of ancestor-communing ('worship' may be down to anthropological over-excitement), while taking a wide view of who our ancestors are. This swims against the mainstream of recent philosophy in this area. Pragmatic theories of truth and value put the main stress on the more or less concealed 'function' of historical enquiry, the hidden needs it answers to and the undeclared interests that it promotes in the contemporary life of a community. I do not doubt that this kind of scrutiny can be illuminating – in reference to academic as well as more popular history. But I shall not accept that all historical interest and study must be motivated primarily in this self-regarding way, that, as the slogan would have it, all history is contemporary history. Nor, indeed, shall I accept that history is best approached in this way. On the other hand, I shall be as much at pains to distinguish my position from the purist view – popular among academic historians until quite recently – that history should be altogether divorced from contemporary causes and concerns.

THE MEANING OF LOVE OF THE PAST

One way in which 'love of the past' easily gets shunted into a subordinate position is by interpreting it as just intellectual curiosity about the past, a love of enquiry into the past more than a love of the past.[1] (The 'history' in 'history for its own sake' is here the study of the past rather than the past itself.) What lent itself to this interpretation was the rigid detachment advocated and practised in some academic circles, for if the historian is not to engage humanly and ethically with her subjects, what backward-looking motive is left but the enjoyment of the play of intelligence and imagination in reconstructing a piece of history? But the way is then clear for making 'love of the past' a mere auxiliary to contemporary relevance as a motive for study – if not for the individual historian at least for history as an institution and as a school subject. For we could not otherwise account for the *importance* we feel history to possess. If it were only, or mainly, a matter of curiosity and the enjoyment of puzzles then it would have the essentially idle character of a hobby like chess or the detective novel. Like them it might indeed contribute to the development of intellectual skills and agility, but this would not be by virtue of its being history specifically.

'History for its own sake' can be interpreted rather more substantially in terms of history being not just another means by which we may achieve our present ends, but something which expands our whole picture of the world and of human beings, and, therefore, of what ends are possible for us.[2] (The 'history' that is 'for its own sake' is still the *study* of history.) Actually, this risks seeing history still as a means, even if to the 'second-order' end of reconsidering our ends in life. More fundamentally, it raises the question of whether it is a *condition* of history opening up new ends for us that we approach the people of the past, not just as important learning resources, but as 'ends-in-themselves'. Is it a matter only of the objectivity that respects evidence and the limits of evidence, seeks to get the account right, and resists capture in advance by particular practical ends and interests in the present? Or is it a matter of a deeper objectivity that seeks also to 'do justice' to the past?

In fact, 'love of the human past' has a plainer yet more substantial sense. It can mean quite simply *brotherly and sisterly love directed to the human beings and the human worlds that are dead and gone*, or at any rate to some of them – piety in its old meaning. Now the 'history' that is valued for its own sake is the significant past itself.

Love of the dead is not necessarily the least bit necrophilic. Don't we have obligations to the human past which parallel those we have to the human present? Doesn't the past, too, engage our attention, respect, admiration, compassion, indignation, sense of justice and so forth? It is obvious that we do in fact adopt such attitudes to past figures, deeds, institutions and movements. When challenged as to their appropriateness in particular cases, we justify them by essentially the same considerations that we use with regard to our contemporary world. Of course the process of coming to the relevant factual judgements is, in significant ways, different in the two cases. With regard to the past it is in some ways easier (the historian can know what contemporaries did not know, can achieve a more rounded view, etc.), and in some ways more difficult (he has to think himself into the times he is studying, etc.). But once the judgements are in they spontaneously evoke or command the same range of feelings, values and attitudes in both cases. And what good reason could we have for blocking these when they relate to the past, unless it be the kind of reason that could also be relevant with regard to the present – that they are in this or that particular case inappropriate, hasty, partial, unjust and so forth? All this seems really very obvious. And it remains obvious even though the contemporary 'now' has, other things being equal, a dramatic and ethical edge over the historical 'then'.[3]

Yet explicit acknowledgements of this level of involvement with history are extremely hard to find. Consider, for example, the Final Report of the National Curriculum History Group. It suggests no fewer than nine purposes of school history: to help understand the present in the context of the past; to arouse interest in the past; to help to give pupils a sense of identity; to help to give pupils an understanding of their own cultural roots and shared inheritances; to contribute to pupils' knowledge and understanding of other countries and other cultures in the modern world; to train the mind by means of disciplined study; to introduce pupils to the distinctive methodology of historians; to enrich other areas of the curriculum; and to prepare pupils for adult life.[4] In this otherwise admirably inclusive list, only the second item, 'to arouse interest in the past', even gestures at 'piety'. Considering the obligations of such a group to consult the way historians actually work, we may safely assume that *pietas* is not a prominent part of the self-image of history as a working discipline.

No doubt, this too may be related to the general influence of positivism in the human sciences and the tendency we criticized in them to depersonalize the scientist–subject relationship. But we must consider a more particular objection to a 'human' involvement with the subjects of research when those subjects are dead and gone. This is that since we cannot *reciprocally* relate to the past and cannot shape and influence it, we cannot therefore take responsibility for it in any real sense. Let us comment in two stages. First, the obvious kernel of truth in it does not render love of the past inappropriate (and throw us back immediately upon 'relevance' and 'usefulness' as the mainsprings of historical enquiry). Many of our responses to present human beings and their ways do not require the setting of a reciprocal relationship, nor do they all seek a practical expression in actions performed in or around the person responded to. Admiration, for instance, can be anonymous, and is not immediately practical. But even in the case of responses like compassion or indignation that do carry a fairly immediate complement of appropriate actions, practical helplessness is frustrating without making the compassion or indignation itself inappropriate. The helpless victim of torture still has the right to her indignation. So does the helpless observer of it. So, too, will the future historian of it. Even non-reciprocal relationships can be 'personal', then, and helplessness would not of itself stop us relating to past people and events in very human ways.

In the second place, we are not *entirely* helpless with regard to the past. There are at least two sorts of thing we can undertake in its regard, each requiring an ethically creative and critical effort of reconstruction. The first is to set the record straight posthumously, to reinstate the stoned prophets and so on. Certainly this is far more difficult, and far less completely accomplished, than we like to think – except where time itself has already yielded the oppressed their revenge in the form of ultimate victory or emancipation. Much history is based on the depositions of murderers about their victims, if for no other reason because the conquerors tend to bury the cultural remains of their victims with their victims themselves. Simone Weil, my source for this reminder, wrote in 1939 that if the Nazis were to win the coming war the historians of two thousand years hence might still be lauding the 'Pax Germanica'.[5] Yet she thought it possible, and a sacred duty, to begin to reconstruct and vindicate civilizations like the Trojan, Carthaginian, Celtic, Inca and American Indian – by a huge effort of attention and imagination with regard to such scraps of them as have survived – and herself contributed to such an effort with regard to the eleventh-century civilization of Languedoc.[6]

We can also allow the light of the past to inform the way we live our lives. This is much more than 'conserving the legacy of the past', there being quick distinctions to remind ourselves of between the mummification and the use of the past and between tradition as a dead weight and tradition as a source of strength and inspiration.[7] We should also distinguish the more general light that history is admitted, perhaps even by academic historians, to cast on the human predicament (e.g. the tendency for victorious might to assume the mantle of right or the frequency with which men propose, but chance, mistake and God dispose) from the more *specific* lessons and inspirations that we can take from particular bits of history, such as a greater devotion to democratic institutions, scientific freedom, the cause of feminism, a particular trade union, a church, etc. Now when we consciously and critically take aboard some specific lesson from a part of history, when our awareness and devotion relating to some cause or value are intensified by a study of the labour, pain and hope that have gone into it, then another mode of 'piety' is at work. We are, and we see ourselves to be, in fraternal and sororal cooperation with some individuals and groups of the past – and in opposition to others.

Someone will insist that 'partnership' with the past remains a fiction in the last analysis, since, for all our creative and critical concern for it and all our efforts to live by the best of it, we still cannot change a jot of it. But that objection overlooks something: though nothing can now change it, the past would have been very different if its individuals and peoples had never worked with an eye to *a future beyond themselves*, never participated in designs which they knew would not be realized in their lifetimes in the faith that others would carry the venture forward, and never been sustained in affection or restrained in power by the reflection that history would judge them (it is even said that we owed Ronald Reagan's military 'restraint' to his wife's desire that he be remembered as a peacemaker).[8] 'Partnership with the past' must have precisely the same validity, indeed, as 'partnership with the future'. These two are aspects of the same ongoing process, so that 'why worry about the past since we can do nothing for it?' is from the same cynical stable as 'what has posterity ever done for me?'

THE PRIMACY OF LOVE OF THE PAST

So far we have been working on the substantial sense and validity of 'love of the human past'. Let us turn now to its primacy in relation to the other main motive for doing history. The idea to ponder here is that only those who love the past for itself can be trusted to mediate it to the present, to draw the *right* lessons from it and indicate its *proper* relevance – and they are precisely those who will not regard such lessons and relevance as the *ground* motive of their concern with the past.

In effect, this idea draws an analogy from our relationships in the present. We distinguish personal relationships from those that are simply cooperative or contractual. In authentic friendship, love and even colleagueship we value the other for himself or herself. The common ventures, exchanges of benefits and lessons learnt are 'spin-off', and they have a value as expressions, symbols and nourishments of the relationship as well as their own utility. Note, however, that their utility is not generally less significant for being indirect. Indeed, the paradox is that there are highly important kinds of 'pay-off' – for instance, in the area of self-knowledge and self-valuation – that can *only* be acquired in relationships in which they are not the primary focus of attention. If someone conducts a personal relationship for the primary purpose of learning from it, perhaps to gain 'experience' in such relationships, we say he is 'using' the other person – but, more to the point, we suspect that such a relationship defeats its own purpose and yields a lower dividend in terms of learning and experience. Does a similar logic obtain in historical study?

Bearing in mind what we have said about the range of our responses and concerns towards the past and the measure of reciprocity, even, between past and present, it seems reasonable to claim that we have relationships with historical individuals that belong more to the personal than the useful category, and that we also have relationships of a quasi-personal kind with whole societies, cultures, institutions and movements of the past (as of the present). It would follow that among the benefits and lessons which the past has for us we may expect some important ones to be ours only if we both enter into such quasi-personal relationships with it and are authentic about this, i.e. do not have the benefits and lessons as our direct and primary object. And surely this is in fact so. No doubt we can, without thus involving ourselves, 'strip mine' the past quite effectively for many of its deposits. We have the beginnings of an idea in philosophy, for instance, and we search the works of past thinkers on the subject for helpful developments of it. We can also keep this 'using' within moral bounds by observing the minimal conventions of respect, acknowledging our sources, avoiding misrepresentation and so on. But we could not mine in this way more precious things that the past can offer us: some steady insight into human heads and hearts, an abiding sense of the fragility of a certain value, a new vitality in some important project – in general, the contribution of history to wisdom and care. For that an altogether more personal commitment seems necessary.

PRE-CRITICAL AND CRITICAL HISTORY

It will be objected that this position returns history to its 'pre-critical' phase since 'piety' is exactly what was characteristic of pre-critical history. Now I doubt if there is any wholly agreed account of the distinction between critical and pre-critical history. But let us work with the following fairly typical set of contrasts. Pre-critical history is (a) ethnocentric, (b) practical and (c) ethical; whereas critical history is (a) universal, (b) explanatory and (c) non-judgemental, even value-free.[9] Considering these three contrasts in turn in relation to our support for 'piety' will also help us to clarify that notion further (and, we might add, rescue it more completely from the Right).

(a) Pre-critical history is largely confined, it is said, to the history of one's own community or society, and where it reaches out to other societies it considers them only in their relevance to one's own. Critical history is universal in its intended scope, and when it addresses itself to other societies it endeavours to do so on their own terms. It may even prefer to work on societies and times that are particularly remote from the historian's own.

This contrast forces us to a vital clarification: there is no need to conceive piety as a duty only to one's own forebears – that would be no more than moral childishness. In fact, the logic of piety replicates the logic of charity. There is an important sense in which each is to be universal, but as 'openness' to all rather than (impossible) realization. On the other hand, piety and charity 'begin at home', both in the sense that they must first be learnt there, and in the sense that unless one goes on loving one's own that is near at hand one's protestations regarding what is distant and not one's own become suspect. In addition to kinship, there are certain other grounds on which actual charity becomes obligatory or specially desirable, and to each of them also there is an analogue for piety. In both there are the special claims upon us of the afflicted and oppressed, of our own urgent needs – in particular as viewed morally and spiritually, of those we have already engaged and become friendly with, and of those that circumstances have just now put squarely in our way. Thus an historian or a student might, in piety, work on a period or society because it had been neglected by other historians – especially if its people had been oppressed and destroyed, or because it possessed virtues that she believed she and her times stood in special need of, or because she was an authority on it and therefore responsible for it, or because she felt a spontaneous affinity with it, or because a school or university syllabus is forcing it on her. Piety, then, does not require a return to the jingoism of pre-critical history. On the other hand, neither does it accord with the flat and *a priori* neutrality of the first proposed canon of critical history. For it does have criteria for judging and assigning priorities, though ones that are broad and generous.

(b) Pre-critical history, like the folk memory from which it evolves, has a *practical* function, namely to promote the society's sense of its own identity and its devotion to its own survival and development. It tells the stories of the society's existing institutions (or perhaps of revolutionary ones being struggled for), contrasts them favourably with those of other societies, refutes the 'calumnies' of neighbours regarding them, and legitimates the power structure embodied in them. Its effectiveness for these ends sometimes requires of it a consummate artistry. Critical history, however, is (or was) said to have no practical function, and to regard political and apologetic aims as fatal to the achievement of its task. That task is simply to discover what was really going forward at a particular place and time, and why, and to set this forth in a significant narrative, preferably in plain prose. So, its explanatory drive is directed not at the present but at the past itself, and it proceeds by a greater and greater concentration on the detail of the past, and an ever more thorough discarding of the historian's contemporary reflexes and presuppositions in favour of an imaginative assumption of those of the times he is studying.[10]

How does piety stand in relation to this purported contrast? Three points may be made. First, and again like charity, piety has critical as well as appreciative modes: it may express itself very well, for instance, in a bitter condemnation of things done by one's country. Second, this account of pre-critical history generalizes unjustly. Folk history has been known to beat its breast rather than justify itself at all costs, to acknowledge some of the people's past crimes rather than glorify them. The Old Testament occasionally achieved this moral objectivity, and the *Iliad*'s sorrowful evocation of the tyranny of war over both victor and vanquished is a remarkable example of it.[11] Third, the polarization in the stated contrast between practical relevance on the one hand and the past for its own sake on the other hand is extreme. Our argument has been that these are organically related: if (and only if) the past is explored for its own sake, its more profound relevance to the present will be realized. (Similarly, the 'functional' analysis of ancestor-communion is disrespectfully reductionist. When I meditate at the graves of my parents and more remote forebears my direct concern is to remember and honour them. I may come away with a stronger sense of my roots and identity or with a new inspiration for some project. But this would be a spin-off from the self-transcending movement of piety.)

(c) Finally, it is said, pre-critical history is *ethical*. As well as narrating, it apportions praise and blame. It is a tribunal before which people and deeds of the past pass in review to be condemned, or excused, or commended. This follows on from its practical function and, so, its ethical criteria tend to be chosen in the interests of contemporary survival and development. But the critical historian professes to eschew ethical judgement and he is severe on those historians who indulge in it. Thus Butterfield condemned Lord Acton and those he called generally 'Whig historians' in a classic essay. In part this was for the arrogance implicit in their wholesale judgements of others. But in addition Butterfield, and critical historians generally, believed that the intrusion of moral judgement in historical enquiry, like the intrusion of political and apologetic purposes of which it was generally an aspect, led to a loss of objectivity in the work: 'It is not clear that moral indignation is not a dispersion of one's energies to the great confusion of one's judgement.'[12] It tended, if not quite to a falsification of the historical details, at any rate to premature and artificial synopses of broad historical developments, based on a simplistic division of historical agents and ideas into 'good' and 'bad', 'progressive' and 'reactionary', or – in other hands – 'loyal' and 'subversive'. This issue seems the most critical for our recommendation of piety.

We shall start with some preliminary points. First, piety, yet again like charity, is not all ethical encounter. It is also fascination with the past, enjoyment of it, aesthetic delight at it, polite tolerance of occasional boredom with it, and so on. (This observation lines up with our placing of ethical values generally inside the much larger whole of love of the world in Chapter 8.) Second, insofar as it is ethical, piety is essentially independent both of an *a priori* belief in historical progress (such as was held by the 'Whig' historians) and of the romanticization of the past. It implies no case, not even a *prima facie* one, for placing the present (and its historians) on a moral eminence in relation to the past – or the reverse. In an ethical encounter with the past that was properly open and critical the *a priori* probability values should be equal of the historian and the present being put in question, and of the past to be studied being put in question. This is indeed to expect impartiality from the historian, but an impartiality that differs from, and strikes deeper than, ethical neutrality. Third, the refusal of an ethical encounter with the past is a denial of spontaneous expectations, a methodical exclusion of a range of responses that naturally seem appropriate. As such it is it that requires justification. The one offered is that these responses impede objectivity. Now it is obvious that certain kinds of moral fervour would distort an historical account. But the claim that moral interest *necessarily* distorts depends on the assumption that a self-critical moral objectivity is an impossible, perhaps incoherent, ideal. If it is only very difficult then one could, perhaps, convict academic history of a failure of nerve: history is made easier at the price of making it less significant.

It might be replied that, at any rate in an age of moral pluralism like ours, history as a cooperative venture requires a *methodological* exclusion of value judgements. And, after all, if professional historians can only get the bald narrative together the readers or audience can still, if they wish, use it towards their own personal ethical encounters with the past. Indeed, we might conceive of a systematic comparative ethics (to be called 'dialectics' perhaps), distinct from history proper but for which history would provide most of the data.[13] There is something in these suggestions. In pluralist societies history writing will be better for taking account of the pluralism of contemporary values, laying special emphasis on the values that are shared, being explicit about relevant more 'personal' values, and so forth – in other words, for adopting the manners and procedures of everyday ethical discourse in this kind of society. Again, there is surely some useful distinction to be drawn between the actual conduct of historical enquiry, to which the (rough) Weberian adage 'value-relevant but value-free' would apply, and our wider and more general relationship with the fruits of that enquiry. In effect, this is to apply to this area the earlier distinction between what we called 'scientific' and 'utopian' discourses, and there may also be something to be said for the idea of a systematic version of the utopian discourse in this context. But these concessions affect only the formulation of the main point. We simply say, now, that a proper historical involvement and a proper historical education have to include *both* the scientific and the normative.

THE NON-NEUTRALITY OF PERSPECTIVE

Historical involvement and historical education should include a sense of the correlativity, as well as the distinctiveness, of these discourses. For the question raised by these exchanges is of the very *possibility* of a complete ethical neutrality in an historical narrative retaining at least some human significance. (Thus we have an opportunity, right at the end of this book, to look again at the scientific–utopian link, this time in one specific context.)

This is the moment to acknowledge that the account of critical history we have been working with is one that would have appealed more a generation ago. Today's historian is more likely to be sceptical about the possibility of value-free history. In particular, the overall organization or *perspective* of a work is now commonly seen as influenced (at least) by factors which the historian has brought to her enquiry from outside history. Perspectives can differ without conflicting, as would the histories of the science and the art of the same period, or they may conflict, as would socialist and non-socialist accounts of the industrial revolution. The sheer bulk and diversity of the materials of history guarantee an endless supply of perspectives in the first sense. Now even this point presents some difficulty for the old-style critical faith that, in Bury's words, 'a complete assemblage of the smallest facts of human history will tell in the end'.[14] It does not seem reconcilable with the atomism of that ideal, suggesting, rather, that 'facts' are only intelligible, and only noticed, in some degree of relationship to perspectives formed or being formed. But the difficulty is clearer in conflicts of perspective. Here the governing differences (that are not, or not in all respects, to be resolved by further historical research and discovery) are not just matters of the historian's personal interests, but of her metaphysical and moral beliefs. The crucial point is that these beliefs and attitudes participate *inevitably* in the shaping of an historical enquiry.

We may broadly distinguish two respects in which they do. First the historian's *views of what is possible*, whether in nature as it impinges on people or for human nature itself, will be more or less remote operators of the interpretation she puts on historical data. They inevitably affect her attitude to testimonies and other sources, limit the hypotheses she is prepared to entertain, and so on. One may say that if these views are right it is perfectly proper that they should do these things. But the question of their rightness is not an historical question, not at any rate an exclusively historical question. The point is at least as old as Hume's reflections on the historian's attitude to miracles.[15] One should be careful, however, not to overstate it. There is no good reason for assuming that historical study itself makes *no* contribution to our views on what is possible. On the contrary, this might well be thought one of its more important values. But though the historical evidence may suggest some reappraisal of our views of the possible, it will not by itself *determine* them.

Second, there is the inevitable influence of the historian's broad moral outlook – that is, of her *view of what is humanly important*. We can see this through a distinction between the *intrinsic* and the *instrumental* importance of an historical event. Instrumentally, an event's importance is measured by the extent of its causal influence on other events (the loss of a horseshoe nail may bring the kingdom down). Intrinsically, its importance is independent of anything that happens afterwards. If one claimed that the French Revolution was the most important event in modern history, one might well have both kinds of importance in mind. Again, if history has shifted its focus from the doings of kings and queens to the common man, it is likely that this reflects both a post-Marx perception of economic and associated social movements as more *influential* than the actions of monarchs, and our *ethical* beliefs about the rights of people and the value of democracy. So, history may be structured by moral values even if it eschews overt moral judgement.[16] But we can surely go further and claim that it must be so structured. For instrumental importance must itself depend on intrinsic importance. Every event has, perhaps, an infinitude of ripples. So the *significance*, as well as the quantity, of actual consequences must be involved in judging instrumental importance, and that means that intrinsic importance, and the broader kind of value, are *always* involved in historical selection and construction.[17]

We have found reason to doubt some standard contrasts between pre-critical and critical history. In the end it may be that the only real differences between them are that a properly conceived critical history is more concerned constantly to expand the story of the past, more concerned with getting the story right, and is methodologically better equipped to achieve that expansion and that fidelity. And those differences, though this is not how it is usually put, could themselves be conceived as developments in piety, expressions of a greater piety!

NOTES

1. An influential and well-known work that does this is W. H. Walsh (1967).
2. See my colleague Peter Lee (1991, pp. 42–3).
3. Note that we are not here addressing the question of the relative importance of (and the relationship between) solidarity with the past and solidarity with the present. That is certainly a distinct question.
4. National Curriculum History Working Report 1990, paragraph 1.7.
5. 'The Great Beast. Some reflections on the origins of Hitlerism', in Weil (1962).
6. 'A medieval epic poem' and 'The Romanesque Renaissance', in Weil (1962).
7. See Nietzsche's classic essay on *The Use and Abuse of History*.
8. I believe I have borrowed some of these purple phrases from Lonergan's works, but I cannot trace the reference.
9. These points of contrast are borrowed from Lonergan (1972, pp. 185ff.). Chapters 6–10 of this distinguished theological study offer an extremely useful survey and analysis of issues relating to the study of history. Note that theology, because of the combination of historical with philosophical and experiential claims that an historical religion involves, has been to the forefront in considering these matters.

10. Lonergan (1972).
11. See Simone Weil's brilliant essay, 'The Iliad, a poem of force', in Weil (1958a).
12. Butterfield (1950).
13. As Lonergan (1972) recommends, in this, I think, echoing Schliermacher in the nineteenth century.
14. Bury, 'The science of history', reprinted in Bury (1927).
15. 'But suppose, that all the historians who treat of England, should agree, that, on the first of January 1600, Queen Elizabeth died, that both before and after her death she was seen by her physicians and the whole court, as is usual with persons of her rank; that her successor was acknowledged and proclaimed by the parliament; and that, after being interred a month, she again appeared, resumed the throne, and governed England for three years: I must confess that I should be surprised at the concurrence of so many odd circumstances, but should not have the least inclination to believe so miraculous an event' (*Essay Concerning Human Understanding*). The Christian apologist will see this as bringing out the importance of *context*: in Christ's case, his religious mission and his life as a whole. Note that this observation would itself be historical, but not exclusively so.
16. I have borrowed both this distinction and these examples from W. H. Walsh (1967, Appendix A, 'The limits of scientific history').
17. This is just to apply to history what we have seen Weber (1949, p. 76) say of cultural sciences in general. See pp. 65–6 above.

Bibliography

Apple, M. (1982) *Education and Power*. London: Routledge & Kegan Paul.

Aquinas, St Thomas: *Summa Theologica*; *Summa contra Gentes*; *In Libro Boetii de Trinitatis Expositio*.

Aristotle: *Ethics*; *Posterior Analytic*.

Ball, S. (1990) *Markets, Morality and Equality in Education*. Hillcole Group paper no. 5. London: Tufnell Press.

Barnes, D. (1976) *From Communication to Curriculum*. Harmondsworth: Penguin.

Bereiter, C. (1973) *Must We Educate?* Englewood Cliffs, NJ: Prentice-Hall.

Bernstein, B. (1971) *Class, Codes and Control*, Vol. 1. London: Routledge & Kegan Paul.

Bernstein, R. (1983) *Beyond Objectivism and Relativism*. Oxford: Blackwell.

Bloom, B. *et al.* (1956) *Taxonomy of Educational Objectives: The Classification of Educational Goals, Handbook I - Cognitive Domain*. New York: David McKay.

Bonnett, M. (1983) 'Education in a destitute time', *Journal of Philosophy of Education* 17(1), 21–33.

Bosanquet, N. (1983) *After the New Right*. London: Heinemann.

Bury, J. B. (1927) *Selected Essays*.

Butterfield, H. (1950) *The Whig Interpretation of History*. London: Bell.

Care, N. S. (1973) 'On fixing social concepts', *Ethics* **84**, 10–21.

Carr, W. and Kemmis, S. (1986) *Becoming Critical: Education, Knowledge and Action Research*. Lewes: Falmer Press.

Chitty, C. (1989) *Towards a New Education System: The Victory of the New Right?* Lewes: Falmer Press.

Clarke, D. R. (1984) 'The role of the videodisc in education and training', *Media in Education and Development*, December, 190–2.

Cotter, R. (1992) 'TVEI in a London borough: a vocational initiative in mainstream secondary education', PhD thesis, University of London.

Crittenden, B. (1982) *Cultural Pluralism and Common Curriculum*. Melbourne: Melbourne University Press.

Cronbach, L. *et al.* (1980) *Toward Reform of Program Evaluation: Aims, Methods and Institutional Arrangements*. San Francisco: Jossey-Bass.

DES (1989) *English for Ages 5 to 16* (The Cox Report). London: HMSO.

DES (1989) *Design and Technology for Ages 5 to 16*. London: HMSO.

DES (1990) *History for Ages 5 to 16*. London: HMSO.

Darling, J. (1978) 'Progressive, traditional and radical: a re-alignment', *Journal of Philosophy of Education* 12, 157–66.

de Castell, S. (1981) 'Literacy and communicative competence', paper read to the Annual Conference of the Philosophy of Education Society of Great Britain.

Dearden, R.F. (1981) 'Balance and coherence', *Cambridge Journal of Education* 11(2), 107–18.

Descartes, R. (1637) *Discourse on Method*.

Dewey, J. (1910) *How We Think*. Boston: D.C. Heath (revised 1933).

Dewey, J. (1916) *Democracy and Education*. Toronto: Macmillan.

Dewey, J. (1938) *Experience and Education*. New York: Collier-Macmillan.

Dewey, J. (1946) *Problems of Men*. Republished in 1958 as *Philosophy of Education*. Totowa, NJ: Littlefield, Adams.

Donaldson, M. (1978) *Children's Minds*. London: Fontana.

Dunlop, F. (1984) *The Education of Feeling and Emotion*. London: George Allen & Unwin.

Eisner, E. (1984) *The Educational Imagination*. New York: Macmillan.

Elliott, J. (1975) 'Objectivity, ideology and teacher participation in educational research', Mimeo, University of East Anglia.

Elliott, J. (1980) 'Implications of classroom research for professional development', in J. Megarry and E. Hoyle (eds), *Professional Development of Teachers: World Year Book of Education*. London: Kogan Page.

Elliott, J. (1985) 'Educational action-research', in J. Nisbet (ed.), *Research, Policy and Practice: World Yearbook of Education 1985*. London: Kogan Page.

Elliott, J. (1988a) 'Teacher evaluation and training as a moral science', in M.L. Holly and C. McLoughlin (eds), *Perspectives on Teacher Professional Development*. Lewes: Falmer.

Elliott, J. (1988b) 'The state v education: the challenge for teachers', in H. Simons (ed.), *The National Curriculum*. Kendal: British Educational Research Association.

Elliott, J. (1989) 'Educational theory and the professional learning of teachers: an overview', *Cambridge Journal of Education* 19(1), 81–101.

Elliott, J. (1991) 'A model of professionalism and its implications for teacher education', *British Educational Research Journal* 17(4), 309–18.

Elliott, R.K. (1974) 'Education, love of one's subject, and the love of truth', *Proceedings of the Philosophy of Education Society of Great Britain* 8(1), 135–53.

Elliott, R.K. (1975) 'Education and human being', in S.C. Brown (ed.), *Philosophers Discuss Education*. London: Macmillan.

Elliott, R.K. (1977) 'Education and justification', *Proceedings of the Philosophy of Education Society of Great Britain* 11, 7–27.

Elliott, R.K. (1982) 'Objectivity and education', *Journal of Philosophy of Education* 16(1), 49–62.

Emmet, D. and MacIntyre, A. (1970) *Sociological Theory and Philosophical Analysis*. London: Macmillan.

Evers, C. and Walker, J. (1983) 'Knowledge, partitioned sets and extensionality', *Journal of the Philosophy of Education* 17, 155–70.

Evers, C. and Walker, J. (1984) 'Epistemology, semantics and educational theory', Occasional Paper no. 16, Sydney University.

Foucault, M. (1975) *Discipline and Punish*. Harmondsworth: Penguin (trans. 1977).

Freire, P. (1970) *Cultural Action for Freedom*. Harmondsworth: Penguin.

Freire, P. (1972) *Pedagogy of the Oppressed*. Harmondsworth: Penguin.

Gadamer, H.G. (1975) *Truth and Method*. London: Sheed & Ward.

Gaden, G. (1983) 'The case for specialisation', *Irish Educational Studies* 3(1), 47–59.

Gallie, W.B. (1955/6) 'Essentially contested concepts', *Proceedings of the Aristotelian Society* 56, 167–98.

Gallie, W.B. (1964) *Philosophy and Historical Understanding*. London: Chatto & Windus.

Geach, P.J. (1956) 'Good and evil', *Analysis* 17, 33–42.

Gellner, E. (1967) 'The concept of a story', *Ratio* 9, 49–66.

Giddens, A. (1976) *The New Rules of Sociological Method*. London: Hutchinson.

Giddens, A. (1982) *Sociology. A Brief but Critical Introduction*. London: Macmillan.

Giroux, H. (1983) *Theory and Resistance in Education: A Pedagogy for the Opposition*. London: Heinemann.

Giroux, H. (1986) 'Politics of student voice', *Interchange* 17(1), 48–69.

Golby, M. *et al.* (eds) (1975) *Curriculum Design*. London: Croom Helm.

Goody, J. and Watt, I. (1968) 'The consequences of literacy', in J. Goody (ed.), *Literacy in Traditional Societies*. Cambridge: Cambridge University Press.

Greenfield, P. (1972) 'Oral or written language: the consequences for cognitive development in Africa, US and England', *Language and Speech* 15, 169–78.

Habermas, J. (1968) *Knowledge and Human Interests*. Boston: Beacon Press/London: Heinemann (trans. 1971/72).

Habermas, J. (1972) 'Towards a theory of communicative competence', in H. P. Dreitzel (ed.), *Recent Sociology*, no. 2. New York: Macmillan.

Hamilton, D. *et al.* (1977) *Beyond the Numbers Game*. London: Macmillan.

Hargreaves, D. (1982) *The Challenge for the Comprehensive School*. London: Routledge & Kegan Paul.

Hart, H. L. A. (1961) *The Concept of Law*. Oxford: Oxford University Press.

Havelock, E. (1973) 'Prologue to Greek literacy', in *Lectures in Memory of Louise Tatt Semple, second series 1966–71*. Oklahoma City: University of Oklahoma Press for the University of Cincinnati Press.

HMI (DES) (1985) *Curriculum Matters 2: The Curriculum from 5 to 16*. London: HMSO.

Hirst, P. (1966) 'Educational theory' in J. Tibble (ed.), *The Study of Education*. London: Routledge & Kegan Paul.

Hirst, P. (1974) *Knowledge and the Curriculum*. London: Routledge & Kegan Paul.

Hirst, P. (1979) 'Human movement, knowledge and education', *Journal of the Philosophy of Education* 13, 101–8.

Hirst, P. (1983) 'Educational theory', in P. Hirst (ed.), *Educational Theory and Its Foundation Disciplines*. London: Routledge & Kegan Paul.

Hirst, P. and Peters, R. S. (1970) *The Logic of Education*. London: Routledge & Kegan Paul.

Hollis, M. (1982) 'Education as a positional good', *Journal of the Philosophy of Education* 16(2), 235–44.

Hollis, M. and Lukes, S. (1982) *Rationality and Relativism*. Oxford: Blackwell.

Holt, J. (1976) *Instead of Education*. Harmondsworth: Penguin.

House, E. (1977) *The Logic of Evaluative Argument*. Los Angeles: Center for the Study of Evaluation, University of California, Los Angeles.

House, E. (1980) *Evaluating with Validity*. Beverly Hills, CA: Sage.

Hume, D. (1748) *Essay Concerning Human Understanding*.

Illich, I. (1971) *Deschooling Society*. Harmondsworth: Penguin.

Jonathan, R. (1985) 'Education, philosophy of education and context', *Journal of Philosophy of Education* 19(1), 13–25.

Kant, I. (1781) *Critique of Pure Reason*.

Kant, I. (1785) *Groundwork of the Metaphysic of Morals*.

Kierkegaard, S. (1843) *Either/Or*.

Kierkegaard, S. (1844) *Philosophical Fragments*.

Kripke, S. (1972) *Naming and Necessity*. Oxford: Blackwell.

Kuhn, T. (1962) *The Structure of Scientific Revolutions*. Chicago: University of Chicago Press (enlarged 1970).

Lakatos A. and Musgrave, P. (1970) *Criticism and the Growth of Knowledge*. Cambridge: Cambridge University Press.

Lawton, D. (1973) *Social Change, Educational Theory and Curriculum Planning*. London: Hodder & Stoughton.

Lawton, D. (1975) *Class, Culture and the Curriculum*. London: Routledge & Kegan Paul.

Lawton, D. (1980) 'Common curriculum or core curriculum', *Westminster Studies in Education* 3, 5–10.

Lawton, D. (1983) *Curriculum Studies and Educational Planning*. London: Hodder & Stoughton.

Lawton, D. (1989) *Education, Culture and the National Curriculum*. London: Hodder & Stoughton.

Lee, P. J. (1984) 'Why learn history', in A. K. Dickinson, P. J. Lee and P. J. Rogers (eds), *Learning History*. London: Heinemann Educational Books.

Lee, P. J. (1991) 'Historical knowledge and the National Curriculum', in R. Aldrich (ed.), *History in the National Curriculum*. The Bedford Way Series, Institute of Education, University of London.

Lessnoff, M. (1974) *The Structure of Social Science*. London: Allen & Unwin.

Levit, M. (ed.) (1971) *Curriculum*. Champaign-Urbana: University of Illinois Press.

Lewin, K. (1952) *Field Theory in Social Science: Selected Theoretical Papers* (ed. D. Cartwright). London: Tavistock Publications.

Lonergan, SJ, B. (1957) *Insight: A Study of Human Understanding*. London: Longman.

Lonergan, SJ, B. (1972) *Method in Theology*. London: Darton, Longman & Todd.

McCarthy, T. (1978) *The Critical Theory of Jurgen Habermas* Cambridge: Polity Press.

MacDonald, B. (1974) 'Evaluation and the control of education', reprinted in D. Tawney (ed.) (1976) *Curriculum Evaluation Today: Trends and Implications*. London: Macmillan.

MacDonald, B. (1977) 'The portrayal of persons as evaluation data', in N. Norris (ed.), *Safari Theory in Practice. Papers Two*. Occasional publications no. 4, CARE, University of East Anglia.

MacIntyre, A. (1973) 'The essential contestability of some social concepts', *Ethics* **84**, 1–9.

MacIntyre, A. (1981) *After Virtue: A Study in Moral Theory*. London: Duckworth.

MacIntyre, A. (1990) *Three Rival Versions of Moral Enquiry*. London: Duckworth.

Maritain, J. (1943) *Education at the Crossroads*. New Haven, CT: Yale University Press.

Mercer, N. (ed.) (1988) *Language and Literacy from an Educational Perspective*, two volumes. Milton Keynes: Open University Press.

Midgley, M. (1979) *Beast and Man*. London: Methuen.

Moy, B. and Raleigh, M. (1988) 'Comprehension: bringing it back alive'. In N. Mercer (ed.), *Language and Literacy from an Educational Perspective*, volume 2, *In Schools*. Milton Keynes: Open University Press.

Myrdal, G. (1970) *Objectivity in Social Research*. London: Duckworth.

Naish, M. (1984) 'Education and essential contestability revisited', *Journal of Philosophy of Education* **18**, 141–53.

Nietzsche, F. W. (1949) *The Use and Abuse of History*. The Library of Liberal Arts. Indianapolis: Bobbs-Merrill. (First published 1874.)

Oakeshott, M. (1962) *Rationalism in Politics and Other Essays*. London: Methuen.

O'Hear, A. (1981) *Education, Society and Human Nature*. London: Routledge & Kegan Paul.

Olson, D. R. (1977) 'From utterance to text: the bias of language in speech and writing', *Harvard Educational Review* 13, 257–81.

Peters, R. S. (1966) *Ethics and Education*. London: George Allen & Unwin.

Peters, R. S. (1973) 'The justification of education', in R. S. Peters (ed.), *The Philosophy of Education*. London: Oxford University Press.

Peters, R. S. (1974) *Psychology and Ethical Development*. London: George Allen & Unwin.

Peters, R. S. (1977a) 'Education and justification: a reply to R. K. Elliott', *Proceedings of the Philosophy of Education Society of Great Britain* **11**, 28–38.

Peters, R. S. (1977b) *Education and the Education of Teachers*. London: Routledge & Kegan Paul.

Peters, R. S. (1981) *Essays on Educators*. London: George Allen & Unwin.

Phenix, P. (1964) *Realms of Meaning*. New York: McGraw-Hill.

Pirsig, R. (1974) *Zen and the Art of Motorcycle Maintenance*. London: Bodley Head.

Plato: *Meno*; *Gorgias*.

Polanyi, M. (1958) *Personal Knowledge*. London: Routledge & Kegan Paul.

Popper, K. (1945) *The Open Society and Its Enemies*. London: Routledge & Kegan Paul (revised 1966).

Popper, K. (1959) *The Logic of Scientific Discovery*. London: Hutchinson (revised 1968).

Popper, K. (1963) *Conjectures and Refutations*. London: Routledge & Kegan Paul (revised 1972).

Popper, K. (1972) *Objective Knowledge*. London: Oxford University Press.

Pring, R. (1976) *Knowledge and Schooling*. London: Open Books.

Pring, R. (1987) 'Vocational education: a philosophical appraisal', in P. Preece (ed.), *Philosophy and Education: Perspectives 28*. School of Education, University of Exeter.

Putnam, H. (1981) *Reason, Truth and History*. Cambridge: Cambridge University Press.

Quicke, J. (1988) 'The "New Right" and education', *British Journal of Educational Studies* **34**(1), 5-19.

Quine, W. (1953) *From a Logical Point of View*. Cambridge, MA: Harvard University Press.

Rahner, K. (1971) 'Ideas for a theology of childhood', in K. Rahner (ed.), *Theological Investigations*, Vol. 8. London: Darton, Longman & Todd.

Rajchman, J. and West, C. (eds) (1985) *Post-analytic Philosophy*. New York: University Presses of Columbia and Princeton.

Reid, L. A. (1962) *Philosophy and Education*. London: Heinemann.

Rose, N. (1985) *The Psychological Complex*. London: Routledge & Kegan Paul.

Sartre, J. P. (1943) *Being and Nothingness*. London: Methuen (trans. 1957).

Scheffler, I. (1967) *Science and Subjectivity*. Indianapolis: Bobbs-Merrill.

Schon, D. (1983) *The Reflective Practitioner: How Professionals Think in Action*. London: Temple Smith.

Schwab, J. (1964) 'Structure of the disciplines: meanings and significances', in G. Ford and L. Pugno (ed.), *The Structure of Knowledge and the Curriculum*. Chicago: University of Chicago Press.

Schwab, J. (1970) 'The practical, I: a language for curriculum', National Education Association, Washington, DC.

Schwab, J. (1971) 'The practical, II: arts of the eclectic', *School Review* **79**, 493-542.

Schwab, J. (1973) 'The practical, III: translation into curriculum', *School Review* **81**, 501-22.

Schwab, J. (1978) *Science, Curriculum and Liberal Education*. Chicago: University of Chicago Press.

Schwab, J. (1983) 'The practical, IV: something for curriculum professors to do', *Curriculum Inquiry* **13**(3), 239-365.

Scollon, R. and Scollon, S. (1981) *Narrative, Literacy and Face in Interethnic Communication*. Norwood, NJ: Ablex.

Sealey, J. (1979) 'Education as a second-order form of experience and its relation to religion', *Journal of Philosophy of Education* **13**, 83-90.

Sexton, S. (1988) 'No nationalized curriculum', *The Times* 9 May.

Simons, H. (1987) *Getting to Know Schools in a Democracy: The Politics and Process of Evaluation*. Lewes: Falmer Press.

Skilbeck, M. and Harris, A. (1975) *Ideology, Knowledge and the Curriculum*, Open University E 203, Units 3-4.

Skilbeck, M. (1984) *School-Based Curriculum Development*. London: Harper & Row.

Smith, B., Stanley, W. and Shores, J. (1957) *Fundamentals of Curriculum Development*. New York: Harcourt, Brace & World.

Stenhouse, L. (1975) *An Introduction to Curriculum Research and Development*. London: Heinemann.

Strawson, P. F. (1966) *The Bounds of Sense: An Essay on Kant's 'Critique of Pure Reason'*. London: Methuen.

Van Manen, M. (1991) 'Reflectivity and the pedagogical moment: the normativity of pedagogical thinking and acting', *Journal of Curriculum Studies* **23**(6), 507-36.

Vazquez, A. S. (1977) *The Philosophy of Praxis*. London: Merlin Press.

Wain, K. (1984) 'Lifelong education: a Deweyian challenge', *Journal of Philosophy of Education* **18**(2), 257-64.

Walkerdine, V. (1984) 'Developmental psychology and the child-centred pedagogy', in J. Henriques *et al.* (eds), *Changing the Subject*. London: Methuen.

Walsh, P. D. (1975) 'The individual and the educational community', in K. Nichols (ed.), *Theology and Education*. Langley, WA: St Paul's Press.

Walsh, P. D. (1978) 'The upgrading of practical subjects', *Journal of Further and Higher Education* **2**(3), 58-71.

Walsh, P. D. (1985) 'Education: one concept in many uses', *Journal of Philosophy of Education* **19**, 167-80.

Walsh, P. D. (1988) 'Open and loaded uses of "education" – and objectivism', *Journal of Philosophy of Education* **22**, 23-34.

Walsh, P.D. (1990) 'Kinds of discourse referring to education', *Irish Educational Studies* **9**(1), 30–44.

Walsh, P.D. (1992a) 'Elementary curriculum maps', *Irish Educational Studies* **11**(1), 99–118.

Walsh, P.D. (1992b) 'Discourses of the reflective educator', *Journal of Philosophy of Education* **26** 139–51.

Walsh, P.D. (1992c) 'History and piety', in P. Lee, J. Raynor, P. Walsh and J. White (eds), *The Aims of School History: The National Curriculum and Beyond*, London File Papers. London: Tufnell Press.

Walsh, W.H. (1951) *An Introduction to Philosophy of History*. London: Hutchinson (expanded edition 1967).

Wasserman, E. and Garrod, A. (1983) 'Application of Kohlberg's theory to curriculum in democratic schools', *Educational Analysis* **5**(1), 5–15.

Weber, M. (1949) *The Methodology of the Human Sciences*. New York: Macmillan Free Press.

Weil, S. (1949) *The Need for Roots*. London: Routledge & Kegan Paul (trans. 1952).

Weil, S. (1958a) 'The Iliad: a poem of force', in *Intimations of Christianity among the Ancient Greeks*. Boston: Beacon Press.

Weil, S. (1958b) *Oppression and Liberty*. London: Routledge & Kegan Paul.

Weil, S. (1962) *Selected Essays 1934–43*. Oxford: Oxford University Press.

Weil, S. (1965) *Simone Weil: Seventy Letters*. Oxford: Oxford University Press.

Weil, S. (1968) *On Science, Necessity and the Love of God*. Oxford: Oxford University Press.

White, J. (1973) *Towards a Compulsory Curriculum*. London: Routledge & Kegan Paul.

White, J. (1978) 'The aims of education: three legacies of the British Idealists', *Journal of Philosophy of Education* **12**, 5–12.

White, J. (1982) *The Aims of Education Restated*. London: Routledge & Kegan Paul.

Whitehead, A. (1932) *The Aims of Education*. London: Benn.

Whitty, G. (1985) *Sociology and School Knowledge*. London: Methuen.

Williams, B. (1972) *Morality: An Introduction to Ethics*. Cambridge: Cambridge University Press.

Williams, R. (1961) *The Long Revolution*. Harmondsworth: Penguin.

Williams, R. (1976) *Keywords*. London: Fontana.

Williams, R. (1981) 'Popular culture, themes', in *Popular Culture*, Open University v.203.

Wilson, B.R. (ed.) (1970) *Rationality*. Oxford: Blackwell.

Wilson, J. (1979) *Preface to the Philosophy of Education*. London: Routledge & Kegan Paul.

Wilson, J. (1981) 'Concepts, contestability and the philosophy of education', *Journal of Philosophy of Education* **15**(1), 3–16.

Winch, P. (1958) *The Idea of a Social Science*. London: Routledge & Kegan Paul.

Wittgenstein, L. (1958) *Blue and Brown Books*. Oxford: Blackwell.

Wittgenstein, L. (1953) *Philosophical Investigations*. Oxford: Blackwell.

Wittgenstein, L. (1967) *Zettel*. Oxford: Blackwell.

Young, M.F.D. (ed.) (1971) *Knowledge and Control: New Directions for the Sociology of Education*. London: Collier-Macmillan.

Young, M.F.D. and Whitty, G. (eds) (1976) *Explorations in the Politics of School Knowledge*. Driffield: Nafferton Books.

Young, M.F.D. and Whitty, G. (eds) (1977) *Society, State and Schooling*. Lewes: Falmer Press.

Name Index

Subject Index